The Ideas of the Woman Suffrage Movement,

1890 - 1920

The Ideas of the
Woman Suffrage Movement,
1890 - 1920

AILEEN S. KRADITOR

W · W · NORTON & COMPANY

New York · London

Copyright © 1981 by Aileen S. Kraditor
Copyright © 1965 by Columbia University Press

Published simultaneously in Canada by George J. McLeod Limited,
Toronto.

Printed in the United States of America

All Rights Reserved

Norton edition first published 1981

Library of Congress Cataloging in Publication Data
Kraditor, Aileen S.
The ideas of the woman suffrage movement, 1890–1920.
Reprint of the ed. published in 1965 by the Columbia University Press,
New York.
Originally presented as the author's thesis, Columbia, 1962.
Bibliography: p.
Includes index.
1. Women—Suffrage—United States.   I.   Title.
JK1896.K7   1981   324.6′23′0973   80–21356
ISBN 0-393-01449-5
ISBN 0-393-00039-7 (pbk.)

W. W. Norton & Company Inc. 500 Fifth Avenue,
New York, N.Y. 10110
W. W. Norton & Company Ltd. 25 New Street Square,
London EC4A 3NT

1 2 3 4 5 6 7 8 9 0

Preface to the Norton Edition

Much has happened to women's history during the more than eighteen years since this book was completed. There was no such field as women's history at the time I chose the topic. Eleanor Flexner's *Century of Struggle* (1959), the score or so of articles on suffragism and closely related topics, the few theses and dissertations, and some biographies of feminists were not regarded as auguring the definition of a whole subfield—much less laying the bases for college majors, degrees, institutes, historical societies, and periodicals. The bibliography, which I have left unchanged, shows the extent of the secondary literature available then on suffragism and cognate subjects.

Nor did I choose this topic as a contribution to a cause. I did not then, nor do I now, think that any aspect of women's history is "what is important to know about women" more than any other,[1] or that a scholar's choice of topics should be guided by didactic motives. The guides should be interest and curiosity. I was—and still am—curious to learn about the relation between a dissenting

[1] In "New Approaches to the Study of Women in American History," *Journal of Social History,* III (1969), Gerda Lerner cites Flexner's and my books and asserts that "modern historians . . . think that what is important to know about women is how they got the ballot." I cannot answer for Flexner, but there is not a word in my book to justify such an assertion.

movement's attitudes and theories, on the one hand, and its strategies and tactics, on the other. The woman-suffrage movement was available for my first such exploration. Since then I have studied other dissenting movements with the same sort of questions in mind.

For this edition I have improved the prose in a very few places, but for economic reasons it was not possible to make many changes in form or any in substance. I therefore welcome this opportunity to point out a few of the things I would do differently if I were rewriting the book.

The main change would be to replace chapter two with one that takes the antisuffragists more seriously, in both tone and content. My graduate student Louise L. Stevenson, in a seminar paper that became "Women Anti-Suffragists in the 1915 Massachusetts Campaign,"[2] pointed out that one should not refer to "the antisuffragists" as though they all thought the same way. I also erred in referring to the antisuffragist "ideology"; antisuffragism was not an ideology but a part of a comprehensive belief-system, and far more complex than I imagined. The attitudes and beliefs of conservative, native-born, middle-class, white Americans were being battered between 1890 and 1920, and what they were defending against social atomizers and Progressives is worthy of respectful study.

I would also adopt a more neutral approach toward the controversy between the National American Woman Suffrage Association and the Congressional Union/Woman's Party over the nature of American party politics. I do not know that a reversal of my bias in favor of the CU/WP would be justified, but the subject requires more study than I gave it. A related question that I did not have the opportunity to investigate and on which I should have been agnostic is "What effects did the two organizations' tactics have on Congressmen's votes on the Nineteenth Amendment?" If someone tabulated the votes of all those Members of Congress who voted both when the amendment lost and later when it passed, and then searched the papers of those who changed their votes, we might know why they did so. Only in this way could we discover whether the NAWSA was right when it contended that the same persuasion that had won the earlier victories would win the ultimate one and that the semimilitant tactics of the CU/WP would alienate potential supporters among both Congressmen and their constituents—or whether the CU/WP was right in insisting that its provocative tactics plus political coercion were essential to the victory.

My speculation (p. 72) about why western states were the first to adopt woman suffrage should be supplemented by some findings in Alan P. Grimes, *The Puritan Ethic and Woman Suffrage* (New York: Oxford University Press, 1967), especially with respect to Utah.

I should also eliminate what Arthur Mann, in his review, called "the foolish Marxist jargon of 'the Robinson Crusoe of the early bourgeoisie escaping from the feudal class relations that confine his energies'" (see p. 48). Professor Mann was right; and I would change several other passages that show a Marxist bias, albeit less blatantly.

Among the changes I would *not* make would be to replace "chairman" and "spokesmen" by "chairperson," or "chair," and "spokeswomen," which seem to me barbarisms.

Another change that I would not make would be to switch the focus from intellectual to social history. Several years ago, a specialist in women's history, in conversation with me, referred to "old-fashioned intellectual history" in a tone suggesting it was, thank heavens, dead. It seems to me that the ideas expressed by articulate women in the past are worthy subjects for a historian to investigate, and that we should encourage research in both social and intellectual history. Like those who assume that a historian's choice of topic is necessarily a statement about what it is "important" to know, the currently influential contemners of intellectual history are implicitly telling scholars what they should and should not study. Unfortunately, a large proportion of the recent literature on women's history has been motivated more by the desire to provide current feminists with a heritage of oppression-plus-achievement than by the desire to find out what happened. It is, consequently, often of poor quality.

As a result of these biases, there are still many lacunae in the intellectual history of women's organizations. When Professor William E. Leuchtenburg of Columbia suggested I work on suffragism, to my surprise he said that it had not been studied extensively. I then found that the only works on it focused on organizational activities, names, and dates, leaving me with far too many topics in the intellectual history of suffragism, even in its last thirty years, to include in one dissertation. I therefore selected just those topics that especially interested me. Most of those I omitted remain unstudied. I look forward to those works, still to be written, that will fill the gaps I left as well as enhance our knowledge about the topics included in this book.

A. S. K.

Wellesley, Mass.
December, 1979

Note: After this book was published, the Radcliffe Women's Archives, abbreviated "RWA" in this book, changed its name to the Arthur and Elizabeth Schlesinger Library on the History of Women in America. The original form has been left unchanged here.

Preface

The woman suffrage movement had no official ideology. Its members and leaders held every conceivable view of current events and represented every philosophical position. Although they all agreed that women should have the right to vote, they disagreed on why they ought to have that right. What, then, was it that united and moved these millions of women into clubs and onto platforms to seek a right that their society said they should not have? What were their notions of the nature of the home, the state, religion, marriage, as they were and as they should be? How would the suffrage help make these institutions what they should be? These and other questions have remained unasked and therefore as yet unanswered.[1]

The struggle for woman suffrage and the circumstances causing that struggle generated the rationale of the movement. Just as suffragists had to battle institutions that impeded women's progress toward equality, they had to fight ideas that buttressed and justified those institutions.

[1] Most secondary works dealing with the suffrage movement are biographies of individual leaders. The only scholarly work that covers the entire movement in all its aspects is the very fine *Century of Struggle,* by Eleanor Flexner, published in 1959 in Cambridge by the Belknap Press of Harvard University Press. Its very breadth, however, prevents it from dealing with ideological questions in great detail.

The ideas of the suffragists reflected their aspirations but were also weapons, and the history of a battle can hardly be understood if some of the most potent weapons used in it are ignored. Thus the history of the woman suffrage movement must be understood as a chapter in the intellectual history of the American people.

Although the suffrage movement as such had no ideology, its spokesmen constantly found themselves forced to answer the arguments that the antisuffragists (usually called "antis") used against the participation of women in government. In time these answers developed into a more or less standardized repertory of suffragist arguments, from which advocates selected those most suited to their own beliefs and the supposed predilections of their intended audience. This arsenal of arguments constitutes one field of study of suffragist ideas. Another is the record of intra- and interorganizational disputes about principles, strategy, and tactics. These two sources of information complement each other; the former tells us what the suffragists consciously considered to be the justifications of their claim to the franchise, whereas the latter makes it possible to examine their implicit ideological assumptions.

An examination of the thinking of several million enrolled suffragists, to say nothing of the unknown millions of their supporters, is manifestly impossible, but a study of the thinking of a small group of national leaders is both possible and instructive. A woman who year after year held national office in the principal suffrage association would come to be known to the general public; her statements in the press and from the platform would be assumed to be the statements of her organization and to represent the ideology of her cause. Such a woman would by her long tenure acquire an influence on the thinking of her constituents, and her repeated re-election would evidently represent a vote of confidence on their part. A study of the thinking of the long-term leaders of the National American Woman Suffrage Association thus constitutes an analysis of what the American public believed "suffragism" to mean and of those ideas which were generally acceptable to the membership.

This book investigates the views of those women who were re-elected to national office in the association at least twice between 1890 and 1918 (after 1918 the imminence of victory caused the membership to hold over the incumbent leaders regardless of their individual merit) and of top leaders in the Woman's Party; the published works that bore the official endorsement of the association and the Woman's Party regardless of author; the testimony before legislative committees in behalf of the two associations; the events within the National Association as recorded in its *Proceedings* and the *History of Woman Suffrage*;[2] and the writings of a few individuals who did not hold national office in suffragist associations but exerted great influence nevertheless.

The enfranchisement of American women did not come

[2] The *History of Woman Suffrage* is a six-volume treasure-house of suffrage information. Its compilation took many years; hence different volumes have different editors. Volumes I-III, which cover the years before 1890, were edited by Elizabeth Cady Stanton, Susan B. Anthony, and Matilda Joslyn Gage. The first two were published in 1881, in Rochester, N.Y., and the third in 1886. Only Volumes IV, V, and VI will be used here. Volume IV was edited by Susan B. Anthony and Ida Husted Harper and was published by Miss Anthony in Rochester in 1902. Mrs. Harper edited Volumes V and VI, which were published in 1922 in New York by the National American Woman Suffrage Association.

easily. The early pioneers for women's rights were subjected to humiliation and occasional violence. Many
women devoted their lives to the cause. No rights were
handed to them on a platter; they fought long and hard
for every victory they won down to and including the
Nineteenth Amendment. Before the final triumph they
suffered heartbreak and despair more often than they
experienced elation and optimism. Yet to what extent
was their tireless work responsible for their victory? The
very industrialization and other changes in American life
that made the victory possible, indeed inevitable, also
brought into being the movement that realized that victory. The triumph would not have been possible without
the movement, but the movement would not have been
possible without the social transformations that permitted
women to participate, outside their homes, in activities
that inevitably led them into politics.

The suffragists assumed that the revolution in women's
political status would constitute a social revolution, but
in fact the enfranchisement of women did not change
the economic or political structure of American society.
Although working-class, Negro, and foreign-born women
received the vote along with the rest, the suffrage movement was essentially from beginning to end a struggle
of white, native-born, middle-class women for the right
to participate more fully in the public affairs of a society
the basic structure of which they accepted. That acceptance, however, left room for a wide variety of opinions
on the significance of their movement and on the strategy
and tactics they ought to pursue. These differences produced a number of separate organizations and sharp disputes within organizations. Alongside the National Amer-

ican Woman Suffrage Association (NAWSA), several smaller associations came into being, to fight for suffrage legislation other than the usual state and national amendments. In addition, one group, the Congressional Union for Woman Suffrage (CU), withdrew from the NAWSA, believing that by that time woman suffrage had been secured in a sufficient number of states to make the federal amendment's passage possible without still more state campaigns. This dispute over tactics, however, was the only important ideological difference between the two associations; in general the attitudes toward other ideological issues that existed among members of the NAWSA existed within the CU too.

During the 1890s the old, mainly abolitionist, pioneers who had begun the suffrage agitation in the 1840s and 1850s died or retired, and a younger group rose to leadership. In ideology most of the leaders of this second stage were more conservative, and in methods more systematic. In this period, too, the first suffrage organizations appeared in the South. The Southern suffragist movement was a white women's movement, and the participation of Southern individuals and organizations in the NAWSA signified a permanent break with the abolitionist tradition from which the women's rights agitation had sprung. A few years before World War I the organized suffragists consciously cultivated a rapport with working women and foreign-born voters in the cities of the East, groups that the suffragists had hitherto ignored or deliberately contemned in their propaganda. The changes in the types of women who joined or led the associations, the changes in the nonsuffragist audiences to whom they appealed and whose opinions they had to take into account, the changes in the prospects of success of the demand for suffrage, and the major events of the times in which the struggle was conducted, all affected the attitudes of the leading spokesmen of the movement toward their own cause.

I wish to thank the librarians and archivists whom I met in the course of my research. Many did far more to help me than any researcher has a right to expect. In particular my deepest appreciation goes to Miss Elizabeth Duvall of the Sophia Smith Collection at Smith College, Dr. Jacqueline Bull and her staff at the Margaret I. King Library, University of Kentucky, and Miss Mary E. Howard of the Women's Archives at Radcliffe College. A talk with Dr. Janet Giele was most helpful in enabling me to deal with a few problems we had both encountered in our respective studies of suffragist thinking. I also wish to thank Miss Eleanor Flexner for permitting me to interview her at her home in the summer of 1961. A special word of thanks is due to Dr. Edward T. James, who furnished me with research leads and much important information.

Professors William E. Leuchtenburg and Robert D. Cross of Columbia read part or all of the manuscript when it was a potential doctoral dissertation, and their criticisms were most helpful. Finally, my deepest thanks go to my friend, Professor Eugene D. Genovese of Rutgers, who generously criticized portions of the first draft.

AILEEN S. KRADITOR

Johnston, Rhode Island
August 1, 1964

Abbreviations

FHL   Friends Historical Library of Swarthmore College, Swarthmore, Pennsylvania

HL   Huntington Library, San Marino, California

LC   Library of Congress, Manuscript Division, Washington, D.C.

NYHS   New-York Historical Society, New York, N.Y.

NYPL   New York Public Library, New York, N.Y.

RWA   Radcliffe Women's Archives, Radcliffe College, Cambridge, Massachusetts

SSC   Sophia Smith Collection, Smith College, Northampton, Massachusetts

UCB   Bancroft Library, University of California, Berkeley, California

UK   Margaret I. King Library, University of Kentucky, Lexington, Kentucky

Contents

The Ideas of the Woman Suffrage Movement,
1890-1920

ONE

The History of
Suffragist Organization

The woman suffrage movement was the child of the woman's rights movement. The origin of the woman's rights movement is commonly dated from 1848 when Elizabeth Cady Stanton, Lucretia Mott, and a few others met in Seneca Falls, New York, and drew up the first public protest in America against women's political, economic, and social inferiority. This protest, modeled after the Declaration of Independence, was called the "Declaration of Sentiments." [1] Mrs. Stanton included in its list of proposed reforms the demand for the ballot, a suggestion so advanced that Mrs. Mott feared its inclusion would hurt the infant movement. But Frederick Douglass supported Mrs. Stanton, Mrs. Mott acquiesced, and the demand for the vote became an official part of the new movement for women's equality with men.

The founders of the women's rights movement were all abolitionists, although not all abolitionists believed in

---

[1] The Declaration may be found in Henry Steele Commager, ed., *Documents of American History* (6th ed., New York, Appleton-Century-Crofts, Inc., 1956), pp. 315-16 (Document No. 172). T. V. Smith reprints it in an appendix to his *The American Philosophy of Equality*, pp. 327-31.

equal rights for women. Some in fact protested against women's speaking from abolitionist platforms because, desiring to persuade as many people as they could to oppose slavery, they shrank from making that task more difficult in a day when any public activity by women was considered shocking and indecent. The problem of how far to go in advocacy of change, which has in all periods plagued reform movements, troubled abolitionists too. An abolitionist might want freedom for the Negro and equality for woman for the same reason: the equal natural right and dignity of each human being. At the same time he might realize that the effort to abolish slavery might be defeated if it were linked to a premature demand for women's rights. Yet he might be troubled by the problem of how far he could play down the cause of women's rights without compromising his principles. For an individual to whom one of the two causes was far more important than the other the solution might be relatively simple, but one who studies the women pioneers for women's rights in the United States cannot easily decide at all times whether the desire for their own emancipation or for the right to work for the emancipation of the slave motivated them more strongly. Probably they could not have sorted out their own motives completely.

When in 1840 the American delegates to the World's Anti-Slavery Convention arrived in London to find the women delegates among them excluded from participation, Mrs. Stanton and Mrs. Mott decided it was time to fight for the right to work for abolition and for other rights for women as well. The 1848 meeting in Seneca Falls was the long-delayed result of this determination.

It was the first of many such conventions, each one of which was greeted in the press with ridicule and from the pulpit with shocked denunciation. Yet other women were taking the same road. Lucy Stone, Susan B. Anthony, and many other women who were to lead the suffrage cause undertook the struggle for women's rights in the same period. When the Civil War began, the women, still abolitionists as much as they were fighters for women's rights, suspended their annual conventions and threw themselves into the war effort, to which they made notable contributions. After the war's end they resumed their demands for equal rights and for the vote, expecting the Republican party, out of gratitude for the women's war activities, to respond more favorably than before. To their dismay and disillusionment, the party leaders informed them that "this is the Negro's hour," and that the women must wait for their rights.[2]

The suffragists disagreed among themselves as to how they ought to view the Fourteenth Amendment, which inserted the word *male* into the United States Constitution for the first time. Some of them, including Miss Anthony and Mrs. Stanton, thought it would be better if the amendment were defeated, while others, including Mrs. Stone, argued that if women could not win their political freedom, it was well that Negro men could win theirs. On this and other issues the suffragists found they could not agree. In 1869 two separate organizations came

[2] The Republicans argued that an attempt to enfranchise women would jeopardize their plans to enfranchise Negro men in the South. Their actual attitudes toward woman suffrage and Negro suffrage are irrelevant here. The Republican leadership included individuals who favored votes for women and others who opposed that reform regardless of its possible effect on the fortunes of the party.

into being: the National Woman Suffrage Association
(led by Mrs. Stanton and Miss Anthony) and the American Woman Suffrage Association (led by Henry Ward
Beecher and Mrs. Stone). The split lasted until 1890
when the two factions merged into the National American
Woman Suffrage Association (NAWSA), and a new era
in woman suffrage history began.[3]

By 1890 the cause of women's rights had come a long
way since 1848, the year of the Seneca Falls convention
and the year in which New York State had given married
women the sole possession of the property they owned
before marriage, although they did not yet have the right
to bequeath it.[4] In 1838 Kentucky had given its women,
under certain conditions, the right to vote in school elections, but it was not until 1861 that the second state,
Kansas, adopted school suffrage. Michigan and Minnesota
adopted a similar reform in 1875, and thirteen other
states and territories had followed suit by 1890. Wider
forms of suffrage had by then been introduced, Kansas
women having received the municipal suffrage in 1887;
more significantly, the territory of Wyoming decreed full
political equality in 1869.[5] In 1890 Wyoming entered the
Union as the first state with full suffrage for women.
Colorado in 1893 and Utah and Idaho in 1896 enfran-

[3] The pre-1890 history of the suffrage movement may be traced in the
first four volumes of the *History of Woman Suffrage*.

[4] If the property was sold, the husband owned the proceeds. Married
women did not yet have legal custody of their own children or legal
ownership of their own earnings or any property acquired after marriage.
The power of a husband legally extended even to the right to prescribe
the medicine his family must take and the amount and kind of food they
ate. These legal disabilities generally disappeared more quickly than the
political disfranchisement of women.

[5] Women in Washington and Utah had won the full vote, but had lost
it again before the two territories had become states.

chised their women, but then a long period began in which no states adopted the reform.

The suffrage movement did not sleep, however. The women conducted many state campaigns, securing signatures on petitions, traveling over the immense western distances in bad weather and with dreadful transportation, speaking again and again before voters and legislators. Defeat after defeat rewarded their efforts. After the first state referendum in Kansas in 1867, which failed, 55 more such popular votes on state woman suffrage amendments took place in the next fifty years. Altogether there were 480 campaigns to induce state legislatures to submit amendments to their electorates; 277 campaigns to persuade state party conventions to include woman suffrage planks in their platforms; 19 campaigns with 19 successive congresses; and the ratification campaign of 1919 and 1920.[6] Between 1869 and 1916 there were 41 state amendment campaigns, with 9 victories and 32 defeats.[7] Between the passage of the Utah and Idaho constitutional amendments in 1896 and the Washington victory in 1910 not one state enfranchised its women.

During that period changes were taking place that made the later triumphs possible. Women's clubs proliferated, women college graduates were almost becoming accepted as normal, women factory workers increased enormously in number and were beginning to organize, and middle-class women were finding that recent household inventions and changes in living patterns gave them more time for outside activities, while their training was making them dissatisfied with traditional middle-class women's activities. Economic and social changes were

[6] NAWSA, *Victory: How Women Won It*, p. 53.   [7] *Ibid.*, p. 72.

drawing the spheres of men and women together; women's political status changed accordingly.

In 1910 the "doldrums" ended, and Washington adopted an amendment to its state constitution enfranchising women. The next year California followed; and in 1912 Oregon, Kansas, and Arizona adopted the reform. The first state east of the Mississippi to enfranchise its women was Illinois, 1913, but instead of giving them the full suffrage it gave them the right to vote for presidential electors, a reform that the state legislatures could pass without consulting their electorates. This event proved a turning point, for it broke the solid antisuffragist East and raised by 29 the number of members in the Electoral College whose constituents included women. It also showed that this manner of enfranchising women was practicable, and unlike other forms of limited suffrage, such as municipal suffrage, it would not prove an obstacle to the further extension of women's right to vote. In the next few years one state after another enfranchised its women, until when in 1917 New York State voters finally approved a full-suffrage constitutional amendment in a referendum, victory throughout the nation was assured. A sufficient number of members of Congress now were responsible to women constituents to secure passage of the national amendment by Congress in 1919; it was ratified by the thirty-sixth state, Tennessee, in August 1920.

The precise number of enrolled suffragists will never be known. Since local affiliates of the NAWSA had to pay a tax of ten cents per capita to National each year, an estimate of the minimum number of members may be derived from the treasurer's annual report, by noting the amount of per capita tax income. However, such a computation would in every case be far below the actual number of members, since the affiliates were extremely lax in sending in their money and reports to the National. Membership can also be estimated from random remarks by leaders. From such sources it may be inferred that the NAWSA grew from 13,150 in 1893; to 17,000 in 1905; to 45,501 in 1907; to over 75,000 in 1910; to 100,000 in 1915; to 2,000,000 in 1917.[8] Exact figures would not prove much, since in many places and for much of this thirty-year period membership in a suffrage club was a mere formality. There were undoubtedly many women outside the association who sympathized with the cause just as deeply as those who were enrolled in clubs. Consequently,

[8] The 1893 figure may be found in *Proceedings* of the Twenty-Fifth Annual Convention of the National American Woman Suffrage Association, held in Washington, D.C., January 16-19, 1893 (Washington, D.C., 1893), p. 16. The report notes that the figures are far too low; many clubs did not send in figures. The 1905 figure appears in Shaw, *Story of a Pioneer*, chap. XVII. Cf. Miss Shaw in *Woman's Journal*, July 29, 1905, where she wrote that if the NAWSA grew by 20 percent a year it would have 100,000 members in 1915. That would set 1905 membership at a bit less than 17,000. The 1907 figure may be found in the report of "Committee on Enrolment," *Proceedings* of the Thirty-Ninth Annual Convention of the National American Woman Suffrage Association, held at Chicago, Ill., February 14 to 19, inclusive, 1907 (Warren, Ohio, n.d.), pp. 31-32. The report said, however, that actual enrollment was far higher. The 1910 estimate was made by Treasurer Jessie Ashley in *Woman's Journal*, July 8, 1911. For the 1915 estimate, see Shaw, *Story of a Pioneer*, chap. XVII. However, another suffragist leader stated in 1914 that the NAWSA had 462,000 members (Mrs. C. W. McCulloch, quoted in clipping from [Washington *Herald*, March 8, 1914], Clay Papers, UK). But Maud Wood Park, a leader of the NAWSA's lobby in Congress, put the 1915 figure at "more than two million" (Park, *Front Door Lobby*, p. 12). The 1917 figure appears in *Woman Citizen*, June 2, 1917. Carrie Chapman Catt gave this figure in [Carrie Chapman Catt] to James P. Hornaday, May 24, 1917, and Carrie Chapman Catt to Inez Haynes Irwin, March 29, 1933, both in Suffrage Archives, LC.

membership figures, even if available, would not reflect sentiment accurately.

This was not, however, the case with the Congressional Union for Woman Suffrage (CU), later known as the Woman's Party (WP), the group of younger women who broke with the NAWSA in 1914 to become a separate organization and who used semimilitant tactics to demand that the federal amendment be passed. Unlike the NAWSA, which was a loose federation of clubs of varying levels of activity, the CU never tried to enroll large numbers of women. It saw itself, rather, as a small disciplined army able to maneuver quickly according to the tactics worked out by its leaders.[9] It had no use for paper members. The NAWSA not only tolerated inactive members; it sought to enroll all women who favored suffrage, believing that one of its main tasks was to disprove the antisuffragist argument that "women do not want to vote." The CU, on the other hand, believed that by 1914 the time for educational work to convince fence-sitters had passed. Instead, it proposed to "teach" the lawmakers that inaction on the woman suffrage amendment would cost them votes in the full-suffrage states. This type of educational work could not be carried on by a large paper membership. The CU, thus, was a small organization of active young women. In 1916 its leaders founded the Woman's Party. For a year thereafter the CU was made up of disfranchised women in the East and a few in the South, and the WP was its sister organization of women voters in the full-suffrage states in the West. When in 1917 the two organizations merged to form the National

[9] The military analogy and this analysis of the nature of the WP are to be found in Irwin, *The Story of the Woman's Party,* p. 315.

Woman's Party, the CU alone had 25,000 members.[10] The combined groups never numbered more than a tiny percentage of the enrolled suffragists in the country, but although the leaders of the NAWSA, who abhorred CU tactics, boasted about the difference in numerical strength, the CU-WP was at least as active and effective as the giant NAWSA in the last eight years of the federal amendment campaign.

The two organizations worked in different ways, and both ways were undoubtedly necessary to the complete victory of 1920. Certainly the NAWSA's educational work and repeated attempts to secure amendments to state constitutions were necessary in the long years before the birth of the CU. By 1912, when Alice Paul organized the CU within the NAWSA, she and other younger members of the NAWSA believed that the association should exert irresistible pressure on Congress to pass the federal amendment. They criticized the Congressional Committee of the NAWSA for half-hearted activity. In 1914 they became a separate association, and while the NAWSA continued to focus its main attention on the states, the CU campaigned chiefly in Washington, D.C. The activity it carried on in the states aimed primarily at mobilizing the voting power of Western women to show congressmen it was in their own interest to support the federal amendment.

In 1916 the NAWSA adopted a new policy toward the federal amendment, ending its long period of almost exclusive concentration on the states. President Carrie Chapman Catt's "Winning Plan," presented to the 1916 convention, assigned specific tasks to the state auxiliaries.

[10] *Ibid.*, p. 201; *Suffragist*, March 10, 1917.

Key parts of the plan were to be the efforts in certain states to secure the presidential suffrage, which had been proved practicable in Illinois. In other states, where prospects looked good, the women were to try for full suffrage. Clubs in hopeless states were not to waste their resources, needed elsewhere, on futile campaigns. Although most NAWSA leaders were extremely hostile toward the WP, this plan supplemented the WP tactic of mobilizing Western women voters and putting direct pressure on officials in Washington via picket lines and deputations; both aimed at the passage and ratification of the federal amendment.

The nature of the leadership of the NAWSA reflected the periods in which that leadership was given, the problems the association faced, and the suffragists' self-image. The first president of the NAWSA was Elizabeth Cady Stanton of New York, who when she took office in 1890 was seventy-five years old. The mother of seven children, she had frequently before the Civil War had to withdraw from active campaigning owing to family duties. At those times Susan B. Anthony helped care for the children and do the household chores to free Mrs. Stanton for her writing. Writing was indeed her main talent. Periodicals of the day are full of her articles on many subjects in addition to woman suffrage. In her last years Mrs. Stanton, for whom woman suffrage had never been more than one means to her goal, the full development of women's potentialities, began to regard the suffrage as less and less important. Her essays on other subjects became more and more frequent, as the columns of the main suffragist paper, the *Woman's Journal*, attest. Her views, never orthodox, became positively shocking to most suffragists, as she publicly denounced the Bible and most clergymen for their alleged contempt for women, and as she began advocating a reorganization of American society along cooperative lines. Mrs. Stanton was the *enfant terrible* of the suffrage cause in the nineteenth century. She forced people to think and was hardly surprised when they failed to agree with her.

In 1892 Mrs. Stanton resigned, and Susan B. Anthony of New York succeeded her as NAWSA's president. A mere seventy-two years old, Miss Anthony had begun her career as a teacher, but while ardently championing abolition of both slavery and liquor, she quickly decided that woman's enfranchisement was the cause to which she must devote her life. That conviction never changed. Lacking Mrs. Stanton's facile pen and easy eloquence, Miss Anthony saw herself as the prosaic day-to-day worker for the cause. She constantly traveled about the country, speaking, organizing, pleading, bit by bit building an organization. In later years she and Mrs. Stanton complemented each other. Mrs. Stanton, a short fat woman with curly white hair, needed prodding to work at her propaganda tasks. Miss Anthony, tall and angular, with straight gray hair tied in a bun at her neck, tirelessly provided her friend with the facts, figures, and prodding. If Mrs. Stanton came to believe that the enfranchisement of women was less necessary as a means of bringing about the full equality of the sexes than she had earlier believed, Miss Anthony to the end of her life contended that the vote was the key to women's emancipation. Her single-minded and selfless devotion to that one cause led her, rather than any of her more brilliant co-workers, to become the greatest individual in the American suffrage movement. Although she lived until 1906, she retired in 1900 and was succeeded as president by Carrie Chapman Catt, a young Wisconsin-born Iowan with a genius for organization and a winning manner on the platform. Like Miss Anthony, Mrs. Catt was a prohibitionist and a schoolteacher in her youth. By 1895, although only thirty-six, she had already become chairman of the NAWSA's Organizational Committee. Owing to her husband's ill-health, however, she withdrew from the presidency in 1902.

Her successor, a short, stocky, and red-cheeked minister, Anna Howard Shaw, was one of the most remarkable in a group of remarkable suffrage leaders. Born in England in 1847, she came to America as a child and spent her early years on the Michigan frontier. She early felt the call to the ministry, an almost unheard-of vocation for women in those days. Over the opposition of her family, she worked her way through college and Boston University's theological school, the only woman in her class at the latter institution. Although by then a licensed preacher, she was denied the financial exemptions accorded to her male fellow-students who were licensed preachers, and suffered from malnutrition throughout her stay at theological school. Thanks to an iron constitution and fierce determination, Miss Shaw survived, was graduated, and in 1880 was ordained by the Protestant Methodist Church, after her own church, the Methodist, refused to ordain her. Her subsequent duties as pastor of two Massachusetts parishes left her with abundant energy that needed an outlet, and having been appalled by the sickness she had encountered in the slums of Boston, she studied medicine and received her M.D. degree in 1885. As a lecturer for the Woman's Christian Temperance Union (WCTU), she came in contact with the suffrage movement and soon became a devoted friend of Susan B. Anthony. Miss Shaw after becoming NAWSA's president devoted her truly great oratorical powers to the suffrage cause, but by then speechmaking was no longer the most important activity for a suffrage leader to engage in. The movement was stagnating, and Miss Shaw's administrative deficiencies made the organization's problems worse. By 1911 its internal splits and dissensions had become public knowledge. Miss Shaw retired as president in 1915, served during the war as the chairman of the Women's Committee of the Council of National Defense, and died in 1919.

In 1915 Mrs. Catt resumed the office of president and immediately began to work out the specific goals and the plans for achieving those goals that the organization had lacked. Mrs. Catt, although she did not have Miss Shaw's oratorical brilliance and keen sense of humor, was the organizer of the suffrage movement. She transformed the huge, disorganized, and aimless group of women into a purposeful organization, each part of which carried out its assigned task in its leader's grand strategy for victory.

TWO

The Rationale of Antisuffragism

The movement of women to secure the vote was a conscious assault on ideas and institutions long accepted by most middle-class Americans. In response to the suffragist challenge, the antisuffragists made those ideas explicit and rationalized those institutions. That antisuffragism was essentially defensive is evidenced by the pattern of its organizational activity, which waxed or waned as the suffragist campaigns intensified or stagnated.[1] Unlike the suffragist movement, antisuffragism was not characterized by mass activity. The antis published several periodicals and organized many societies, but their activity was sporadic. It was their ideology that was significant. The antis defined the context within which suffragist ideas developed, posed the problems the suffragists had to solve, and asked the questions they had to answer. They even inadvertently pointed out which parts of the fortress

[1] See, for example, the letter from the leaders of the New York and Massachusetts Associations Opposed to the Extension of Suffrage to Women, to the International Congress of Women, reprinted in the New York *Sun*, July 2, 1899. The letter recounts the history of antisuffragist organizations and notes that they did not begin in earnest until the period of state amendment campaigns in the 1890s.

could be taken with ease and which parts could not be captured without ingenious new weapons. Their propaganda will be examined to discover what the world, real and ideal, looked like through the antisuffragists' eyes, and what they considered woman's place in it to be.[2]

Close to the heart of all antisuffragist orators, particularly congressmen, was a sentimental vision of Home and Mother, equal in sanctity to God and the Constitution. Although all four entities regularly appeared in various combinations in antisuffragist propaganda, it was the link of woman to the home that underlay the entire ideology. The antis regarded each woman's vocation as determined not by her individual capacities or wishes but by her sex. Men were expected to have a variety of ambitions and capabilities, but all women were destined from birth to be full-time wives and mothers. To dispute this eternal truth was to challenge theology, biology, or sociology.

The commonest form of the theological argument was

[2] The analysis of the antisuffragist literature does not attempt to assess the validity of all the arguments it contains or to discuss motives. Nor have I discussed the antisuffragist sentiment that may have existed among immigrant groups who brought with them to America a conservative attitude toward woman's place, and the ulterior motives for antisuffragism of brewing interests or other businessmen. This study is concerned only with the ideas of those who took to the press and platform to oppose the suffrage movement, and who in the process developed a more or less coherent set of arguments. Every effort was made to secure a sampling of the antisuffragist propaganda which is representative of both the thinking of the leaders of the movement and the arguments to which the intended audience was exposed. The footnote citations are intended to be representative rather than exhaustive. Within the thirty-year period, 1890-1920, the antis used the same basic handful of arguments—though with changes of emphasis—with the exception of the "states' rights" objection to a federal amendment. The states' rights argument appeared only in the few years before 1920, in response to the need for an argument that could still win support.

no argument at all, but the mere announcement that God had ordained man and woman to perform different functions in the state as well as in the home, or that he had intended woman for the home and man for the world.[3] For those to whom assertion was not tantamount to proof, however, more detailed analyses of divine intentions were furnished, based mainly on Genesis and St. Paul. A clear statement of the ostensibly antisuffragist implications of Genesis was provided by Grover Cleveland, in an article that brought an avalanche of protests from women, suffragists and nonsuffragists, all over the country. The ex-president wrote that

Those who . . . [seek] to protect the old and natural order of things as they relate to women reverently appeal to the division of Divine purpose clearly shown when Adam was put in the Garden of Eden to dress it and keep it, and Eve was given to him as a helpmeet and because it was not good that man should be alone . . . and . . . they . . . fortify their position by referring to the fact that, as part of the punishment visited upon their first parents for their disobedience, it was decreed that in the sweat of his face should the man eat bread, and in sorrow should the woman bring forth children.[4]

[3] Rep. Webb of North Carolina, in *Cong. Rec.*, 63d Cong., 3d Sess. (1915), p. 1421; *Extracts from Addresses* of the Rt. Rev. Wm. Croswell Doane, D. D., Bishop of Albany, to the classes graduated from St. Agnes' School, Albany, June 6, 1894 and June 6, 1895; *Copy of Preamble and Protest* signed by twenty-one women; *Revised Record of the Constitutional Convention of the State of New York*, May 8, 1894, to September 29, 1894, pp. 295, 432-33, 541; Johnson, *Woman and the Republic*, p. 263; " 'Mars' Henry Watterson, the Noblest Roman of Them All Speaks in Meetin'," leaflet in Alabama Folder, Box 243, Suffrage Archives, LC.

[4] Cleveland, "Woman's Mission and Woman's Clubs," *Ladies' Home Journal*, XXII (May, 1905), 3. The punishment referred to was turned into an argument for equal rights by the suffragists, who interpreted it as a prediction unfortunately fulfilled throughout history, rather than as a command to be obeyed. See chap. IV.

Cleveland believed that the division of labor between men and women decreed by the Creator, as far as the suffrage was concerned, happened to correspond exactly to that which existed throughout the United States in 1905 (except in Wyoming, Colorado, Utah, and Idaho).[5]

St. Paul was the other religious authority for antisuffragism; the relevant passages were those in the Epistles to the Corinthians and to the Galatians, in which the apostle enjoined women to silence in the church and obedience to their husbands.[6] One scholarly essayist declared that "The first principle of religion is obedience. The woman who does not rightly obey her husband will not obey the God who enjoins her submission. Her rightsism is simly sex-atheism, and can only generate atheistic minds."[7] But since the religious argument against woman suffrage was intended to persuade women and must also appeal to men who approved of higher education and other nineteenth-century advances in women's status, the antis had to demonstrate that the divinely ordained division of labor and male headship in the family did not imply male superiority. How well the attempt to reconcile the antis' interpretation of the Bible with their own conception of the equality of the sexes succeeded may be judged from the following analysis:

In the origin of civilization there is every evidence (*see Genesis*) that woman was given by the Creator a position that is inseparable from and is the complement of man. She was made man's helper, was given a servient place (not

[5] See also Cleveland, "Would Woman Suffrage Be Unwise?" *Ladies' Home Journal*, XXII (October, 1905), 7.

[6] See, for example, Rep. Clark of Florida, in *Cong. Rec.*, 63d Cong., 3d Sess. (1915), p. 1414.

[7] Holland, "The Suffragette," *Sewanee Review*, XVII (June, 1909), 282.

necessarily inferior) and man the dominant place (not necessarily superior) in the division of labor.[8]

In fact, the antis maintained that this division, far from implying woman's inferiority, actually insured her supremacy as long as she remained in the sphere to which she had been assigned. The division of labor required men to work, govern, and protect and women to bear and raise children and create for their men a refuge from the cares of the world.[9]

The biological argument, designed to appeal to people who needed a scientific sanction for their beliefs, rested on two assumptions: that souls as well as bodies had sexual attributes, and that women were physically incapable of undertaking the various duties concomitant with voting. The first assumption underlay those antisuffragist arguments which identified femininity with inherent emotionalism and illogicality, traits inconsistent with the proper exercise of the suffrage. Octavius B. Frothingham explained the difference between masculine and feminine characteristics:

[8] Man-Suffrage Assoc., *The Case against Woman Suffrage*, p. 31. A Florida congressman, after quoting St. Paul's command to wives to be subject to their husbands, added that women were not inferior—only different (*Cong. Rec.*, 63d Cong., 3d Sess. [1915], p. 1414). See also speech of Rep. Webb cited in footnote 3. Similar views may be found in John H. Vincent to Ida Husted Harper, Jan. 4, 1898, Harper Collection, HL; and in *Revised Record of the Constitutional Convention of New York*, 1894, pp. 297 and 433.

[9] Cuyler, *Shall Women Be Burdened with the Ballot?* See also Parkman, *Some of the Reasons against Woman Suffrage; Copy of Preamble and Protest*; "Letter of Prentiss Cummings, Esq.," in *Woman Suffrage Unnatural and Inexpedient*, a compilation of antisuffragist statements by six eminent men (Boston, 1894), p. 104; Women Remonstrants of Illinois, *To the Honorable the Senate and House of Representatives of the State of Illinois*; Root, *Address* on August 15, 1894; "Nebraska Men's Association Opposed to Woman Suffrage," a manifesto published in 1914 and reprinted in *History of Woman Suffrage*, VI, 874.

The masculine represents *judgment*, the practicable, the expedient, the possible, while the feminine represents *emotion*, what ought to be, the dream of excellence, the vision of complete beauty. . . . The predominance of sentiment in woman renders her essentially an idealist. She jumps at conclusions. . . ., She can make no allowance for slowness, for tentative or compromising measures. Her reforms are sweeping. She would close all the bars and liquor saloons, and make it a crime to sell intoxicating drink.[10]

Antis who resorted to this argument frequently took care to disclaim any implication of contempt for illogical woman. On the contrary, woman had a higher faculty than logic, "woman's intuition," which yielded a perception of truth beyond that possible to man, provided the intuition was employed in its proper sphere. Just as women were superior to men in the feminine sphere, so their own method of arriving at truths was also superior to men's, but was useless in the political realm.[11] Since feminine illogic was believed to be an attribute of sex, the antis felt that the possession of it made women especially attractive to men. A minister spoke of that "logical infirmity of mind which constitutes one of the weaknesses, and I might also say, one of the charms of the feminine

[10] Frothingham, "The Real Case of the 'Remonstrants' against Woman Suffrage," *The Arena*, II (July, 1890), 176, 179. See also Mrs. M. E. Sherwood, in New York *Herald*, May 6, 1894, clipping in Woman Suffrage Scrapbooks, NYPL; Man-Suffrage Assoc., *The Case against Woman Suffrage*, p. 34; Parkman, *Some of the Reasons against Woman Suffrage*, pp. 4, 12; Holland, "The Suffragette," *Sewanee Review*, XVII (June, 1909), 278; C. W. Clark, "Woman Suffrage Pro and Con," *Atlantic Monthly*, LV (March, 1890), 315, 320; Buckley, "The Wrongs and Perils of Woman Suffrage," *The Century*, XLVIII, new series XXVI (August, 1894), 614.

[11] See, for example, Alice Hill Chittenden, "Woman Suffrage a Mistaken Theory of Progress," *The Woman's Protest*, I (September, 1912), 8; Man-Suffrage Assoc., *The Case against Woman Suffrage*, p. 34.

constitution."[12] Thus the innate emotional differences made it imperative for women to use their "feminine intuition" and visions of abstract justice to instill the proper ideals in their young sons who would then grow up into fine citizens, employing their masculine logic and reasonableness to govern wisely, tempering idealism with practicality.

The second variety of the biological argument described woman's physical constitution as too delicate to withstand the turbulence of political life. Her alleged weakness, nervousness, and proneness to fainting would certainly be out of place in polling booths and party conventions.[13] The following pronouncement combined both types of biological argument in charming fashion and bore the endorsement of both a scientist and a priest:

A woman's brain evolves emotion rather than intellect; and whilst this feature fits her admirably as a creature burdened with the preservation and happiness of the human species, it painfully disqualifies her for the sterner duties to be performed by the intellectual faculties. The best wife and mother and sister would make the worst legislator, judge and police.

The excessive development of the emotional in her nervous system, ingrafts on the female organization, a neurotic or hysterical condition, which is the source of much of the female charm when it is kept within due restraints. In . . . moments of excitement . . . it is liable to explode in violent paroxysms. . . . Every woman, therefore, carries this power

[12] Parkhurst, "The Inadvisability of Woman Suffrage," in *Significance of the Woman Suffrage Movement, Annals* of the American Academy of Political and Social Science Supplement, XXXV (May, 1910), 36.

[13] Max G. Schlapp, "The Enemy at the Gate," *The Woman's Protest,* I (September, 1912), 6; Massachusetts Man Suffrage Association, *Why Should Suffrage Be Imposed on Women?* (Boston, n.d.); Buckley, "The Wrongs and Perils of Woman Suffrage," *The Century,* XLVIII, new series XXVI (August, 1894), 619; Root, *Address.*

of irregular, illogical and incongruous action; and no one can foretell when the explosion will come.[14]

A different sort of biological argument purported to deduce antisuffragism from the theory of evolution which was then rapidly becoming respectable. Darwinism was cited to demonstrate that the highest forms of life were the most specialized. Therefore, the proposal that woman invade man's sphere must be retrogressive rather than progressive.[15]

Suffragists often expressed amused perplexity at the antis' inconsistency. The latter insisted that the eternal differences between the sexes were so great that women *could* not participate in government, and in the next breath assumed that those differences were so fragile that to preserve them women *must* not participate in government. Perhaps the antis were manifesting something more than inconsistency. They were living in a period in which the traditional roles of men and women, hitherto clearly defined and separated, were changing. Men were performing women's tasks, as chefs, tailors, and laundry

[14] Walsh, *Protest against Woman Suffrage:* Address Delivered at a Mass Meeting Called by the Anti-Women's Suffrage Association of Albany, N.Y. (reprinted as a pamphlet and bound in 1896 with a number of others). Walsh was paraphrasing a Dr. William A. Hammond, whom he identified as "the distinguished nerve and brain specialist." It is not clear from the text how much of this passage is Hammond's and how much is Walsh's. See also Alice Stone Blackwell, "Rose Terry Cooke on Suffrage," *Woman's Journal*, April 25, 1891.

[15] Chittenden, "Woman Suffrage a Mistaken Theory of Progress," *The Woman's Protest*, I (September, 1912), 8; Bissell, *A Talk with Women*; Mrs. W. F. Scott, "Women's Relation to Government," *North American Review*, CXCI (April, 1910), 551; Root, *Address*. A variant of this argument may be found in Dos Passos, *Equality of Suffrage*, a copy of which is in the Antisuffrage Box, Suffrage Collection, ssc. Dos Passos wrote that the "political amalgamation" of the sexes would break down the refining barriers and let loose the "smothered brutality of both sexes."

operators. Women were entering the male sphere as voters, scholars, and breadwinners. The literature of antisuffragism understandably contains few explicit statements of the widespread confusion that existed in that period as to the social implications of sex differences. But perhaps that confusion may help to explain both the antis' inconsistency and their fierce determination to maintain the traditional distinctions, whatever the source of those distinctions might be.

This "separate but equal" doctrine of the respective spheres of man and woman was a central part of the sociological argument against woman suffrage, which declared that social peace and the welfare of the human race depended upon woman's staying home, having children, and keeping out of politics. Voting implied much more than simply dropping a ballot in a box once a year. It meant on the part of woman an entire intellectual reorientation. Having the right to vote imposed the duty of exercising that right competently, which required doing whatever was necessary to become politically intelligent. At the very least it meant that women must become informed on political issues, and the inevitable discussions on such subjects between spouses would cause disagreements which in turn would raise the divorce rate.[16] Woman suffrage would lead to neglect of children

[16] "Letter from Richard H. Dana, Esq.," in Frothingham and others, *Woman Suffrage Unnatural and Inexpedient*, p. 21; Buckley, "The Wrongs and Perils of Woman Suffrage," *The Century*, XLVIII, new series XXVI (August, 1894); Doane, "Why Women Do Not Want the Ballot," *North American Review*, CLXI (September, 1895), 257-67; L. Abbott, "The Profession of Motherhood," *The Outlook*, August 10, 1909, pp. 836-40; Holland, "The Suffragette," *Sewanee Review*, XVII (June, 1909); L. Abbott, "Why the Vote Would be Injurious to Woman," *Ladies' Home Journal*, XXVII (February, 1910), 21-22; *Cong. Rec.*, 63d Cong., 1st Sess. (1913), p. 3459 (Sen. Tillman of

by politically active mothers and, thereby, to increased juvenile delinquency,[17] because the franchise would inexorably draw women into political organization and even into office.[18] And, of course, women's political activity would inject sex into politics.[19] To illustrate this danger, the Massachusetts Anti-Suffrage Committee warned that woman suffrage meant "pretty girls buttonholing strange men on the streets on Election Day in behalf of the 'Handsome' candidate" and that it meant women on juries listening to shocking testimony which they would then have to discuss with strange men behind locked doors through the night; such things, the committee concluded, were of course "unthinkable."[20] The rewards of office, which interfered with maternal duties, would put a premium on singleness and childlessness. Women who thus invaded the masculine sphere would forfeit their right to chivalry, that mode of male behavior which ennobled society.[21] Such activity would also encourage that spe-

---

S.C.); 3d Sess. (1915), p. 1414 (Rep. Clark of Fla.); p. 1421 (Rep. Webb of N.C.); Appendix, p. 163 (Rep. Parker of N.J.); Man-Suffrage Assoc., *The Case against Woman Suffrage*, p. 33; Massachusetts Anti-Suffrage Committee, *The Case against Woman Suffrage*, p. 15; Parkman, *Some of the Reasons against Woman Suffrage*; Cuyler, *Shall Women Be Burdened with the Ballot?*; Walsh, *Protest against Woman Suffrage.*

[17] Holland, "The Suffragette," *Sewanee Review*, XVII (July, 1909), 272-88; M'Intire, *Of No Benefit to Woman.*

[18] L. Abbott, "The Profession of Motherhood," *The Outlook*, August 10, 1909, pp. 836-40; Buckley, "The Wrongs and Perils of Woman Suffrage," *The Century*, XLVIII, new series XXVI (August, 1894); M'Intire, *Of No Benefit to Woman; * Wells, *An Argument against Woman Suffrage.*

[19] *Cong. Rec.*, 63d Cong., 3d Sess. (1915), Appendix, p. 163 (Rep. Parker of N.J.); Parkman, *Some of the Reasons against Woman Suffrage;* Holland, "The Suffragette," *Sewanee Review*, XVII (June, 1909).

[20] Massachusetts Anti-Suffrage Committee, *The Case against Woman Suffrage*, pp. 43-44.

[21] Doane, "Why Women Do Not Want the Ballot," *North American Review*, CLXI (September, 1895); Buckley, "The Wrongs and Perils

cious independence of woman slyly advocated by supporters of free love and socialism.[22]

To comprehend the horror with which the antis con-
templated these possibilities, it is necessary to understand their belief that the unit of society was not the
individual but the family.[23] A man voted not for himself
alone but for all the members of his family, as their political representative. Social stability depended upon the
existence of many tightly knit families, each of which
was, in the antisuffragist view, a state in miniature, relatively isolated from outside influences and interests. An
extreme expression of this was in a leaflet entitled "Household Hints," which read in part:

Housewives! You do not need a ballot to clean out your
sink spout. A handful of potash and some boiling water is
quicker and cheaper. . . . Control of the temper makes a
happier home than control of elections. . . . Good cooking
lessens alcoholic craving quicker than a vote on local option.
Why vote for pure food laws, when you can purify your
ice box with saleratus water?
To shine cut glass, rub it over with a freshly peeled potato
and then wash. . . .

of Woman Suffrage," *The Century*, XLVIII, new series XXVI (August,
1894); Holland, "The Suffragette," *Sewanee Review*, XVII (June,
1909); M'Intire, *Of No Benefit to Woman*; Root, *Address; Cong. Rec.*,
63d Cong., 2d Sess. (1914), p. 4145 (Sen. Martine of N.J.); 3d Sess.
(1915), Appendix, pp. 91-92 (Rep. Stephens of Tex.); Gibbons, "The
Restless Woman," *Ladies' Home Journal*, XIX (January, 1902), 6.
  [22] Massachusetts Anti-Suffrage Committee, *The Case against Woman
Suffrage*; Illinois Assoc., *To the Voters of the Middle West*; Bissell,
A Talk with Women; Cong. Rec., 64th Cong., 1st Sess. (1916), pp.
4987-88 (Statement of the District of Columbia Association Opposed
to Woman Suffrage, hereafter referred to as DCAOWS Statement); *Remonstrance* (1892), p. 2, and *ibid.* (July, 1919), p. 1.
  [23] C. W. Clark, "Woman Suffrage Pro and Con," *Atlantic Monthly*,
LV (March, 1890); *Copy of Preamble and Protest;* Dana, in Frothingham and others, *Woman Suffrage Unnatural and Inexpedient*.

Clean houses and good homes, which cannot be provided by legislation, keep children healthier and happier than any number of laws.[24]

The head of each family was its sole link to the outside world and its spokesman in the state. The family's leader within each home was the wife and mother. To endow that wife and mother with the franchise, therefore, would dissolve society into a heterogeneous mass of separate persons, whose individual rather than family interests would thenceforth receive political representation.[25] For this reason, the vote would not be merely a quantitative addition to all the other rights women had acquired in the preceding two generations. The franchise was not just another new right to add to higher education, equal guardianship of children, and ownership of one's own earnings in the march of women toward full equality with men. Suffrage meant a qualitative change in the social and familial role of women, antis believed, and the demand for it consequently met with more determined resistance than did women's struggles for other rights.

In working out the implications of the proper relation of the home to the state, the antis concluded that the welfare of society demanded that woman should restrict her "political" activity to training her sons to be good citizens and to inspiring and influencing man by being above politics rather than in it.[26] Members of Congress

[24] Published by Women's Anti-Suffrage Association of Massachusetts. A copy is in the Laidlaw Collection, RWA, Box 8. Contrast it with Jane Addams's theory as set forth in chap. III, pp. 68-71.

[25] See, for example, New York *Tribune*, May 4, 1901, semiannual report of the Illinois Association Opposed to the Extension of Suffrage to Women.

[26] John H. Vincent to Ida Husted Harper, January 4, 1898, Harper Collection, HL; *Cong. Rec.*, 63d Cong., 1st Sess. (1913), p. 3460) (Sen. Tillman of S.C.); Mrs. W. F. Scott, "Women's Relation to Govern-

often dwelt reverently on this theme. One such oratorical flight was taken by Rep. Clark of Florida in 1915:

> I do not wish to see the day come when the women of my race in my state shall trail their skirts in the muck and mire of partisan politics. I prefer to look to the American woman as she always has been, occupying her proud estate as the queen of the American home, instead of regarding her as a ward politician in the cities. As the mother, as the wife, as the sister she exercises a broader and deeper and mightier influence than she can ever exercise or hope to on the stump and in the byways of politics in this land. The American mother, the American woman, has my admiration, my respect, and my love—
>
> THE SPEAKER. The time of the Gentleman from Florida has expired.[27]

Suffragists were fond of noting publicly the inconsistency between man's prizing the suffrage so highly that its deprivation was considered a terrible punishment and man's ardent desire to save women from the political mire. Although this inconsistency existed, the men who wished to keep women away from dirty politics were frequently sincere idealists. Suffragists did not deny that politics was dirty; they expected to clean it up, at least

---

ment," *North American Review*, CXCI (April, 1910); Gilfillan, "The Disadvantages of Equal Suffrage," *Publications* of the Academy of Social Sciences, VIII (1915), 170-74; Frothingham, "Real Case of the 'Remonstrants'," *The Arena*, II (July, 1890), 176; Chittenden, "Woman Suffrage a Mistaken Theory of Progress," *The Woman's Protest*, I (September, 1912); "Women Who Want to Vote," New York *Times*, December 20, 1908 (Woman Suffrage Scrapbooks, NYPL); Illinois Assoc., *To the Voters of the Middle West*; Root, *Address; Cong. Rec.*, 63d Cong., 3d Sess. (1915), Appendix, p. 91 (Rep. Stephens of Texas); 2d Sess. (1914), p. 4145 (Sen. Martine of N.J.).

[27] *Cong. Rec.*, 63d Cong., 3d Sess. (1915), p. 1413. For many excellent examples of soaring prose and poetry in honor of the Queens of the Household, see *Revised Record of the Constitutional Convention of the State of New York*, 1894, *passim*.

partially. The idealists among the male antis wished to preserve women from this disagreeable task, hoping they could clean up politics without feminine help.

It was, therefore, wrong to say that woman did not have the right to vote; rather, she had the right *not* to vote.[28] The suffragists erred in complaining that antis classed woman with idiots, aliens, and criminals; *they* were deprived of the privilege of the franchise; *she* was exempt from the burden of it.[29] She was exempt so that she could devote her mind and her energies to those vocations which most benefited society: in the home, bringing up her many children; outside the home, philanthropy. So many antisuffragist writers included the latter activity in the enumeration of woman's duties that it must be considered an essential element in their picture of the ideal woman and family. One tract speaks of "women who have their hands full and more than full of home and social and philanthropic duties." [30] Another asks sympathy for those engaged in "the charitable work, that now so fills the lives of good women that they are often overburdened, and break down beneath the strain." [31] A group of New Hampshire women, claiming

[28] Jamison, "The Wrong of Suffrage," *American Woman's Journal,* May 4, 1894, reprinted as a pamphlet (n.p., n.d.).

[29] *Ibid.;* Buckley, "The Wrongs and Perils of Woman Suffrage," *The Century,* XLVIII, new series XXVI (August, 1894); Frothingham, "Real Case of the 'Remonstrants'," *The Arena,* II (July, 1890), 176, 177; *Copy of Preamble and Protest;* "Rev. O. B. Frothingham's Argument," in Frothingham and others, *Woman Suffrage Unnatural and Inexpedient,* p. 6; Carpenter, "The Disadvantages of Equal Suffrage," *Publications* of the Minnesota Academy of Social Sciences, VIII (1915), 186-98.

[30] Illinois Assoc., *To the Voters of the Middle West.*

[31] Crannell, *Address* before the Committee on Resolutions of the Democratic National Convention, at Chicago, July 8, 1896; reprinted as a pamphlet by Mrs. Crannell's organization.

to represent "women of every station in life," stated that "with the demands of society, the calls of charity, the church, and philanthropy constantly increasing, we feel that to add the distracting forces of political campaigns would wreck our constitutions and destroy our homes." [32]

What was the nature of that society from which the antis were so concerned to isolate the home and mother? Outside the sheltered calm of the home they saw a society racked by social unrest that convinced them that force was still, in their America, the ultimate basis of government. Peace was insured, they felt, only because the out-voted minority knew that an appeal to arms could not succeed. If women were to vote, the thesis continued, half the electorate would be incapable of enforcing its mandate and vicious elements would be encouraged to resort to violence. A vote was not simply the registering of an opinion; it was a demand and consequently would be meaningless unless exercised only by the mus-cular portion of the community. A Columbia University professor of jurisprudence assured his fellow antis that history was on their side. He stated that " 'the consent of the governed' has meant, historically, the consent of those who were actually or potentially fighting units." He noted that throughout European history the propor-tion of the population which could vote had grown or diminished with the right or duty of fighting, and he concluded that "such matters should be left to the adult

[32] "Memorial" from 205 women of Newport, New Hampshire, in-serted by Rep. Gallinger in *Cong. Rec.*, 63d Cong., 1st Sess. (1913), p. 6011. See also L. Abbott, "Why Women Do Not Wish the Suffrage," *Atlantic Monthly*, XCII (September, 1903), 295; *Why Should Suffrage Be Imposed on Women?*; Bissell, *A Talk with Women on the Suffrage Question.*

males."[33] This argument was sometimes linked with the theory of inherent feminine mental traits: since the minds of women worked differently from men's, it was not inconceivable that the majority of women and a few men should vote for a declaration of war, and in that case the minority (the men) would be sent to fight against their will. Anarchy, naturally, would promptly ensue.[34]

If the electorate, in effect, constituted a militia on inactive duty, there must have been a potential internal enemy. This enemy is omnipresent in antisuffragist literature. To the Southern antis it was the Negro.[35] To North-

[33] M. Smith, "The Consent of the Governed," *Proceedings* of the Academy of Political Science, V (1914), 82-88. See also Parkman, *Some of the Reasons against Woman Suffrage*; L. Abbott, "Why the Vote Would Be Injurious to Women"; Jamison, "The Wrong of Suffrage," *American Woman's Journal*; Man-Suffrage Assoc., *The Case against Woman Suffrage*, pp. 31-34; Fred A. Ewald, "Some Reasons for Opposition to Woman Suffrage," *The Woman's Protest*, I (September, 1912), 8-9; DCAOWS Statement, p. 4987; Frothingham, in *Woman Suffrage Unnatural and Inexpedient*; M'Intire, *Of No Benefit to Woman*; Dodge, "Woman Suffrage Opposed to Woman's Rights," *Annals* of the American Academy of Political and Social Science, LVI (November, 1914), 99; Frothingham, "Real Case of the 'Remonstrants'," *The Arena*, II (July, 1890), 177; Johnson, *Woman and the Republic*, chaps. II, III, X; "The Anti-Suffragists," New York *Sun*, July 2, 1899, reprinting a letter from antisuffragist associations to the International Congress of Women meeting in London.

[34] G. Smith, *Woman Suffrage*. See also L. Abbott, "Why Women Do Not Wish the Suffrage," *Atlantic Monthly*, XCII (September, 1903), 293; Ewald, "Some Reasons for Opposition to Woman Suffrage," *The Woman's Protest*, I (September, 1912), 8-9.

[35] A Southern representative inserted an article from the Macon *Daily Telegraph* in *Cong. Rec.*, 63d Cong., 3d Sess. (1915), pp. 1427-28. After warning that a woman suffrage amendment would revivify the Fifteenth Amendment and thus bring about male as well as female Negro suffrage in the South, the editorialist intoned: "There will be political night meetings of negro men and negro women. . . . Southern Congressmen know, and should protect our women on the farms, without police protection, from the return of those days when the farmer's wife sat in her home with fear and trembling—her vine and fig tree being but the crouching place of the brute ready to pounce upon her and take advantage of her helplessness. . . . These flippant city girls, singing airily, 'Votes for women,' know not the disasters they invite

easterners it was Democratic machines, the immigrant, and the Negro. To the Western remonstrants it was prostitutes, frontier riff-raff, and political machines. Unanimously the pamphleteers pointed out that the poor, ignorant, and immoral elements in society (equating the three) already outnumbered the patrician, intelligent, and impeccably proper. Doubling the electorate would increase the preponderance of the "undesirable" voters. Typical of the dire warnings that filled antisuffragist literature is one which appeared in the periodical *Remonstrance*:

It is the influx of foreign ignorance *en masse* that threatens our country hourly. . . . There are millions of men in the world for whom despotism is a necessity, and it is this class who immigrate to us every day, who are undermining our institutions and shaking the very pillars whereon the house standeth, like their vengeful prototype. If Woman Suffrage is to be allowed, we double not only the numerical force of this threatening majority, but its moral—or immoral—influence.[36]

___

by this reckless movement." See also remarks by Rep. Dies and other Southern Members, on pp. 1430, 1448, 1464-65, 1479-80, and Appendix, pp. 91-92; also, DCAOWS Statement, p. 4985. It must not be inferred that the antis alone used racist arguments. One technique of the suffragists was to print a picture of a brutish-appearing Negro porter next to a photo of a refined-looking white lady, over a caption which might say, "*He* can vote; why can't I?" The antis usually answered that query, in effect: Certainly you are more qualified than he, but if you are given the franchise, so is his wife, and their class by far outnumbers the class of "intelligent" women. For other racist arguments used by the suffragists, see chap. VII.

[36] Rose Terry Cooke, "Average Women," *Remonstrance* (1892), p. 1. There are many passages in suffragist literature that equal or surpass this in contempt for the immigrants. Many suffragists reacted to the new immigration either by pointing out that white, Anglo-Saxon, native-born women outnumbered men and women of other groups, so that woman suffrage would increase the proportion of fit voters; or by advocating an educational qualification for the vote, which would dis-

The evil to be feared from this threatening majority was quite specific. One anti warned her fellow Bostonians, "If the great mass of ignorant women's votes are added to the great mass of ignorant men's votes, there will be constant demands for work, money, bread, leisure, in short, 'all kinds of laws to favor all kinds of persons.'" [37] Evidently the antis' benevolent feelings toward the beneficiaries of their philanthropy were tempered by fear lest their wards render the philanthropy unnecessary. Some antis even professed to fear that suffragists would do away with the philanthropists themselves. Mrs. Caroline Fairfield Corbin, leading Illinois anti, for instance, constantly identified woman suffrage with socialism, and other antis

---

franchise both men and women of unfit sections of the population. See chap. VI.

[37] M'Intire, *Of No Benefit to Woman*. Another typical passage is the following: "We have suffered many things at the hands of Patrick; the New Woman would add Bridget also. And—graver danger—to the vote of that fierce, silly, amiable creature, the uneducated Negro, she would add (if logical) the vote of his sillier, baser female." (Deland, "The Change in the Feminine Ideal," *Atlantic Monthly*, CV [March, 1910], 299.) For other expressions of fear of enfranchising ignorant women, and for many passages in which poor, ignorant, and immoral are equated, see Wheeler, *Home Rule*; "Woman Suffrage," *Harper's Weekly* (June 16, 1894), p. 554; Wells, *An Argument against Woman Suffrage*; Sherwood, in New York *Herald*, May 6, 1894; *Copy of Preamble and Protest*; Illinois Assoc., *To the Voters of the Middle West*; Bissell, *A Talk with Women on the Suffrage Question*; Gilfillan, "The Disadvantages of Equal Suffrage," *Publications* of the Minnesota Academy of Social Sciences, VIII (1915), 176; Carpenter, "The Disadvantages of Equal Suffrage," *Publications* of the Minnesota Academy of Social Sciences, VIII (1915), 186-87; *Remonstrance* (July, 1919), p. 1; Cuyler, *Shall Women Be Burdened with the Ballot?*; C. W. Clark, "Woman Suffrage Pro and Con," *Atlantic Monthly*, LV (March, 1890); Parkman, *Some of the Reasons against Woman Suffrage*; Man-Suffrage Assoc., *The Case against Woman Suffrage*, pp. 53-54; Massachusetts Anti-Suffrage Committee, *The Case against Woman Suffrage*, pp. 6-7; Prof. William W. Goodwin of Harvard, letter in Frothingham and others, *Woman Suffrage Unnatural and Inexpedient*, pp. 14-15; Buckley, "The Wrongs and Perils of Woman Suffrage," *The Century*, XLVIII, new series XXVI (August, 1894), 619.

exultantly publicized evidence that Socialists favored
woman suffrage.[38]

The preceding arguments suggested that instead of
broadening the suffrage, legislatures ought to restrict it
by imposing educational and property requirements. Proposals strikingly reminiscent of the old "stake-in-society"
theory actually appear in anti literature as well as in the
writings of those suffragists who believed that nonwhites
and the foreign born were unfit to vote. Although such
suffragists sometimes advocated suffrage for taxpaying
women alone, for "taxation without representation is
tyranny," their antisuffragist counterparts opposed suffrage for all women in order to bar from the electorate
as many as possible of those citizens who did not contribute by money or muscle to the support of the state.
What divided the suffragists from the antis on this subject was the suffragists' recommendation for dealing with
the threat of undesirables at the polls, not their attitude
toward the undesirables. Suffragists insisted that the enfranchisement of women would insure the preponderance
of fit voters; the antis contended that woman suffrage
would virtually hand the reins of government over to the
unfit.

The antis' unanimous contempt for the unwashed multitude also found expression in their repudiation of the

[38] C. F. Corbin, "The Reasons for Remonstrance," *Remonstrance*
(1892), p. 2; leaflet published in 1915 in New York, a copy of which
is in the Laidlaw Scrapbooks, NYHS; *Woman Suffrage*. Hearing before
the Committee on the Judiciary, House of Representatives, Sixty-Second
Congress, Second Session, March 13, 1912, pp. 85-92; *Extending the
Right of Suffrage to Women*. Hearings before the Committee on Woman
Suffrage, House of Representatives, Sixty-Fifth Congress, Second Session,
on H. J. Res. 200, January 3, 4, 5, and 7, 1918, pp. 97-140, including
charts prepared by a statistician, purporting to prove that the New
York State suffrage victory of 1917 was due to the Socialist vote.

natural right theory which suffragists invoked to justify their demand. No, said the antis, the question is not one of principle but of expediency. "Society" bestows the franchise on that section of the population which can best exercise it in the interest of all. The question of whether women should vote is not "to be settled by the citation of any such aphorism as that which bases the powers of government on the consent of the governed."[39]

Suppose that the populations of Turkey, the Soudan, or Zulu-land were to attempt to . . . govern themselves by universal popular suffrage. The consequences would be anarchy, and a quick return to despotism as a relief. . . . The air-blown theory of inalienable right is unworthy the good sense of the American people.[40]

The theory that only those who could fight should vote implies that when the antis spoke of *society* they meant only that section of it which had the power to enforce its decisions. There could be no natural right appeal from

[39] M. Smith, "The Consent of the Governed," *Proceedings* of the Academy of Political Science, V (1914), 82. See also Dana, in Frothingham and others, *Woman Suffrage Unnatural and Inexpedient*; Man-Suffrage Assoc., *The Case against Woman Suffrage*, pp. 31-32; Carpenter, "The Disadvantages of Equal Suffrage," *Publications* of the Minnesota Academy of Social Sciences, VIII (1915); "Women Who Want to Vote," New York *Times*, December 20, 1908; M'Intire, *Of No Benefit to Woman*; Root, *Address*; Mrs. W. F. Scott, "Woman's Relation to Government," *North American Review*, CXCI (April, 1910); Doane, "Why Women Do Not Want the Ballot," *North American Review*, CLXI (September, 1895), 260; Holland, "The Suffragette," *Sewanee Review*, XVII (July, 1909), 272.

[40] Parkman, *Some of the Reasons against Woman Suffrage*. It should be remembered that the last thirty years of the suffrage agitation were contemporaneous with the debate over imperialism and the new immigration. Many suffragists repudiated their own natural right argument for the ballot at this time. After the turn of the century they stressed the expediency argument for suffrage, but their interpretation of what was expedient differed from that of the antis. See chap. III, pp. 52-56.

the bullet-backed ballots of any electorate which legally existed even if that electorate was only a small part of the population. The logic that would disfranchise women because they lacked the strength to enforce their mandate would also justify disfranchisement of any portion of the population unable to prevail by brute force over the rest. In short, only those who possessed the *might* to secure the vote had the *right* to vote. Logical analysis, however, only elucidates the implications of the antis' views; it does not explain the source of those views. In antisuffragist social philosophy, the disfranchisement of women was necessary to the governmental stability that depended upon the exclusion of "unfit" men.

Those who could not be convinced that extension of the suffrage was dangerous might be persuaded that the vote was not worth fighting for. Antis repeatedly insisted that the suffragists overestimated what the vote could accomplish. The suffrage could not help the working girl get higher wages and better working conditions, for instance, because if it could, male workers would long before have used it for that purpose. Wages and conditions were determined by the inexorable laws of supply and demand. Any legislated improvement would bring an influx of new workers into the affected industry, and the resulting competition would soon cause a reversion to the old conditions.[41] Some writers advised working-

[41] Doane, "Why Women Do Not Want the Ballot," *North American Review*, CLXI (September, 1895); Mrs. W. F. Scott, "Woman's Relation to Government," *North American Review*, CXCI (April, 1910); DCAOWS Statement, p. 4986; Gilfillan, "The Disadvantages of Equal Suffrage," *Publications* of the Minnesota Academy of Social Sciences, VIII (1915), 179; Man-Suffrage Assoc., *The Case against Woman Suffrage*; Chittenden, "Woman Suffrage a Mistaken Theory of Progress," *The Woman's Protest*, I (September, 1912), 7-8; Jamison, "The Wrong

women to shift their attention, rather, to trade unions as a means for economic betterment.[42] None of them chose to explain why unions could affect the laws of economics when legislatures were powerless to do so. Neither did they explain the contradiction between this argument addressed to workers and the argument addressed to their own class, to the effect that workingwomen would use their votes to join with workingmen to demand "work, money, bread, and leisure." The legislation which workers were told would be useless was precisely what the patricians were told would be a danger to be feared from a doubling of the working-class electorate.

The antis minimized the value of the vote also by explaining that elections did not create public policy, but simply registered decisions already formed by the evolution of public opinion.[43] Evidence of this was that laws which disregarded public opinion became dead letters. Hence, woman's influence on public affairs suffered no diminution from her inability to vote, since her status as mother, wife, sister, and inspirer assigned her an influential role in the creation of the consensus, which her men then registered at the polls. Thus the reformers' chronic overvaluation of the formal processes of democracy here evoked an expression of the conservatives' un-

---

of Suffrage," *American Woman's Journal* (May, 1894); Crannell, *Address*; L. Abbott, "Why the Vote Would Be Injurious to Women," *Ladies' Home Journal*, XXVII (February, 1910).

[42] M'Intire, *Of No Benefit to Woman*; Jones, "The Position of the Anti-Suffragists," Supplement to the *Annals* of the American Academy of Political and Social Science, XXXV (May, 1910), 16-22.

[43] Mrs. W. F. Scott, "Woman's Relation to Government," *North American Review*, CXCI (April, 1910); Gilfillan, "The Disadvantages of Equal Suffrage," *Publications* of the Minnesota Academy of Social Sciences, VIII (1915).

dervaluation of them.[44] If any skeptic had inquired how the conception of the ballot-as-registrar-of-public-opinion gibed with the theory of the ballot-as-expression-of-potential-force, he might have been met with the argument of woman's irrationality. Perhaps women voters could not be trusted to vote consistently with public opinion as already evolved, whereas men could be relied upon to vote conservatively; such a view would be consistent with the fears of antis such as Frothingham that women voters would legislate sweeping reforms. In reality, however, this contradiction between the two antisuffragist definitions of the ballot probably remained undetected, for like suffragism, antisuffragism was not a systematic ideology; it dealt with opposition arguments as they arose, without much regard for consistency.

Antisuffragist women who subscribed to this picture of society provided antisuffragist propaganda with the additional argument that "women do not want to vote." The suffragists, declared the antis, were a small minority of women, and humanity was fortunate that they were, for if they were to achieve their goal, women would become large-handed, big-footed, flat-chested, and thin-lipped.[45] The qualities of emotionalism and sensitivity

[44] Cf. Hofstadter, *Age of Reform*, p. 263. Writing of the differences between direct-government reformers and ultraconservatives, Hofstadter says: "The conservatives moaned and admonished as though each new reform proposal portended the end of the nation, while many Progressives seemed to imagine and often, indeed, said that these reforms, once achieved, would open the way to a complete and permanent victory over the machines and corruption." Although this tendency toward extremes did characterize the suffrage debate, the one exception noted (the antis' single argument directed at workers) is significant. The suffragists' overvaluation of the power of the vote is noted in chap. III.

[45] Holland, "The Suffragette," *Sewanee Review*, XVII (July, 1909), 275.

which disqualified most women for the political life became, when thrown into the political arena, the unlovely traits of the shrew.[46] History proved that when women participated in government, their nations suffered: consider Cleopatra, Marie Antoinette, and Catherine de Médicis. Even Queen Elizabeth I's reputation was beginning to crumble under the weight of new historical discoveries.[47] The *womanly* woman who knew her true vocation did not want to vote. She would not insult her men by implying that they had failed to protect her interests.[48] She insisted that the American colonists' arguments against the theory of virtual representation were misapplied to this question, for woman was not a class apart but a part of every class.[49] Since she was adequately represented by her menfolk, why should two do what one could do at least as well? The colonists' argument against "taxation without representation" was like-

[46] Root, *Address*; DCAOWS Statement, p. 4988; *Cong. Rec.*, 63d Cong., 3d Sess. (1915), p. 1414 (Rep. Clark of Fla.). Sen. Martine of N.J., *Cong. Rec.*, 63d Cong., 2d Sess. (1914), p. 4145, said, "I want woman as my mother was. I would rather have the mild, tender voice of my mother bidding me, as my father did, to vote whenever the Commonwealth gave me the privilege to vote linger in my ears than to hear the high, shrieking voice of woman around the polls dragging her sisters to the ballot box."

[47] Walsh, *Protest against Woman Suffrage*; G. Smith, *Woman Suffrage*; Holland, "The Suffragette," *Sewanee Review*, XVII (July, 1909). The inventory of female tyrants varied somewhat from writer to writer. Occasionally an anti would list a few woman sovereigns who had ruled well, and in each case he would discover a wise male adviser behind the throne.

[48] Massachusetts Anti-Suffrage Committee, *The Case against Woman Suffrage*.

[49] Carpenter, "The Disadvantages of Equal Suffrage," *Publications* of the Minnesota Academy of Social Sciences, VIII (1915); Mrs. W. F. Scott, "Woman's Relation to Government," *North American Review*, CXCI (April, 1910); DCAOWS Statement, p. 4987; G. Smith, *Woman Suffrage*; Dana, in Frothingham and others, *Woman Suffrage Unnatural and Inexpedient*.

wise irrelevant, since minors, corporations, and aliens paid taxes, but did not vote. Moreover, for every tax-paying woman who would vote, there would be many nontaxpaying women whose votes would more than cancel hers.[50] For all these reasons, contended the antis, the majority of women did not want the ballot; to force it upon them would be undemocratic.[51]

A different sort of appeal to democracy was made by those antis who argued, in the last few years before ratification of the Nineteenth Amendment, that it would be undemocratic for 36 states to force a woman suffrage amendment on 12 states, some of which had by referenda rejected similar amendments to their own constitutions. Suffragists frequently expressed pleasure upon hearing this argument, for two reasons. First, they believed that the states' rights argument was the last refuge of an anti who had exhausted all his reasons for opposing woman suffrage and was reduced to opposition to the amendment. Second, suffragists felt that the states' rights argument was the easiest to demolish, especially after the Southern congressmen who cited it most frequently became the most consistent supporters of the prohibition

[50] Massachusetts Anti-Suffrage Committee, *The Case Against Woman Suffrage*; Doane, "Why Women Do Not Want the Ballot," *North American Review*, CLXI (September, 1895); Jones, "The Position of the Anti-Suffragists," Supplement to the *Annals* of the American Academy of Political and Social Science, XXXV (May, 1910); Man-Suffrage Assoc., *The Case against Woman Suffrage*; M'Intire, *Of No Benefit to Woman*; C. W. Clark, "Woman Suffrage Pro and Con," *Atlantic Monthly*, LV (March, 1890).

[51] DCAOWS Statement. It should be remembered that the antis considered that their own class of women, when they *could* vote, *must* vote, to counteract, as far as possible, the votes of the poor and vicious. That is why they could speak of the suffrage as being forced on themselves.

amendment.[52] However, some antis contended that there was a principled difference between the Eighteenth and the Nineteenth amendments, the former inserting an expression of the public will into the fundamental law, and the latter changing the very basis of that public will.[53]

When the antis spoke of the majority of women who did not want the suffrage, they meant the majority of middle-class, white, native-born women. That is the only interpretation which reconciles their appeal to majority will with their demand that immigrant, poor, and Negro women be prevented from voting.[54] They were saying, in effect, that the majority of that class of women who alone could use the suffrage wisely did not want it, not

[52] There was, however, a brief period in which the states' rights objection troubled suffragists enough to induce the NAWSA to drop the traditional Susan B. Anthony amendment and advocate instead a substitute amendment designed to meet the states' rights objections. This episode, which lasted only a year, is discussed in chap. VII.

[53] For instances of the states' rights argument, see *Annual Message of Richard I. Manning, Governor,* to the General Assembly of South Carolina at the Regular Session, beginning January 8, 1918, p. 12; *Remonstrance* (July, 1919), p. 1; *Cong. Rec.,* 63d Cong., 2d Sess. (1914), p. 4148 (Sen. Borah of Idaho); 3d Sess. (1915), p. 1421 (Rep. Webb of N.C.); other congressmen on pp. 1444-45, 1448, 1449-53, 1464-65, Appendix, pp. 91-92, 163. Sen. Borah favored woman suffrage but opposed the national amendment.

[54] Cf. Wells, *An Argument against Woman Suffrage:* "I had occasion one winter to be connected with some work at the North End. The women were too careless and wretched in their lives and in their dress to be here described. They talked with each other in little groups; many a one spoke of the time when she could vote, as the only vengeance left her to exercise upon the wealthy classes." Mrs. Wells went on to explain that these women would vote themselves higher pay, and that their men would also vote for woman suffrage so that the women would be able to put through the eight-hour law. It is interesting to note that men and women such as those described by Mrs. Wells frequently were mentioned in suffragist literature as constituting a solid bloc against woman suffrage. Could it be that each side in an intra-middle-class dispute was attributing "unsavory" allies to its adversaries?

only because their time was already fully occupied with home and charity but also because it was unfortunately no longer possible to give *them* the vote and deny it to the others.[55] Further, the woman whose time was taken up by home and philanthropy was obviously not the beneficiary of that philanthropy. The woman who was too weak to survive the emotional and physical stresses of political campaigns could not be the woman who had to stand ten hours a day before a machine-loom. The woman who shrank from entering a polling-place filled with inelegant workers was certainly not the wife of one of them. The frequency with which *ignorant* and *poor* and *immoral* were used as equivalent terms shows that the combination fitted easily into the thinking of anti-suffragist propagandists and formed an integral part of their ideology.[56] The fact that most suffragists in this

[55] Note that the argument that women with charitable work to do had no time for political activity raises the question of how much time for political activity male workers had after a ten-hour day in factories. Suffragists who sympathized with workingwomen's need for the vote inferred that the antis who used this argument were really being consistent, inasmuch as they allegedly favored the disfranchisement of the entire working class although they could not say so publicly.

[56] This entire complex of ideas should be thought of against the background of various events and thought currents in the United States in the period 1890 to 1920. See Higham, *Strangers in the Land*, chaps. IV-VII, and Hofstadter, *Social Darwinism in American Thought*, chaps. V-IX, for discussions of Social Darwinism, eugenics, pragmatism, imperialism, and reactions to immigrants, all of which gave additional meaning to the antisuffragist arguments. Higham subtitles one of his sections "Patricians on the Defensive," a phrase which is a peculiarly appropriate designation for the antisuffragist movement. (The antisuffragist sentiment among immigrant groups reflecting a conservative attitude toward woman's place, and the ulterior motives of brewing interests or other businessmen are outside the scope of a study of the ideas of those organized antis who propagandized against suffrage.) Goldman, *Rendezvous with Destiny*, p. 66, writes, in regard to this period's conservatism in general, "The ideas, of course, were no deliberate contrivance on the part of evil men. The dominant groups in

period belonged to the middle class and made the same identification of poverty with vice does not deprive this central aspect of antisuffragist thinking of its significance. On the contrary, the suffragists argued most fervently that woman suffrage was the solution to the problems that suffragists and antis alike believed were created by the enfranchisement of Negroes and immigrants.

To understand the debate between suffragists and antis it is necessary to avoid two errors, each of which may be made by focusing attention on one part of a wide-ranging assortment of arguments. The debate was not merely a disguised form of a political struggle between liberals and conservatives who devised arguments on the question of woman's enfranchisement that suited their primary purposes; nor was the debate a superficial bout between women who wanted to vote and women who did not want to vote, with each group attempting to justify its position by appeals to the welfare of society and the home. Instead, the public polemics on woman suffrage manifested profound and often unconscious differences in social philosophy and the nature of woman. Few suffragists were radicals; the vast majority of them simply wanted the right to participate more fully in the affairs of a government, the basic structure of which they accepted. Within the broad area of agreement between them and the antis, there was room for widely differing

---

America had simply done what dominant groups usually do. They had, quite unconsciously, picked from among available theories the ones that best protected their position and had impressed those ideas on the national mind as Truth." This observation applies also to those members of the dominant groups who propagandized against woman suffrage. Chapter VI describes how suffragists also equated *ignorant, poor,* and *immoral*; how that equation was also of utmost importance in their thinking; but how they drew different conclusions.

conceptions of the role of women in public life. The rise of the suffrage movement challenged the antis to formulate the traditional assumptions of woman's place, and these formulations in turn defined the context of ideas within which the suffragists must plead their case.[57]

[57] Many essays evoked by particular antisuffragist arguments may be found among the immense number of suffragist speeches and writings. Many of the articles cited in the foregoing pages were specifically discussed by Alice Stone Blackwell in the *Woman's Journal.* Her replies may be found by noting the dates of publication of the antisuffragist articles and then turning to the issues of the *Woman's Journal* of the next two or three weeks.

THREE

The Two Major Types of Suffragist Argument

From the early days of the woman's rights movement to 1920 when the Nineteenth Amendment was ratified, American society underwent drastic changes that were reflected in the thinking of the movement. In the middle of the nineteenth century the United States, with the exception of the slave South, was a nation of relative class fluidity, a nation in which men believed themselves equal, if not in fortune, certainly in natural right. The task of the pioneers of women's rights was to prove that this equality applied to women too. A half century later the nation was attempting to understand the implications of the growth of trusts, the influx of immigrants from unfamiliar cultures, the acquisition of colonies populated by "inferior" races, the class strife of the 1890s, and the sharpening demarcation between city and country. The equality of all men was no longer taken for granted, and those to whom it remained a fundamental principle began to see it not as a statement of present fact but as an ideal to be realized in the future. The meaning of the claim that all women were created equal to men altered accordingly.

In the earlier period suffragists had based their demand for political equality with men on the same ground as that on which their men had based their demand for political equality with their English rulers two generations before. If all men were created equal and had the inalienable right to consent to the laws by which they were governed, women were created equal to men and had the same inalienable right to political liberty. In asserting that natural right applied also to women, the suffragists stressed the ways in which men and women were identical. Their common humanity was the core of the suffragist argument. By the end of the century, however, many men of the older American stock were questioning the validity of the principle of "the consent of the governed" as it applied to the new immigrants, the populations of the islands acquired by the United States in 1898, and the workers in the cities. The suffragists, belonging to the same native-born, white, Anglo-Saxon, Protestant, middle class as the men who were rethinking the meaning of natural right, also began to put less emphasis on the common humanity of men and women. At the time when the men of their group were taking new cognizance of the ways in which men differed from each other, new arguments for suffrage evolved, emphasizing the ways in which women differed from men. If the justice of the claim to political equality could no longer suffice, then the women's task was to show that expediency required it.[1] The claim of women to the vote

[1] The terms *justice* and *expediency* are used in this chapter as shorthand expressions to designate the two major categories of arguments for woman suffrage. The first includes arguments based on the principle of the "consent of the governed," the natural equality of all human beings, and other ways of setting forth the belief that women ought

as a natural right never disappeared from the suffragist rationale, but the meaning of natural right changed in response to the new realities, and new arguments enumerating the reforms that women voters could effect took their places alongside the natural right principle that had been the staple plea of the suffragists in the early days of the movement. In 1894 Mrs. Stanton wrote a pamphlet entitled *Suffrage a Natural Right*;[2] in 1918 Mrs. Catt said that she did not know what it was, a right, a duty, or a privilege, but that "whatever it is, the women want it."[3] Mrs. Catt's remark illustrates in two ways the change from justice to expediency. First, she was recognizing the validity of claims to the vote other than natural right and justice. Second, the fact that she could ask for the vote on whatever grounds might bring the most favorable response was itself an indication of the triumph of expediency. This double meaning of the expediency argument appeared time and again. Some suffragists used the expediency argument because social reform was their principal goal and suffrage the means. Other suffragists used the same expediency argument because the link of woman suffrage to reform seemed to be the best way to secure support for their principal

---

to have political equality because justice required it. Under the term *expediency* are subsumed arguments that claim that woman suffrage would benefit society. The term *expediency* was used in this manner by Putnam-Jacobi in *"Common Sense" Applied to Woman Suffrage*, pp. 60 and 219. The fact that all the arguments could be placed under these two headings was occasionally recognized by the suffragists, especially during the period when *expediency* was supplanting *justice* as the principal sanction for suffrage, although they sometimes employed different terms to describe the two types of arguments.

[2] The manuscript of this essay may be found in the Elizabeth Boynton Harbert Papers, RWA.

[3] House *Hearings*, 1918, p. 50. According to the reporter, Mrs. Catt's remark was followed by "laughter and applause."

goal: the vote. To these women the expediency argument was itself an expedient. The difference between Mrs. Stanton's and Mrs. Catt's standpoints was the difference between not only two generations of suffragist spokesmen but also two periods of American history.

On January 18, 1892, Mrs. Stanton's address, "The Solitude of Self," was read for her at a congressional committee hearing.[4] This paper may be considered the epitome of the natural right argument for woman suffrage in the form it took at the start of our thirty-year period.

The point I wish plainly to bring before you on this occasion [wrote the elder statesman of the movement] is the individuality of each human soul; our Protestant idea, the right of individual conscience and judgment; our republican idea, individual citizenship. In discussing the rights of woman, we are to consider, first, what belongs to her as an individual, in a world of her own, the arbiter of her own destiny, an imaginary Robinson Crusoe, with her woman Friday on a solitary island. Her rights under such circumstances are to use all her faculties for her own safety and happiness.

Secondly, if we consider her as a citizen, as a member of a great nation, she must have the same rights as all other members, according to the fundamental principles of our government.

Thirdly, viewed as a woman, an equal factor in civilization,

---

[4] The paper was reprinted in *Woman's Journal*, January 23, 1892. It may also be found, though with minor differences in wording and punctuation, in *Hearings* of the Woman Suffrage Association before the Committee on the Judiciary, Monday, January 18, 1892 (House of Representatives), pp. 1-5. See also Anthony and Harper, eds., *History of Woman Suffrage*, IV, 189-91, and San Francisco *Examiner*, September 6, 1896. Susan B. Anthony wrote of this essay: "It is the speech of Mrs Stanton['s] life— I think—" (Susan B. Anthony to Elizabeth Boynton Harbert, August 12, 1901, Harbert Papers, RWA).

her rights and duties are still the same; individual happiness and development.

Fourthly, it is only the incidental relations of life, such as mother, wife, sister, daughter, that may involve some special duties and training. . . .

Mrs. Stanton then explained why she listed the roles of woman in this order. Before a woman was a citizen or woman or wife, she was a human being, the possessor of a unique soul. The solitude and personal responsibility of her own individual life demanded she be given the fullest opportunity to develop her faculties, to escape the bondage of superstition and custom, to exercise the fullest freedom of thought and action. Inasmuch as each human being comes into the world alone and leaves the world alone and under circumstances peculiar to himself, every individual is unique. The solitary responsibility each individual bears for his own destiny demands that he have the training to cope with whatever life brings him.

To throw obstacles in the way of a complete education is like putting out the eyes; to deny the rights of property, like cutting off the hands. To deny political equality is to rob the ostracized of a self-respect; of credit in the market place; of recompense in the world of work; of a voice in [the choice of] those who make and administer the law; a choice in the jury before whom they are tried, and in the judge who decides their punishment.

The responsibilities of life, Mrs. Stanton declared, rest equally on men and women. It would be a mockery to talk of sheltering woman from the fierce storms of life, for they beat upon her from every point of the compass and with more fatal results, for man has been educated to protect himself, to resist, and to conquer. Who, she

asked, dared take on himself the rights, the duties, or
the responsibilities of another human soul?

Here is the classic natural right theory on the verge
of change. At the core of the argument is the Robinson
Crusoe of the early bourgeoisie escaping from the feudal
class relations that confine his energies, a solitary human
soul in the Protestant tradition responsible for its own
destiny. But unlike the eighteenth-century Robinson
Crusoe, the female Robinson Crusoe of the nineteenth
century could not create her own destiny. Equal in natural right, she was unequal in condition. Her equality
was in the future, not something given but rather a
potentiality to be developed. Mrs. Stanton was demanding for woman not the right to manifest her equality
but the right to become equal. For this she needed education and the vote. Hence the claim to equality for
women could not rest upon an abstract assertion of
equality; it required concrete demands for specific social
and political rights.

Yet the claim for rights had first to be established on
the foundation of right. Here is seen the significance of
the order in which Mrs. Stanton enumerated the attributes of woman: first, she was an individual, identical
in that respect with a man; second, she was a citizen,
identical in that respect also with man; third, she was
feminine, different from man but still equal in contribution to civilization and in her duty of self-development;
and, fourth and last only, was she a mother, wife, sister,
or daughter, roles which no man could play. The fourth
category Mrs. Stanton, mother of seven children, disposed of quickly not because she slighted its importance,
but because she did not consider it a fundamental basis

for the claim to equality. If the principles of the Declaration of Independence applied to men, they must also apply to women in those respects in which women were the same as men. It was peculiarly appropriate that the suffragists found their sanction in the Declaration of Independence, that eighteenth-century formulation of natural right by which American Robinson Crusoes had asserted their title to their own new world. Their women descendants now insisted that the charter by which they claimed their inalienable right to do so applied to them too.[5] Although they sometimes admitted that the men who wrote "all men are created equal" were not thinking of women,[6] they declared that the principle of "the con-

[5] A few of the numerous instances in which suffragists cited the Declaration of Independence by name or principles such as that of the consent of the governed or that taxation and representation ought to be linked are: Lucy Stone on p. 5 of the 1892 hearing cited in footnote 4; Blackwell in *Woman's Journal*, May 6, 1893; Anthony in San Francisco *Examiner*, July 5, 1896; *Proceedings* of the Twenty-Eighth Annual Convention of the National American Woman Suffrage Association held in Washington, D.C., January 23 to 28, 1896 (Philadelphia, n.d.), p. 90, quoting first resolution passed by the convention; *Proceedings* of the Thirty-First Annual Convention of the National American Woman Suffrage Association at . . . Grand Rapids, Mich., April 27-30 and May 1-3, 1899 (Warren, Ohio, n.d.), p. 56, quoting first resolution; *Proceedings* of the Thirty-Fourth Annual Convention of the National American Woman Suffrage Association held at Washington, D.C., February 14-18, 1902 (Warren, Ohio, n.d.), p. 2, quoting Call to the convention, signed by all the national officers; Corr. Sec'y Kate M. Gordon, on p. 14 of *Proceedings* of the Thirty-Fifth Annual Convention of the National American Woman Suffrage Association, held at New Orleans, La., March 15 to 25, inclusive, 1903 (Warren, Ohio, n.d.); Laura Clay, *ibid.*, p. 41; "Declaration of Principles" prepared by Mrs. Catt, Miss Shaw, Miss Blackwell, and Mrs. Harper, and adopted by the NAWSA, in *Proceedings* of the Thirty-Sixth Annual Convention of the National American Woman Suffrage Association, held at Washington, D.C., February 11 to 17, inclusive, 1904 (Warren, Ohio, n.d.), p. 19.

[6] At the House Hearing referred to in footnote 4, Lucy Stone cited the Declaration of Independence and the principle that those who obey the laws should help to make them. Then she added, "Now it is easy to say that our fathers announced that principle but did not apply it.

sent of the governed" must necessarily apply to women, for women were governed. The revolutionists' cry, "No taxation without representation!" pertained to women, for women were taxed. Whereas the Founding Fathers, in asserting their inalienable right to govern themselves, were arguing that their actual rights as subjects of the British sovereign were inconsistent with their theoretical rights as parties to the social contract or with their actual ability to govern themselves, the American suffragists a century later sometimes acknowledged that their subjection to men had stunted their development and had made them indubitably inferior.[7] The humanity that they shared equally with their men, implied in their Protestant and republican principles, now gave them the right to demand that they be permitted to participate in activities conducive to their development up to actual equality.[8]

Of course they were in no condition to do so, and they could not. In the white heat of the struggle of the war of the Revolution these men declared bettter things than they could do. They saw the great truth that a complete government must be a just government; but they were too near the throne; they had the idea of the one man power, and so they were unable to carry out the principle of a just government."

[7] That inferiority could be eradicated within a generation, according to most suffragists. Charlotte Perkins Gilman being the exception. Thus it was a question not of evolution but of education. See chap. V for a discussion of this difference between Mrs. Gilman and most suffragists and of the conflict between the suffragists' desire to portray women as perfectly capable of self-government and their desire to demonstrate that disfranchisement restricts one's outlook and stunts one's mental development.

[8] The following are a few instances in which suffragists predicted that the vote would broaden women's minds by placing part of the responsibility of government upon them: Alice Stone Blackwell in *Woman's Journal*, May 6, 1893; Jane Addams, speaking before the Massachusetts Woman Suffrage Association, as quoted, *ibid.*, February 20, 1897; "For Beginners" (a weekly column), *ibid.*, June 3, 1911 (the eleventh of sixteen reasons "Why Women Should Vote"); Shaw, *Passages from Speeches*, p. 13; Elizabeth Cady Stanton, testifying

The antis also used natural right to argue that women should remain in the sphere naturally and divinely marked out for them. To the antis, *natural* meant customary, and the suffragists thus had an additional reason for transferring natural right from the present to the future. They suggested that woman's natural sphere had not yet been discovered and could be discovered only after women had had the opportunity to find it in practice.

However, throughout the entire campaign of women for the franchise, the argument based on natural right most frequently took the form not of the request to be allowed to become equal but of the simple assertion that the logic of the Declaration of Independence made its principles universal.[9] Whenever a state gave its women the vote, suffragists hailed the appearance of a "true republic"[10] and criticized the rest of the states for being

before a Senate Committee in 1890, as quoted in Anthony and Harper, eds., *History of Woman Suffrage*, IV, 160; Carrie Chapman Catt, in Oakland *Tribune* [1896?], clipping in Catt Collection, NYPL. One leader in the New York Men's League for Woman Suffrage stated in a speech: "The great thing to my mind is not that women will improve politics but that politics will develop women." (Max Eastman of Columbia University, as quoted in Harper, ed., *History of Woman Suffrage*, V, 285-86.)

[9] Note one ingenious argument by Ellen Battelle Dietrick, writing in the *Woman's Journal* of March 31, 1894, in answer to an anti: "Dear Sir:— In your recent speech opposing the right of half the people to exercise self-government, you say, 'The right to vote is not a natural right.' As the right to vote, in our present form of government, constitutes those who vote rulers over those who are not allowed to vote, your admission is equivalent to a confession that the male half of the people have no natural right to rule over the female half of the people."

[10] See, for example, Stanton, "Wyoming Admitted as a State," *Westminster Review*, CXXXIV (September, 1890), 284. In the Olivia B. Hall Papers, LC, there is a songsheet with the words and music of "Oh! Sing of Wyoming: The First True Republic," by J. H. DeVoe, dedicated to Susan B. Anthony.

untrue to the principles they claimed to uphold. After the turn of the century, when most suffragists were claiming the vote on the basis of the good that women's votes would allegedly accomplish, some women, notably Miss Shaw, tried to avoid this new addition to the suffragist rationale, feeling that both American democracy and American women were degraded by such reasoning. Miss Shaw contended that no matter how women would use their political power, their right to it was the same; further, no other group that had won the franchise had had to justify its claim to the ballot by exhibiting its qualifications.[11] But Miss Shaw belonged to a diminishing minority of suffragists, and even she occasionally linked woman suffrage with needed reforms.

The start of the twentieth century may be taken as the turning point in the change from justice to expediency as the chief argument of the suffragists, but the transition came about gradually, forms of the expediency doctrine having appeared even before Mrs. Stanton wrote "The Solitude of Self." In a period in which, as Merriam has observed, political liberty was becoming linked with political capacity,[12] women could prove their capacity either as members of the "superior race" or as women. In that context they found that the "best" argument of native-born, white, middle-class women was one which would prove their own capacity but not that of men or women of other sections of the population.

[11] For example: Anna Howard Shaw, "Equal Suffrage—A Problem of Political Justice," in "Women in Public Life," the *Annals* of the American Academy of Political and Social Science, LVI (November, 1914), 94-96.

[12] Merriam, *A History of American Political Theories*, p. 313. Also, see chaps. VI and VII below for further discussion.

The decline of arguments on the basis of principles that must logically be universal in application was accompanied by the ever more frequent claim by many suffragists, including Mrs. Stanton herself, that their own enfranchisement could counteract the votes of the undesirable part of the electorate. When even Mrs. Stanton acknowledged the right of legislatures to define the electorate by barring illiterates from the polls, the natural right argument for woman suffrage lost much of its cogency.

The antis did not fail to note the contradiction between the suffragists' claim to the vote as a natural right and their frequent appeals to legislatures, in the late 1890s, to limit the franchise to the desirable elements in the population.[13] Suffragists occasionally in this period complained of the declining faith in democracy, which was becoming an obstacle to women's enfranchisement. If appeals to the principles of democracy fell on deaf ears, then women seeking the vote would have to use other arguments. Hence, declining faith in democracy may have been a cause of the relative decline in importance of suffragist arguments based on the principles of democracy, in two ways: the women shared their men's skepticism as to the capacity of workers and nonwhites for self-government; and whether they shared that skepticism or not, they were forced to use arguments which could find a favorable hearing from the men from whom they sought their political liberty.

The relative decline of the natural right argument was possible also partly because of the long period in which women *had* claimed the vote as human beings and had by their tremendous progress in education and the pro-

---

[13] See, for example, Johnson, *Woman and the Republic,* pp. 49–50.

fessions demonstrated their hitherto unsuspected capabilities. It was no longer necessary to prove what was now obvious. Even the antis were basing their arguments on the "equality" of the sexes or on the alleged superiority of the gentle, law-abiding, temperate, and moral sex. It was a rare anti, too, who now dared to rest his religious argument on woman's being the source of evil or the cause of the Fall. Thus, the issue of abstract equality had been settled, and the debate now concerned the meaning of equality and whether such separate spheres as the antis advocated for women and men could in fact be equal. Once the abstract equality of the sexes had been established beyond public dispute, the differences could be spelled out in greater detail without fear of inferences' being drawn therefrom that women were inferior to men. The assertion of women's common humanity with men had always been accompanied by explicit recognition of innate differences between men and women, and the natural right claim had always included the demand for the right of women to protect their special interests and to legislate for themselves because one sex could not legislate justly for the other.

The chief form the expediency argument took in the earlier period was the insistence that women needed the ballot for self-protection. This was consistent with the individualistic emphasis of the justice argument, as contrasted to the social consciousness expressed in most of the later expediency arguments. Lucy Stone, until her death in 1893, wrote articles in almost every issue of the *Woman's Journal* explaining that women could use the franchise to protect themselves better than men were protecting them. One of her main themes was the scandalously light punishment meted out to rapists because male legislators simply could not understand the seriousness of sex crimes. She also repeatedly called attention to the ridiculously low "age of consent" in many states. After suffragists began to include the needs of workingwomen in their arguments for the vote, they pointed out that those women must have the vote to protect themselves against the special hazards to health and morals which women in factories faced. Florence Kelley wrote many articles on this subject. Catharine Waugh McCulloch, a lawyer, emphasized the need of women to protect themselves against the effects of discriminatory man-made laws.[14] This self-protection theory was the main version of the expediency argument during the period in which natural right held first place in suffrage propaganda.

To show that the ballot would help create that concrete equality that was woman's natural right, the later suffragists had to discuss specifically what the vote would do for woman and what woman would do with the vote. In this manner, the logic of the natural right claim itself and the transference of equality from the present to the future compelled them to discuss the utility of the ballot. The vote, contended the suffragists, would enlarge woman's interests and intellect by placing upon her part of the responsibility of running the government; it would make her a better mother by enabling her to teach her children from firsthand experience the meaning of

[14] See especially Catharine Waugh McCulloch, "The Protective Value of the Ballot," a paper read at a hearing of the House Committee and reprinted in *Woman's Journal*, February 24, 1900. See also *Woman Suffrage*. Hearing before the Committee on the Judiciary of the House of Representatives, Tuesday, February 13, 1900, pp. 14-20.

citizenship; it would make her a better wife by permitting her to become her husband's equal, thus destroying the warped relationship that bred servility in one spouse and tyranny in the other. In these and other ways political equality would be good for woman, but woman would also be good for government; the development of this proposition dominated their propaganda from about the turn of the century until victory crowned their efforts twenty years later.

If logic alone had motivated this concentration of effort to prove that woman suffrage would benefit society, the endeavor could hardly have lasted as long or produced as voluminous a bibliography as it did. Even had logic not favored the development, the events of the period between the Spanish-American War and World War I would have provided sufficient explanation for the new turn in suffragist propaganda.

The reform surge that eventuated in the Progressive party and the various reform administrations in American cities seemed to liberate a tendency that had always been present to some degree in the suffrage movement. When the movement threw itself enthusiastically into the struggle for the initiative and referendum, for laws to prohibit child labor and excessive working hours, and for sundry other reforms that could be accomplished by legislation (and therefore only by those who had the right to vote), it was expressing an affinity for reform bequeathed to it by the pioneer suffragists. Those pioneers had begun the fight for more rights for women partly to be able to speak for the abolition of slavery. After the rise of the temperance movement in the 1870s, the fight against liquor and the struggle for women's rights came together again and again. Reformers of that day took it for granted that prohibition of liquor was as desirable as prohibition of child labor and other reforms. Many women came into the suffrage movement through their prior interest in temperance, and many members of the NAWSA belonged also to the WCTU.[15] At a time when the suffragist organization was claiming the vote principally as a matter of simple justice, the WCTU was asking for the ballot on the basis of what the teetotaling portion of the population could accomplish with it. With that motive, the temperance women worked in behalf of suffrage amendments in various states, welcomed by some suffragists, but shunned by others. The latter felt that most temperance men would vote for woman suffrage in any case, but that the wets could hardly be induced to vote favorably after being told that the beneficiaries of their ballots would promptly deprive them of their glass of wine. Miss Anthony, for example, was a prohibitionist who nevertheless believed that the cause of woman suffrage could not win without the votes of many wets. As she put it,

The strongest argument to win the Prohibition men to vote for W. S.– is the very strongest one to drive from us the high license men– So the strongest testimony showing how all women's voting will lessen the ratio of the foreign vote & of the Catholic vote– is just the worst thing– in fact wholly estops all hope of winning the foreign born mens vote– & the Catholic vote— We are between two distracting dilemma's at every step— So I try to keep my talk on general

[15] A few leaders in the NAWSA who came to suffrage via temperance were Carrie Chapman Catt, Susan B. Anthony, Anna Howard Shaw, Catharine Waugh McCulloch, and Ella Seass Stewart.

principles– the bettering of women's chances for work &
wages tyranny of taxation– &c &c— But it is hardly possible
to say anything– that will not hurt somebody– so each of
us must be governed by our own true inwardness– as to
what & how to present our claims– [16]

It is impossible to estimate what proportion of organized suffragists were prohibitionists, but it is evident
that the "true inwardness" of a great many led them to
advocate woman suffrage partly on the supposition that
women's votes would help abolish the curse of alcohol.
Evidently few suffragists were as hostile to prohibition
on principle as was Abigail Scott Duniway, pioneer suffragist in the Far Northwest, who believed in the freedom of women to vote on the same ground as she believed in the freedom of a sober man to buy a drink.[17]
The clashes between suffragists and WCTU'ers during
state suffrage referendum campaigns were largely matters of pride or of tactics,[18] and since both antis and

[16] Susan B. Anthony to Olympia Brown, September 9, 1890, Brown
papers, RWA.
[17] Duniway, *Path Breaking*, p. 136. In addition to this autobiography,
many letters from Mrs. Duniway in the Laura Clay Papers, UK, set
forth her unusual views.
[18] For an illuminating discussion of the relations between the two
movements, see Giele, "Social Change in the Feminine Role." Dr. Giele
points out that the temperance women were usually better organized in localities than the suffragists and were hence in a better
position to do effective work in behalf of suffrage amendments to
state constitutions in many places. This created a problem for the
suffragists: if they gave the WCTU'ers credit for their accomplishments
they alienated the wets; if they did not give the WCTU'ers the credit
they merited, the latter resented the suffragists' unfairness. (See *ibid.*,
p. 83.)
Some suffragists such as Anna Howard Shaw, Ella Seass Stewart, and
Laura Clay, all national NAWSA leaders, were also active in the WCTU
and must have known that the public would link their two roles together. On the other hand, a prominent Mississippi suffragist wrote to
Miss Clay, "We WCTU women think it best not to be prominent. I
mean best for the suffrage. . . ." (Nellie N. Somerville to Laura

suffragists generally took it for granted that women voters would tend to vote for prohibition in greater numbers than men voters, it is not surprising that the abolition of the liquor traffic found a prominent place in the suffragist rationale. Though suffragists occasionally took the trouble publicly to deny the existence of an alliance between their organization and the Prohibition party or the wctu,[19] to the wets it mattered little whether two movements that obviously had many members and ideas in common had come to a formal understanding. The opposition of the wets to woman suffrage caused frequent complaint, but it was also a matter of pride on the part of many suffragists. Alice Stone Blackwell, for example, wrote that "in the main suffrage and prohibition have the same friends and the same enemies," [20] and the chairman of the nawsa's Committee on Church Work stated,

There are two reasons why clergymen should support the woman suffrage movement: First, because it is just and right, and in accordance with the golden rule, and, second, because it would augment the power of the churches to have an enfranchised womanhood to aid in carrying on the warfare

Clay, February 16, 1895, Clay Papers, uk.) In 1909 the South Dakota suffragists split, the insurgents accusing the leaders of making the South Dakota Equal Suffrage Association a mere tool of wctu policy. See "Memorial" to the National American Woman Suffrage Association from the Executive Committee of the South Dakota Political Equality Association [April 19, 1909], and other correspondence of that period in the Clay Papers, uk. Similar difficulties were experienced in other states, though without open breaks.

[19] See, for example, Ida Husted Harper in New York *Sun*, July 7, 1901; Anne Martin to "Dear Suffrage President" (addressing presidents of Nevada suffrage clubs), October 14, 1914, Martin Papers, ucb; manuscript article by [Ella Seass Stewart, 1913] in Stewart Papers, rwa; Carrie Chapman Catt, "The Suffrage Platform," *Woman's Journal*, June 12, 1915.

[20] *Ibid.*, November 11, 1916.

against the liquor traffic, the white-slave traffic, child labor, impure food, and many other existing evils that depend upon legislative enactment, that is now being waged with only one-third the power of the churches.[21]

With the advent of the Progressive era the suffragists saw the liquor evil not merely as an individual failing of individual men threatening individual homes but as a Vested Interest. Many suffragists now believed Liquor formed an invisible power in joining with Big Business and Commercialized Vice to control government and rule society. According to suffragist polemics, the new trusts, impersonal and heartless, supplied the money to buy legislators. Part of their funds came from saloons, which provided their link to ignorant voters who voted the way saloonkeepers and their Big Business patrons dictated. One very Big Business was prostitution, which degraded all women and demoralized all society and thus helped perpetuate the hegemony of evil in government. All three monsters cooperated to support and direct their tool, the Political Machine. Naturally, acknowledged the suffragists, these forces strenuously opposed woman suffrage, for voting women would destroy their power.

The two dominating influences in politics today are the corporations, or "trusts," and the liquor interest, the latter indeed constituting one of the greatest of "trusts." The Government finds in it an inexhaustible source of revenue. It controls millions of votes. There are few members of the Congress or the State Legislatures who do not owe their election in a greater or less degree to its influence, or whom it could not defeat. No village is so small as not to feel its touch on local

[21] Mary E. Craigie, quoted in *Proceedings* of the Forty-First Annual Convention of the National American Woman Suffrage Association, held at Seattle, Wash., July 1 to 6, 1909 (Warren, Ohio, n.d.), p. 39.

affairs. It is grounded in politics, and to it and its collateral branches, the gambling resort and the house of ill repute, woman is believed to be an implacable foe. Therefore, it decrees that she shall not be a political factor. The hand of the great moneyed corporations is on the lever of the party "machines." They can calculate to a nicety how many voters must be bought, how many candidates must be "fixed," how many officials must be owned. The entrance of woman into the field would upset all calculations, add to the expenses if she were corruptible, and spoil the plans if she were not.[22]

In order to take power away from Big Business, the Liquor Interests, political machines, and the drinking masses of the cities, and restore it to "the people," suffragists along with other reformers advocated the initiative, referendum, recall, and other reforms in the machinery of government.[23] At the same time the NAWSA began advocating other reforms designed to emancipate

[22] Harper, "Why Women Cannot Vote in the United States," *North American Review*, CLXXIX (July, 1904), 37. Other suffragist discussions, stressing one or more of the elements in this antisuffragist cabal, include: "Mrs. Catt's Address," *Woman's Journal*, February 20, 1904, a reprint of Carrie Chapman Catt's presidential speech to the NAWSA convention; Blackwell in *ibid.*, September 8, 1906; Harper, "Status of Woman Suffrage in the United States," *North American Review*, CLXXXIX (April, 1909), 505-8; *Woman's Journal*, October 14 and 21, 1911, two editorials by Miss Blackwell; cartoon reprinted from *The Woman Voter*, in *Woman's Journal*, September 21, 1912; *ibid.*, April 15, 1916, and a number of other issues during that spring; Mrs. Catt in *Eminent Opinions on Woman Suffrage* (n.p., n.d.), p. 19; leaflet entitled "Facing Facts," put out by the New York State Woman Suffrage Party in August, 1917, a copy of which is in the box labeled "S. U.S. (N.Y.)" in the Suffrage Collection, SSC; Harper, ed., *History of Woman Suffrage*, V, xviii-xix.

[23] See, for example, *Proceedings* of the Thirty-Seventh Annual Convention of the National American Woman Suffrage Association, held at Portland, Oregon, June 28 to July 5, inclusive, 1905 (Warren, Ohio, n.d.), p. 89; *Proceedings* of the Thirty-Eighth Annual Convention of the National American Woman Suffrage Association, held at Baltimore, Md., February 7 to 13, inclusive, 1906 (Warren, Ohio, n.d.), p. 78; and later conventions.

those drinking masses of the cities from the domination
of their oppressors. Calls for child-labor legislation, pure-
food laws, and other such reforms began appearing in
suffrage propaganda. The faith of pre-Prohibition reformers in their ability to legislate their own conceptions of
morality led the suffragists to advocate a number of "reforms" that to modern thinking may seem unworthy to
be listed with child-labor legislation and pure-food laws.
One "Editorial Note" in the *Woman's Journal* of August
1, 1891, in its entirety, read:

> During the past week several Boston newspapers have given
> great prominence to the details of a brutal prize fight, ac-
> companying these with appreciative editorial comments. The
> streets were vocal with the shrill cries of the newsboys,—
> "All about the prize fight!" If women were voters and had a
> voice in legislation, this brutal business would be promptly
> suppressed.

It was not long, however, before more modern-sounding
reforms were being advocated. The fourth resolution
passed by the 1894 convention of the NAWSA read: "That
woman's disfranchisement is largely responsible for her
industrial inequality and therefore for the degradation
of many women, and we advocate the just principle of
'Equal Pay for Equal Work.'" [24] In all conventions thereafter speakers such as Florence Kelley advocated the ap-
pointment of women factory inspectors, restrictions on
night work for women, and the like.[25] Advocacy of prohibition also acquired a new social significance in ad-

[24] *Proceedings* of the Twenty-Sixth Annual Convention of the National American Woman Suffrage Association held in Washington, D.C.,
February 15–20, 1894 (Warren, Ohio, n.d.), p. 168.

[25] See, for example, Mrs. Kelley's address to the 1905 convention,
entitled "The Young Breadwinners' Need of Women's Enfranchisement," reprinted in *Woman's Journal*, July 22, 1905.

dition to its earlier meaning as an aid to individual reformation. All these improvements, it was claimed, could
be brought about if women were enfranchised.

As might have been expected, the suffragists overestimated what they could accomplish with the vote. One
frequent metaphor to be found in their propaganda was
that of the doctor treating the causes of disease (voters)
contrasted to the nurse whose job was to patch and
bandage after the damage had been done (disfranchised
women doing the philanthropic work to which the antis
would have relegated women permanently). The suffragists were not simply overestimating the power of a
woman; they were overestimating the power of the vote
to cure the ills of society. Comparatively modest fore-
casts of the results of woman suffrage were the statements of Alice Stone Blackwell that if women had voted
in New York City, Tammany would not have been returned to power in the 1903 election,[26] and of Florence
Kelley that "the enfranchisement of women is indispensable to the solution of the child labor problem." [27] Anna
Howard Shaw declared, after quoting an anti who had
said that if women voted they would have little time for
charity, "Thank God, there will not be so much need of
charity and philanthropy!" [28] The outbreak of World War
I evoked a more debatable prediction of the probable
effects of woman suffrage. A leaflet published by the
Congressional Union for Woman Suffrage said in part:
"A government responsible to all women, as well as all
men, will be less likely to go to war, without real neces-

[26] *Ibid.*, November 14, 1903.
[27] Letter to the editor of *The Outlook*, March 17, 1906.
[28] Shaw, *Passages from Speeches*, p. 3.

sity." [29] Alice Stone Blackwell wrote, "Let us do our utmost to hasten the day when the wishes of the mothers shall have their due weight in public affairs, knowing that by so doing we hasten the day when wars shall be no more." [30]

Perhaps the historic exclusion of middle-class women from politics itself had laid the basis for the new demand that they be given the vote to help in the good work of men reformers. Since those women could not vote, their energies had been channeled into philanthropic and reformatory activities. Once those activities had acquired political significance in the Progressive era, the women could turn to the men who had made those projects the subjects of legislation and offer their experienced aid in accomplishing the reforms. The men, in their turn, could more easily see the wisdom of enfranchising the women whose history of benevolent enterprise would render them probable allies in the reform crusade. This does not mean, of course, that male reformers all became suffragists. But reform parties had historically endorsed woman suffrage; the Progressive party in 1912 was the first major party to do so.

The woman suffrage movement was linked with the Progressive movement in still another way. Middle-class women who had never felt strongly about suffrage before probably felt the same reform impulses as men of their group, but while the men moved into political action, either in their old parties or by forming a new one, to achieve their reforms, the women were blocked by the wall of disfranchisement. They therefore had to seek

[29] A copy is in the box labeled "U.S. #1," Suffrage Collection, ssc.
[30] *Woman's Journal*, August 8, 1914.

the franchise to carry on their reform activities on a political level. The growth of the women's club movement around the turn of the century had encouraged this development, by broadening middle-class women's interests and bringing home to them the need of the vote as a tool for realizing their objectives.[31]

The advent of the Progressive era saw a change not only in the arguments the suffragists used to justify their claim to political equality and in their motivations for claiming it but also in the framework of ideas within which that claim was expressed. Although the link between temperance and suffrage had provided an early and strong motivation for demanding the vote as a means to reform, some of the expediency arguments used in the Progressive period were based on a radically different philosophy from that of the wctu. The temperance women had been concerned with the reform of individuals. They had attempted to make their own ideals of private morality universal by legislation, as did many reformers after the turn of the century. This motive did not disappear, even from suffragist ideology, but it was

[31] An analysis of the impact of the women's club movement on the suffrage movement in one state may be found in Beldon, "A History of the Woman Suffrage Movement in Illinois" (a copy of this thesis is in the NYPL). Miss Beldon notes that a new period in suffrage history began around 1900. The wctu was no longer the only women's organization. Civic and other clubs of women now found that they could not realize their objectives without the ballot, and by 1902 the change in the outlook of these associations had become so great that the Illinois Federation of Women's Clubs, at its eighth annual meeting, declared itself in favor of a taxpaying-woman suffrage bill. Within a few years the women's clubs had declared for full suffrage for women (p. 44). One Illinois woman, Ella Seass Stewart, who became a national suffrage leader, told Miss Beldon that this process explained her own entrance into the suffrage movement (see especially pp. 42–43).

supplemented by the new concern for public morality characteristic of many reformers of that time.[32] The individualism which "Solitude of Self" expressed could no longer be the most compelling argument for woman suffrage in an era in which a new consciousness of social cohesiveness was forcing changes even in that Protestantism to which Mrs. Stanton had appealed in her description of the solitary soul. The rise of the social gospel reflected a change in the framework of ideas of the men of the suffragists' own class. The suffrage rationale no longer emphasized what benefits women could derive from the vote, or what the government could do for them. A new argument appeared, stressing what enfranchised women could do for the government and their communities. When the state ceased being regarded as a mere restrainer of men's interference with one another's rights and became a social welfare agency, woman suffrage ceased to be advocated primarily *as* a reform and became in addition a *means to* reform. To the wctu, it had, of course, been a means to individual reformation. To the last generation of suffragists it became in addition a means to the reform of society. Hence, the new era saw a change from the emphasis by suffragists on the ways in which women were the same as men and therefore had the *right* to vote, to a stress on the ways in which they differed from men, and therefore had the *duty* to contribute their special skills and experience to government.

That this was more than simply a rationalization is proved by the new activities in which the federal and

[32] For a sociologist's discussion of this change, see Giele, "Social Change in the Feminine Role," pp. 38–39.

state governments engaged around the turn of the century. Whereas in the middle of the nineteenth century women spun, wove, and sewed the clothing for their families, churned their own butter, baked their own bread, and generally grew their own food, a generation later all these functions had become social activities and by the dawn of the Progressive era had become the subjects of legislation. Many men were performing traditional feminine tasks, as chefs, laundry operators, bakers, garment workers, and food processors. Thousands of women in fact followed these activities out of their homes and into the factories and mills.[33] More and more Americans were living in cities and buying their food and clothing without knowledge of the sanitary conditions under which they had been produced. Their children were attending public schools administered by men who were not responsible to the mothers of their charges.

At a time when large numbers of women were entering professions, working in factories and offices, and earning college degrees, suffragists acknowledged gladly that the home was indeed woman's sphere, but they insisted that the spheres of men and women were not as separate as they had hitherto been. The historic sphere of woman was more and more influenced by political life, as governments passed laws concerning food, water, the production of clothing, and education. Thus the statement that the home was woman's sphere was now an argument not against woman suffrage but in favor of it, for government was now "enlarged housekeeping," [34]

[33] For a full discussion of the changes in industry that brought women out of the home and revolutionized family life, see Smuts, *Women and Work in America.*

[34] Twentieth-century suffragists who frequently called government

and needed the experience of the nation's housekeepers. As the functions which they had previously performed as isolated individuals at home became social functions, women's claim to political equality changed from a demand for the right to protect themselves as individuals to an assertion of their duty to serve society as women. They assumed that their training as cooks, seamstresses, house cleaners, and mothers qualified them to help in legislation concerned with food inspection, sweatshop sanitation, street-cleaning, and public schools.

Just as Mrs. Stanton's "The Solitude of Self" embodied the philosophy of suffragism at the start of our thirty-year period, Jane Addams' "Why Women Should Vote," [35] first published in 1909 in the *Ladies' Home Journal,* may be considered the ideal expression of the new philosophy. Miss Addams began by stating that many women were failing to discharge their duties to their own households simply because they did not perceive that as society grew more complicated it was necessary that women should extend their sense of responsibility to many things outside their own homes if they wanted to continue to preserve their homes. A woman's simplest duty, said Miss Addams, was to keep her house clean and wholesome and feed her children properly. Yet if she

housekeeping on a broad scale were using a phrase that Frances Willard of the wctu had used earlier. In both cases the phrase was an expression of the expediency type of argument for the vote, although, as indicated, the contexts differed. Miss Willard had written: "Men have made a dead failure of municipal government, just about as they would of housekeeping, and government is only housekeeping on the broadest scale." (Frances Willard to Susan B. Anthony, January 26, 1898, Harper Collection, HL.)

[35] The article is reprinted in Addams, *A Centennial Reader,* pp. 104–7, and may also be found in Björkman and Porritt, eds., *Woman Suffrage,* pp. 110–29.

lived in an apartment house her efforts to fulfill these duties depended entirely upon the city administration.

Women who live in the country sweep their own dooryards and may either feed the refuse of the table to a flock of chickens or allow it innocently to decay in the open air and sunshine. In a crowded city quarter, however, if the street is not cleaned by the city authorities no amount of private sweeping will keep the tenement free from grime; if the garbage is not properly collected and destroyed a tenement house mother may see her children sicken and die of diseases from which she alone is powerless to shield them, although her tenderness and devotion are unbounded. She cannot even secure untainted meat for her household, she cannot provide fresh fruit, unless the meat has been inspected by city officials, and the decayed fruit, which is so often placed upon sale in the tenement districts, has been destroyed in the interests of public health. In short, if woman would keep on with her old business of caring for her house and rearing her children she will have to have some conscience in regard to public affairs lying quite outside of her immediate household. The individual conscience and devotion are no longer effective. . . . If women would effectively continue their old avocations they must take part in the slow upbuilding of that code of legislation which is alone sufficient to protect the home from the dangers incident to modern life.

Miss Addams went on to explain that the ready-made clothing that city women bought was frequently manufactured in germ-ridden sweatshops, and that the purchasers could control the conditions under which it was made only by participating in the lawmaking process. She illustrated her thesis by the example of a woman living in a comfortable house in a neighborhood that was becoming a slum. The woman kept aloof from the immigrants who were her new neighbors, believing that the problems of sanitation rapidly growing critical were no concern of hers. Her daughters came home from college at a time when typhoid was sweeping the area owing to the bad plumbing; one of them died and the other was sick for two years. The tragedy struck this family not because the mother was not devoted to her children but because the individual devotion of one woman to her isolated family was no longer enough to protect them.

In a book written in the same period, Miss Addams gave her thesis an historical background by arguing that cities had originally been formed for common defense against aggression, and their problems of government had then been those of relations with potential external enemies. In that era, she wrote, it was fair that the fighters should decide policies; but modern cities no longer fight, and the ancient test of an elector is no longer valid. The modern city is a stronghold of indus-trialism, involved in problems like child labor, unsani-tary housing, infant mortality, adulterated food, and so on, problems that women from experience are prepared to deal with. "May we not say," she asked, "that city housekeeping has failed partly because women, the tra-ditional housekeepers, have not been consulted as to its multiform activities?" [36]

Miss Addams' argument may be contrasted with one used by Alice Stone Blackwell in the *Woman's Journal*, July 25, 1891. Miss Blackwell had written that women as well as men had the right to vote in municipal gov-ernment because they breathed the same polluted air,

[36] Addams, *Newer Ideals of Peace,* chapter entitled "Utilization of Women in City Government." The passages referred to above are also reprinted in *A Centennial Reader* (see footnote 35), pp. 113-14.

drank the same contaminated water, and suffered the same long-range effects of saloons permitted by city law and therefore should have the same degree of political influence. Miss Addams, on the other hand, instead of arguing that women should have an equal influence because they suffered equally, declared that women ought to have the vote because they were specially fitted for modern municipal business, inasmuch as that business was large-scale housekeeping. Here is an excellent example of the change from justice to expediency as an argument for suffrage with the identical facts used for support in both cases. The suffragists who argued as Miss Addams did emphasized the need for municipal suffrage, although they also favored full suffrage. The functions of government in which they desired women's participation were taken over first in municipalities, and it is not merely coincidental that the Progressive movement realized its objectives most fully in the reform administrations in cities.

The inference may be drawn, from these and other arguments used at the time, that in the period when Americans were a rural people, when there had been no garbage disposal problem, no disease-causing congestion of populations, and when consumers had known the craftsmen who produced the commodities they bought, women had neither needed the vote nor had anything essential to contribute to government. Although suffragists of course never drew this inference and continued to include statements of the natural right principle in their propaganda, the expediency arguments that dominated that propaganda during the last generation of the suffrage campaign were themselves expedients, tailored to fit the realities of an industrial age. This fact may suggest that woman suffrage came to the East for reasons different from those which brought it earlier to the West. Henry B. Blackwell, in the *Woman's Journal* of May 2, 1903, suggested that the suffrage victories in Western states had been due to the absence there of vested interests allied with ignorant foreign voters, while enlightened middle-class Americans who respected women and favored reforms migrated westward. Whether or not this negative argument contained truth, the advent of woman suffrage in Western states may have been due in part to the positive fact that in pioneer farming settlements the contributions of women *as individuals* to the community were more apparent than in the older areas of the East in the same period. During the Progressive era the contributions of women *as women* to their highly integrated urban communities became clear when local governments began taking over many of the functions that women had hitherto performed in their separate households. The need of government for women's participation and women's duty to participate in the legislative process became the core of the suffrage rationale of a generation of middle-class women who wanted the vote in order to reform their society and not simply because they sought freedom for themselves.[37]

[37] Advocacy of reform as a justification of the claim for the vote may be found in virtually every issue of the *Woman's Journal* after 1900, and by random leafing through almost every collection of suffragist manuscripts dated after 1900. There are few leaflets or pamphlets of suffragist organizations in this period which do not also contain these arguments. Instances are so numerous that citation of specific examples is unnecessary. Giele draws conclusions similar to those offered here. In her content analysis of articles in *Woman's Journal*, she found that from 1875 to 1895 only 13 percent of the articles advocated some

The woman suffrage movement was part of the larger women's rights movement, but it must also be seen as a reflection of changing conceptions of government. Since it was a demand for a role in government, the claim to suffrage had to be justified on the ground of the right or duty of women to participate in those activities that the government carried on at the time the claim was made. If the main function of a government had been to carry on external war, as Jane Addams suggested, women's claim to suffrage would have had to be argued on the basis of an alleged right and capacity of women to bear arms. In a day when government was allegedly becoming more and more housekeeping on a large scale, women's demand for the vote could and did change from a claim based on abstract principle to a very practical demand to participate in governmental activities that had theretofore been considered the special province of women both in their separate homes and in their volunteer aid societies. In the earlier period, none of the benefits that women expected the government to derive from their enfranchisement would have been approved of by the men in power. In the Progressive period, on the other hand, at the time when women could argue that their enfranchisement could help stamp out the liquor traffic, help pass pure-food laws, abolish child labor, and contribute to other reforms, there were groups of men in or near power who needed allies and who could be

humanitarian reform, whereas from 1895 to 1915 the percentage was 26. She adds, "At the same time that the suffrage reform objectives were broadening to include greater emphasis on the use of the ballot for humanitarian purposes, the emphasis on the pure equalitarian arguments for suffrage showed sharp decline." ("Social Change in the Feminine Role," pp. 178-179.)

brought over to their cause by precisely those arguments. The change from justice to expediency as the main suffragist argument reflected: first, the logic of the justice argument as it was developed; second, the entrance of socially conscious women into the suffrage movement; third, a change in the conception of the functions of government; fourth, a change in the groups of men in or near power to whom the appeal for suffrage could be directed; and fifth, the brightening prospects of victory for suffrage itself.

FOUR

Woman Suffrage and Religion

No sooner had the woman suffrage movement begun than it found itself confronted by a problem identical to one that had faced its parent, the abolitionist movement. In the middle of the nineteenth century, most Americans accepted the "plenary inspiration" of the Bible, believing that the Scriptures were literally the word of God, infallible not only in matters of moral and religious truth but also in regard to statements of scientific, historical, and geographical fact. The issue of slavery had had to be fought out partly on the level of Biblical interpretation, with each side marshaling its evidence by Bible exegesis. An individual's interpretation of the Scriptural view of slavery might determine his opinion of slavery in America; or his opinion of slavery in America might influence what he thought the Bible said on the subject. Regardless of which factor was determining, the felt need of most Americans to live according to the Word of God affected both the ideology of abolitionism and the current interpretations of the Scriptures' position on slavery. The suffragists faced a harder challenge than had the abolitionists. By 1890, the number of people who believed that the Bible sanctioned woman suffrage was far smaller than the number of people who, in 1830, thought it con-

demned slavery. Three possible solutions were open to
the suffragists: they could meet Bible-based antisuffragism head on; they could point out those parts of the
Scriptures that seemed to favor the equality of the sexes;
or they could ignore religion in their rationale altogether. All three tactics were used.

A reinterpretation of the Bible's statements on woman
became possible only because of a development that had
nothing at all to do with the woman's rights movement.
To the suffragists, the theological controversies of the
1880s came, as it were, as a gift from Heaven. The higher
criticism that had long been respectable first in Germany
and then in England had crossed the Atlantic.[1] Throughout the 1880s and 1890s books appeared and new theological publications were founded which approached the
Scriptures historically. Heresy trials of ministers received
attention in the press. Popular preachers such as Henry
Ward Beecher, Washington Gladden, and Lyman Abbott
wrote and spoke in opposition to a literal interpretation
of the Bible. The mere appearance of the Revised Version of the Bible in 1881 and 1885 helped to undermine
faith in the Book's infallibility. Discussion of evolution
helped to weaken faith in literalism. Although the vast
majority of American Christians had hardly been affected
by this growing freedom of religious discussion by the late
1880s, it now became possible for suffragists to argue pub-

[1] I am indebted to Ira V. Brown, "The Higher Criticism Comes to
America, 1880–1900," *Journal* of the Presbyterian Historical Society,
XXXVIII (December, 1960), 193–212, for information concerning
religious developments in the United States at that time. See also
Schlesinger, "A Critical Period in American Religion, 1875–1900," *Proceedings* of the Massachusetts Historical Society, LXIV (June, 1932),
523–47, and G. B. Smith, "Theological Thinking in America," in G. B.
Smith, ed., *Religious Thought in the Last Quarter-Century*, pp. 95–
115.

licly against what virtually everybody believed to be the Biblical definitions of woman's place and functions.

Most suffragists found all they sought in the pages of the Old and New Testaments, but a few of them, led by Elizabeth Cady Stanton, had become so bitter at the Scriptural arguments against suffrage that they took the new opportunity to denounce the Bible publicly and completely. Mrs. Stanton's radical rejection of the Bible was rooted in her early career as one of the small group of women who had founded the woman's rights movement. She had insisted on including a demand for the vote in the "Declaration of Sentiments" of 1848, but had never considered suffrage anything more than one of a long list of reforms that women must obtain to achieve that full equality which was her goal. During the 1880s she gradually came to believe that not disfranchisement but the Bible and the churches were the main obstacles to the equality of the sexes.[2] She felt that if she could demonstrate that the subjection of women was not divinely ordained, men would be more willing to admit women to an equal place in government, and women themselves would feel less hesitant in asserting their rights.

Susan B. Anthony, who had entered the woman's rights movement a few years after Mrs. Stanton, when

[2] Mrs. Stanton expressed this opinion on many occasions. For example, in 1893 she remarked that "the most powerful influences against woman's emancipation can be traced to religious superstitions." ("The Sunday Opening," letter to the editor of the *Woman's Journal*, March 18, 1893.) In 1897 she wrote approvingly of "Dr. Andrew D. White, former President of Cornell University, [who] in his new work, 'History of the Warfare of Science with Theology in Christendom,' shows that the Bible has been the greatest block in the way of progress." Stanton, "Reading the Bible in the Public Schools," *The Arena*, XVII (June, 1897), 1034.

the demand for the ballot was somewhat more respectable among the women reformers, never swerved from her conviction that the root of the subjection of women was their lack of the vote. When Mrs. Stanton wrote to invite her to serve on a committee that would prepare a volume of commentaries on those parts of the Bible that referred to women, Miss Anthony wrote in reply,

No– I don't want my name on that Bible Committee— *You* fight that battle— and leave me to fight the secular– the political fellows. . . . I simply don't want the enemy to be diverted from my practical ballot fight– to that of scoring me for belief one way or the other about the bible.[3]

A little more than three years later, after the commentaries had been published as the *Woman's Bible*,[4] Miss Anthony drove this point home in more detail. Expressing her horror at recent instances of racism at home and abroad, she wrote earnestly to her friend,

On every hand *American civilization* which we are introducing into isles of the Atlantic & Pacific– is putting its heel on the head of the negro race. Now this barbarism does not grow out of ancient Jewish Bibles– but out of our own sordid meanness!! And the like of you ought to stop hitting poor old St. Paul– and give your heaviest raps on the head of every Nabob– man or woman– who does injustice to a human being– for the crime! of color or sex!! . . . I do wish you could center your big brain on the crimes we, ourselves, as a

[3] Typed copy of Susan B. Anthony to Elizabeth Cady Stanton, July 24, 1895, Anthony Family Collection, HL.

[4] E. C. Stanton and others, *Woman's Bible*. Part I: Comments on Genesis, Exodus, Leviticus, Numbers, and Deuteronomy was published in 1895 by the European Publishing Company, New York, and contained 152 pages of text. Part II: Comments on the Old and New Testaments from Joshua to Revelation, published by the same company in 1898, was 217 pages long. Copies may be found in the NYPL and RWA.

people are responsible for– to charge *our* offenses to false books or false interpretations– is but a way of seeking a *"refuge of lies."* [5]

Despite Miss Anthony's entreaties, Mrs. Stanton gathered a group of women and proceeded to sow the wind. Although accustomed to being the center of controversy, even she was taken aback by the whirlwind of denunciation she encountered when the *Woman's Bible* appeared.[6] In view of the reading public's familiarity with, although not acceptance of, the new critical approach to the Bible, it is probable that Mrs. Stanton and her co-workers were denounced not only for what they

[5] Typed copy of Susan B. Anthony to Elizabeth Cady Stanton, December 2, 1898, Anthony Family Collection, HL. During her campaign work in California in 1896, Miss Anthony had written to Mrs. Stanton: "You say 'women must be emancipated from their superstitions before enfranchisement will be of any benefit,' and I say just the reverse, that women must be enfranchised before they can be emancipated from their superstitions. Women would be no more superstitious today than men, if they had been men's political and business equals and gone outside the four walls of home and the other four of the church into the great world, and come in contact with and discussed men and measures on the plane of this mundane sphere, instead of living in the air with Jesus and the angels. So you will have to keep pegging away, saying, 'Get rid of religious bigotry and then get political rights;' while I shall keep pegging away, saying, 'Get political rights first and religious bigotry will melt like dew before the morning sun;' and each will continue still to believe in and defend the other." (Harper, *Life and Work of Susan B. Anthony*, II, 857. The punctuation was evidently corrected by Mrs. Harper, as it does not conform to Miss Anthony's style in her manuscript letters.)

[6] Miss Anthony wrote to a friend, "I visited Mrs. Stanton before coming home, and found her, as you may well understand, thoroughly indignant over the petty action of the convention." (Typed copy of Susan B. Anthony to Clara B. Colby, February 10, 1896, Colby Papers, HL.) Miss Anthony was referring to the repudiation of the *Woman's Bible* by the suffragist organization. The Topeka, Kansas, Federation of Woman's Clubs banned the book from its library on the ground that it was "written in a flippant, coarse and inelegant style." (New York *Tribune*, August 27, 1896.) The Greenville *Daily News* of November 23, 1895, devoted more than a column to a sarcastic review of the first volume (clipping in Laura Clay Papers, UK).

wrote but also for the fact that they, women, dared to comment on the Bible at all. Mrs. Stanton believed that the assumption that women had no such right was evidence of that religious attitude toward women which constituted the principal obstacle to their emancipation. Two years after Part I of the *Woman's Bible* appeared, Mrs. Stanton wrote:

The criticisms on "The Woman's Bible" are as varied as they are unreasonable. . . . [One] clergyman says: "It is the work of women and the devil." This is a grave mistake. His Satanic Majesty was not invited to join the Revising Committee, which consists of women alone. Moreover, he has been so busy of late years attending Synods, General Assemblies and Conferences, to prevent the recognition of women delegates, that he has had no time to study the languages and "higher criticism." . . . The Old Testament makes woman a mere after-thought in creation; the author of evil; cursed in her maternity; a subject in marriage; and all female life, animal and human, unclean. . . . Now, to my mind, the Revising Committee of "The Woman's Bible," in denying divine inspiration for such demoralizing ideas, shows a more worshipful reverence for the great Spirit of All Good than does the Church. We have made a fetich of the Bible long enough. The time has come to read it as we do all other books, accepting the good and rejecting the evil it teaches.[7]

The "Revising Committee" responsible for Part I of the *Woman's Bible,* published in November, 1895, consisted of 23 women, including 3 ordained ministers.[8] The com-

[7] *Woman's Bible,* Part II, pp. 7–8.
[8] The Revising Committee consisted of: Mrs. Stanton, the Rev. Phebe Hanaford, Clara Bewick Colby, the Rev. Augusta Chapin, Mary A. Livermore, Mary Seymour Howell, Josephine K. Henry, Mrs. Robert G. Ingersoll, Sara A. Underwood, Catherine F. Stebbins, Ellen Battelle Dietrick, Cornelia Collins Hussey, Lillie Devereux Blake, Matilda Joslyn Gage, the Rev. Olympia Brown, Frances Ellen Burr, Carrie Chapman Catt, Helen H. Gardener, Charlotte Beebe Wilbour, Lucinda B.

mentaries constituting Part I, on the Pentateuch, were actually written by only 8 women.[9] One or more of them wrote a brief commentary on each of the verses singled out for discussion. Although the commentators held differing viewpoints, some of them very much at variance with those of Mrs. Stanton, a composite commentary culled from Part I might read as follows: The two accounts of the creation contradict each other,[10] the rib story obviously being a later interpolation; [11] God created man, male and female, in his own image and gave them together dominion over the earth.[12] Eve was less to blame for the Fall than Adam because in the eating of the fruit of the tree he broke a commandment received from God; she disobeyed an order received from Adam. When con-

Chandler, M. Louise Thomas, Louisa Southworth, Martha R. Almy. Most of them were very well-known suffragists. Note that the word *revising* is used here in its rare sense of "viewing again." The unfortunate title and perhaps also the word *revising* caused many people to assume that these women had rewritten the Bible. Some contemporary comments on the book show that the critics had read no farther than the title.

[9] The commentators were: Mrs. Stanton, Mrs. Blake, the Rev. Miss Hanaford, Mrs. Colby, Mrs. Dietrick, Ursula N. Gestefeld, Mrs. Southworth, and Miss Burr.

[10] Part I, pp. 16–18, by Mrs. Dietrick. The two accounts are Genesis 1:26–28 and 2:7, pp. 15–18, 21–25. The first account tells of the creation of man, male and female, in the image of God. The second chapter begins the story anew and tells of the creation of Adam first and Eve later from Adam's rib.

[11] *Ibid.*, p. 21, by Mrs. Stanton. On at least one other occasion, Mrs. Stanton explained the significance of the "interpolation." In a letter to the editor of *The Critic* (New York), March 28, 1896, p. 219, she wrote, "Take the snake, the fruit-tree and the woman from the tableau, and we have no fall, nor frowning Judge, no Inferno, no everlasting punishment,—hence no need of a Savior. Thus the bottom falls out of the whole Christian theology. Here is the reason why in all the Biblical researches and higher criticisms, the scholars never touch the position of women." She implied that that was also the reason why scholars and the public denounced the group of women who set out to interpret the Bible for themselves.

[12] *Ibid.*, pp. 14–16, by Mrs. Stanton; see also p. 19, by Mrs. Blake.

fronted with his disobedience, Adam tried to blame his wife.[13] The temptation to which Eve succumbed was not the promise of jewels or pleasure but the desire for knowledge and wisdom.[14] God's statement that her husband was to rule over her was a prediction, not a curse; in the same way, God predicted rather than commanded that Adam should eat his bread in the sweat of his face.[15] The story of the patriarchs was one long tale of war, corruption, rapine, and lust. Women were scarcely mentioned except when the advent of sons was announced. From Abraham through Joseph there were just seven legitimate descendants in the first generation, so that the great harvest so recklessly promised would have been meager indeed if it had not been for polygamy and concubinage.[16] "The texts on Lot's daughters and Tamar we omit altogether, as unworthy a place in the 'Woman's Bible.' "[17] Two different kinds of Bible exegesis may be traced through these commentaries: some passages are cited as proving that the Bible was indeed the enemy of woman's progress, and other passages were reinterpreted to show that they really portrayed woman as man's equal. Mrs. Stanton herself wrote both types of comment, illustrating her belief that the Bible ought to be read as any other book containing both good and bad, but her reaction to the Bible as a whole was extremely hostile.

[13] *Ibid.*, pp. 26–27, by Mrs. Blake.

[14] *Ibid.*, pp. 23–26, by Mrs. Blake.

[15] *Ibid.*, p. 27, by Mrs. Blake. This interpretation of the "curse" was one of the favorite religious arguments for suffrage. Man's supremacy over woman turns out, then, to be not a desirable state of affairs with divine sanction, but a product of sin, to be overcome by human effort. A theory of progress and woman's emancipation were thus reconciled with religious orthodoxy. Instances of this type of reasoning will be discussed later.

[16] *Ibid.*, pp. 66–67, by Mrs. Stanton.   [17] *Ibid.*, p. 67.

Part II of the *Woman's Bible*, covering both Testaments from Joshua to Revelation, was published in 1898, with a somewhat different "Revising Committee" of 25, including the 3 ministers, and this time including several distinguished foreign members.[18] No explanation was given for the absence of Mrs. Catt and Mrs. Livermore, but the fact that they both disagreed with Mrs. Stanton's entire approach to the subject may provide a clue.

The appearance of Part II was anticlimactic. Part I had proved more than enough for Mrs. Stanton's critics within the suffragist movement, who had felt that the cause could not survive public identification with heresy. Consequently, at the 1896 convention of the NAWSA, the Resolutions Committee offered a proposal designed to demonstrate to a suspicious public their innocence of religious heterodoxy.[19] The resolution declared: "That this Association is non-sectarian, being composed of persons of all shades of religious opinion, and that it has no official connection with the so-called 'Woman's Bible,' or any theological publication."[20]

In the course of the heated debate that followed the

[18] Mrs. Dietrick was still listed although she died almost immediately after Part I appeared. Missing from Part II's "Revising Committee" were Mesdames Livermore, Hussey, Catt, Thomas, and Almy. The new members were Miss Gestefeld, Mrs. Clara B. Neyman, and the overseas members: Baroness Alexandra Gripenberg, Finland; Ursula M. Bright, England; Irma von Troll-Borostyani, Austria; Priscilla Bright McLaren, Scotland; and Isabelle Bogelot, France.

[19] The originators of the resolution anticipated Miss Anthony's opposition and arranged for the repudiation to be included as a paragraph in the recording secretary's report. Mrs. Colby led the fight to have the paragraph deleted, and it then appeared in the report of the Resolutions Committee. The incident is mentioned in Dorr, *Susan B. Anthony*, p. 312; K. Anthony, *Susan B. Anthony: Her Personal History and Her Era*, pp. 436–37; Lutz, *Created Equal*, pp. 302–5; Harper, *Susan B. Anthony*, II, 852–53.

[20] NAWSA, *Proceedings*, 1896, pp. 20, 29, 91.

introduction of the "Bible Resolution," Susan B. Anthony
relinquished the chair to plead with the delegates to drop
this totally unnecessary repudiation of a privately published work by their eighty-one-year-old honorary president and her co-workers. Miss Anthony said in part:

From the beginning the distinct feature of our Association
has been the right of individual opinion for every member.
We have been beset at every step with the cry that somebody was injuring the cause. You have never repudiated me
and I was born a heretic. . . . I always distrust people who
know so much about what God wants them to do to their
fellows. . . . The question is whether you will sit in judgment
on a woman that has written views different from yours. If
she had written your views you would not object. . . . When
this platform is too narrow for people of all creeds to stand
on, I shall not be on it. . . . If you fail to teach women a
broad catholic spirit, I would not give much for them after
they are enfranchised. . . . You had better organize one
woman on a broad platform than 10,000 on a narrow platform of intolerance and bigotry.[21]

The "Bible Resolution" passed nevertheless, by a vote of
fifty-three to forty-one. Among the majority were Carrie
Chapman Catt, Anna Howard Shaw, and other women
who were to lead the suffrage cause in the next twenty
years.[22] Mrs. Stanton had ceased being active in the association; Miss Anthony would retire from the presidency
in 1900; Mrs. Catt was already showing the genius for
leadership and organization that was to stamp the movement with her personality.

When woman suffrage was a radical cause, a handful
of pioneers who were willing to brave public censure
were its leaders. During the period in which suffragists

[21] *Ibid.*, pp. 91–93.   [22] *Ibid.*, pp. 93–95.

could expect to be pelted with eggs and fruit as well as verbal insults, an unconventional mind was indispensable to the women who dedicated their lives to pleading their case before a hostile public. The treatment they received in turn encouraged their tendency to question all that their society held sacred in the realm of religion, as well as in the field of politics. But, by the last decade of the nineteenth century, woman suffrage had become respectable, and women who held orthodox opinions on every other issue could now join a suffrage organization without fear of ostracism. Hence, a dual movement toward the "middle of the road" may be discerned at this time, of which the "Bible Resolution" was symptomatic. At the one end, a new generation of conservative [23] women came into the suffrage movement to achieve the victory that the Stantons and Anthonys had made possible.[24] At the other, the men who had it in their power to grant the women their demand were now more sympathetic to their appeals, and the younger suffragists felt they could not afford to offend the voters' sensibilities. In

[23] "Conservative" compared to Mrs. Stanton and Miss Anthony, that is. The younger women's conservatism in that context was completely compatible with their strong support of the reforms advocated by the Progressives. It must be noted, incidentally, that not all the pioneers were iconoclasts on subjects other than the woman question. It is the general tendency only which is here noted.

[24] Without a detailed investigation of public reaction to early suffragist propaganda, a task outside the scope of this study, it is manifestly impossible to state authoritatively the degree to which early suffragist radicalism paved the way for later suffrage victories. Pending such an analysis, however, it may be legitimate to postulate that changes in women's economic and social activities laid the foundations for changes in ideological attitudes toward women and that the early unconventional suffragists gradually accustomed the public to ideas which were still ahead of their time, but which circumstances were beginning to render realistic. The victory of suffrage might have come much later than it did if the Stantons had not spread their extremely advanced doctrines in the face of public opposition.

the 1890s suffragism was obviously changing from a vi-
sionary movement, whose sole task was to educate the
public, to a practical cause with a real chance for success.

Although the Association repudiated the *Woman's
Bible*, that book represented one method of arguing for
woman's equality in a period in which most people believed that the Bible opposed any change in the status
of women. In reality, Mrs. Stanton agreed fully with the
antis that this was the "true" interpretation of the Scriptures. Those suffragists who repudiated her work acted
not simply from a desire to curry favor with a funda-
mentalist public but rather from a belief that the Bible,
rightly interpreted, supported their claim. Most suffragists could hardly be expected to surrender the Bible to
their enemies, even if they believed that it was essentially an antisuffragist tract; but, sharing the Christianity
of their antisuffragist neighbors and benefiting from the
new possibility of reinterpreting the sacred texts, they
had both the incentive and the faith to find Biblical sanction for the equal dignity of all human beings in the
state, as well as in the home.

Of course they found this sanction in the first chapter
of Genesis, and in the many other passages that portrayed women as men's equals, as well as in those stories
in which women played heroic or honorable parts.[25]

[25] The Rev. Anna Howard Shaw delivered a major speech to the
National Council of Women in 1891 entitled "God's Women." She
replied to an anti's contention that God's women were the Ruths,
Rachels, and Marys, meek and submissive, and suggested instead that
the Deborahs, Miriams, and other strong women with minds of their
own were God's women. One of the Biblical women most admired by
suffragists was Vashti, who disobeyed her husband's command to ex-
hibit her beauty to his guests although it cost her her queenship. Dr.
Shaw's address is in *Woman's Journal*, March 7, 1891, and in *Trans-*

Sometimes, however, they frankly discussed the verses on which the antis relied most heavily, such as St. Paul's injunction, in the first Epistle to the Corinthians, that women were not to speak in church. Suffragists bold enough to tackle the problem had several recourses. They could find an error in the translation; they could discover that the context in which the Epistle had been written gave it meanings not applicable to modern times; or they could argue that Paul was expressing his own opinion in this letter, an opinion with which a modern Christian could disagree.

Women who chose the first explanation argued that the question involved the correct translation of the original word rendered in the King James version as "speak." Some women alleged that a truer translation would have been "babble," as Paul was expressing his dismay at the tendency of the women of Corinth to chatter and gossip inside the church, as well as at home.[26] Suffragists subscribing to this interpretation were evidently willing to admit that women as a sex gossiped more than men, in order to avoid the worse alternative of having to accept an apostolic injunction with even more uncomplimentary implications. Another passage the disputable translation of which could be turned to suffragist advantage was Acts 2:1–18, the subject of an anecdote by the Rev. Anna Howard Shaw. During her student days she had had a slight disagreement with a professor of Greek.

One day [she recalled] we came to the chapter in the New

---

actions of the National Council of Women of the United States, assembled in Washington, D.C., February 22 to 25, 1891, pp. 242–49.

[26] See, for example, C. W. McCulloch, *The Bible on Women Voting* (Evanston, Ill., n.d.), in McCulloch Papers, RWA.

Testament where, on the mountain-top after Pentecost, the people declared that the Christians were drunk, and Peter defended them by saying: "These are not drunken; this is the fulfillment of your own Scriptures, of your own prophet Joel, who said: 'In the last days, I shall pour out my spirit upon all flesh, and your sons and daughters shall prophesy.'"

I asked the professor what it meant by prophecy. . . .

"Well," he said, ". . . in the New Testament it is used wholly in the sense of preaching."

"Oh," I said, "then women preached at the time of the Pentecost?" The professor was bitterly opposed to women's preaching, and didn't like to have me in his class. "No, no," he said, "the women talked to each other."

"What did the men do?" I asked. "Did they talk to each other?"

"No, no," said he, "they preached."

And I said: "But the two are connected by a conjunction, 'men and women,' and when the women talked they talked, and when the men talked they preached. Is that the way it was?"

He said, "We will resume." [27]

The second way of interpreting St. Paul was exemplified in an essay by the young Carrie Chapman Catt written in 1890 before she became a national suffrage leader.[28] She argued that the Bible was an infallible guide for the true Christian life, but many passages in

[27] "Dr. Shaw Predicts Presidential Issue," the New York *Evening Post*, February 25, 1915, clipping in ssc. Among the many other examples of translation being used as a suffragist weapon was an article in the *Woman's Journal*, August 16, 1902, in which a minister was quoted to the effect that "rib" was an inaccurate rendering of the Hebrew word "tsela," in Genesis. He said a truer translation would have been "counterpart" or "complement," and the passage in question really meant, "The Lord saw that it was not good for man to be alone. So He placed woman by man's side," not above or beneath, but alongside.

[28] MS speech, "Woman-Suffrage and the Bible," in Catt Collection, NYPL.

it simply could not be applied literally to modern times. The attempt to use it as a guide in government, politics, or economics, she wrote, had caused its misuse as a justification for polygamy, slavery, intemperance, and the subjection of women. Since Paul's mission was to preach to the soul rather than to the body, he accepted the institutions of the day as he found them. He commanded men and women to accept whatever circumstances they found themselves in and to be Christians there. Thus slaves were enjoined to obey their masters, and wives their husbands.[29] There was no reason to believe that if Paul should come to modern America to preach, he would command colleges to bar women and every woman speaker to put a seal upon her mouth.

The third way of dealing with St. Paul, adopted by only the boldest suffragists, was to discredit him altogether. For example, Ida Porter-Boyer, a suffragist field organizer, wrote a religious argument for suffrage as late as 1914. She discussed various scriptural passages to support woman's equality and then, turning to St. Paul, disposed of him in the simplest possible way: "Paul never possessed the democratic spirit of Christ." After portray-

[29] A similar viewpoint was expressed by Sallie Clay Bennett, of Kentucky, speaking on "The Authority of Women to Preach the Gospel of Christ in Public Places," *Woman's Journal*, April 11, 1903. She believed that the command that women keep silent referred to some laws of heathen Corinth. She added that men could refuse to ordain women but when God called a woman to preach she did not need man's ordination.

As in so many other cases in which suffragists answered antisuffragist arguments without stopping to make sure that the answers gibed with other suffragist writings, Mrs. Catt evidently did not notice that her interpretation of St. Paul could give aid and comfort to the antis. Paul, she said, commanded men and women to accept their circumstances and be Christians there; antis could point out that suffragists were certainly not accepting their disfranchised circumstances with Christian resignation.

ing the apostle in an extremely unflattering light she asked triumphantly, "Do you wonder that it took a miracle to convert him?" But, she concluded, the miracle did not change *all* his traits, and this accounted for his antiwoman strictures.[30]

The suffragists could hardly be blamed for ignoring St. Paul when possible and concentrating on two passages in the Old Testament frequently cited by antis, but which really buttressed their claim to equality conclusively—provided they were "rightly" interpreted. The first was the familiar "rib story" of the origin of woman. Suffragists often pointed out that the tale of how God put Adam to sleep and fashioned Eve from his rib contradicted the chapter of Genesis in which, as Miss Shaw paraphrased it,

He created man, male and female man, and called their name Adam, and to this male and female man, whom he called Adam, He gave all things, and bade this man Adam, male and female, to subdue all things, even the world, to themselves.[31]

Miss Shaw and most of the other suffragists simply ignored the chapter that described what Mrs. Stanton had called "a petty surgical operation." [32] The second passage in the Old Testament that the suffragists reinterpreted in support of their cause was the "curse," that is, God's statement to Eve, "Thy desire shall be to thy husband, and he shall rule over thee," and the corresponding declaration to Adam that he should eat his bread in the sweat of his face. When suffragists explained

[30] "The Scriptural Authority for Woman's Equality," *"Woman's Journal*, April 18, 1914.
[31] "God's Women," speech cited in footnote 25.
[32] *Woman's Bible*, Part I, p. 20.

that the curse was a prediction rather than a command, they had the satisfaction of turning an important anti-suffragist weapon against its wielders. They argued that if the curse were a command, it would be sacrilegious for men to invent machinery to lighten their labor. This *reductio ad absurdum* proved that the inferior status of women belonged only in the primitive and barbaric society in which men produced their food with the wooden plow and the bow and arrow. Sometimes the theory of progress thus linked with the woman question was given additional support by suffragist theorists who pointed out that Christ came to wipe out the curse, and when St. Paul himself could be quoted to the effect that "There is neither Jew nor Greek, there is neither bond nor free, there is neither male nor female; for ye are all one in Christ Jesus,"[33] the suffragists felt that they had proved that the sexes were equal before God and hence ought to be equal in a God-fearing commonwealth.[34]

Suffragists doubtless welcomed the tendency in some religious circles at the dawn of the twentieth century to use the New Testament as a guide to the good life rather than as a source of rules for religious observance. No longer need they find new translations or interpretations for troublesome passages. More and more they could point out the consistency between the ethics of Christianity and freedom for modern woman to serve her fellow

[33] Galatians 3:28.

[34] Examples of this line of thought may be found in McCulloch, *The Bible on Women Voting;* Laura Clay, letter to the "editor of the Evening Telegram" [1906?], typed copy in Clay Papers, UK (the manuscript does not further identify the newspaper); and Bashford, *The Bible for Woman Suffrage,* reprinted in *Woman's Journal,* December 13, 1913.

human beings in any way her talents permitted. Bible
exegesis took second place in suffragist arguments on
religious themes, and the ethical teachings of Jesus became the principal religious argument for woman suffrage.

The Rev. Anna Howard Shaw expressed this point of
view repeatedly in her speeches. She declared on one
occasion,

The democracy of Christianity teaches us that religion must
become more personal and more human, and the more one
studies the life of Jesus the more he is impressed with the fact
that the one permanent basis of the spiritual life is that community of soul in which each earnestly strives to the attain-
ment of the highest life, yet each in loving fellowship with
the whole.

The great defect in the religious teaching to and accepted
by women is the dogma that self-abnegation, self-effacement,
and excessive humility were ideal feminine virtues. . . . But
we are learning from the teaching and example of Jesus that
life itself is a religion, that nothing is more sacred than a
human being, that the end of all right institutions, whether
the home or the church or an educational establishment, or a
government, is the development of the human soul.[35]

---

[35] "The Women Who Publish the Tidings Are a Great Host," in
Linkugel, "The Speeches of Anna Howard Shaw" (Ph.D. dissertation,
University of Wisconsin, 1960, II, 83–84; copy of original speech in
folder No. 82 of the Anna Howard Shaw Papers, Dillon Collection,
RWA, and quoted by permission of Dr. Mary Earhart Dillon). Linkugel
dates the speech 1914 or later because of its reference to the war, but
the fact that it also refers to the upheaval in Russia probably indicates
that it was given in 1917 or later. See also suggestion of NAWSA's Committee on Church Work, that suffragists point out that "Jesus never
discriminated against sex. In his ideals of life woman has an individuality just as sacred as man's. He came to make man–'male and female'
–*free* so that a Christian civilization *is* one where no law limits a
woman's freedom any more than a man's. As an Association we should
voice this fundamental principle with no uncertain sound." (NAWSA,
Proceedings, 1904, pp. 39–40.)

Elizabeth Cady Stanton also preached the duty of self-development and the dignity of every human soul. Her heresy resulted from her conviction that the Bible taught precisely the reverse. Miss Shaw and most other suffragists, on the other hand, insisted that the principles that Mrs. Stanton could not find in orthodox Christianity were in fact its essence.[36]

Alice Stone Blackwell, as editor and chief editorial writer of the *Woman's Journal*, occasionally expressed opinions in its columns similar to those of Dr. Shaw. In the issue of October 26, 1895, for example, she brushed aside the standard antisuffragist arguments with this explanation:

If we do not give much space to discussion of the scriptural argument in our columns, it is because we are convinced by experience that this objection is not now the practical obstacle in the minds of most people. . . . As good an argument can be made from isolated texts of Scripture, for the divine right of kings or for human slavery, as for the subjection of women. Tory parsons and pro-slavery preachers did not fail to make it. The one unanswerable and all-sufficient text of Scripture in behalf of woman suffrage, as in behalf of all other reforms, is the Golden Rule. Every man knows at the bottom of his heart that he would not like to be taxed without representation, and governed by law makers whom he had no voice in choosing. If he would not like others to do it to him, he ought not to do it to them. Plain people can

[36] It must not be inferred from Mrs. Stanton's anti-Bible and anti-clerical views that she was an atheist. In the Stanton Papers, LC, is a manuscript in her writing, evidently written in her old age, entitled, "My Creed." In it she explains that the complex structure of the world and natural laws cause her to believe in a Supreme Intelligence, although her description of it seems to indicate that she saw it as impersonal and equivalent to "Supreme Law." Evil and pain result from violation of this law. She believed in immortality, but not in special Providence.

well afford to let the doctors of divinity fight out the battle of doubtful texts, and to plant themselves meanwhile squarely on the Golden Rule, secure that in the long run all the doctors of divinity will come around and range themselves on the same side.

Suffragists had an additional motive for following Miss Blackwell's advice to avoid futile arguments about doubtful texts. Quite plainly, clergymen supported woman suffrage in far greater proportion than did men of any other profession.[37] They constituted the most influential and respectable allies among the men suffragists. Furthermore, suffragists frequently said that the vast majority of practicing Christians in the United States were women, who thus provided sympathetic ministers with a ready audience for suffragist sermons. Therefore, once Mrs. Stanton's anticlericalism had ceased to be an issue and once suffragists had satisfied themselves that the spirit of Christianity was on their side, they inaugurated a campaign to secure prosuffrage sermons and public endorsements by ministers as a regular part of their propaganda work. In 1902 the NAWSA established a Committee on Church Work to carry out this task.[38] Although dis-

[37] In 1901 the Massachusetts Woman Suffrage Association sent a questionnaire to clergymen in that state and received 264 replies. One hundred eighty-three were unqualifiedly in favor of equal suffrage; 19 were for municipal, license, or some other form of limited suffrage; 31 were opposed; and 31 were noncommittal or undecided (*Woman's Journal*, January 25, 1902). A few years earlier Miss Blackwell had written, "No class of men knows the scriptures so well, or is influenced by them so strongly, as the ministers; and we find there are six ministers ready to speak for woman suffrage at our meetings to one man of any other profession. It is because the ministers are especially interested in questions of practical righteousness, in which they know that the women's votes would help; and the solidity of the vicious elements against woman suffrage has gone far to solidify the ministers in its favor." (*Ibid.*, October 26, 1895.)

[38] NAWSA, *Proceedings*, 1902, p. 61. The executive committee set up

cussions of Biblical texts still occasionally appeared in suffragist writings and speeches, the movement paid relatively little attention to religious arguments after that time. Suffragists and antis both preferred other battlegrounds.

---

the committee at its closing meeting on February 19, and instructed it to report at the next convention on "ways and means of interesting conservative church women." Subsequent convention *Proceedings* indicate that the committee worked to reach ministers and religious societies also, as well as to publicize what it believed to be Biblical support of women's claim to equality.

FIVE

Woman and the Home

A strategic battleground between suffragists and antis was the definition of *woman* and *the home*. Suffragist spokesmen, who in most cases had benefited from educational and economic opportunities far beyond the average and who demanded the vote in order to bring their political status up to their social, economic, and educational status, were constantly confronted by the antisuffragist argument that such a change would contradict the inherent nature of woman and would destroy the home. The suffragists were certain, of course, that they were perfectly normal women and that their homes were not endangered, but having been challenged they had to make their countertheories explicit. The antis' argument was circular in that they had defined *home* and *woman* in such a way as to make suffrage inadmissible and then proclaimed that definition to be proof of the inadmissibility of woman suffrage. The suffragists thus had to reject the antis' very definitions.

They replaced those definitions with definitions of their own that portrayed the nature of woman as perfectly consistent with political activity and that broke down the wall of isolation around each home that the antis had erected. The various suffragist spokesmen went about

this task in different ways. In most cases they were
content to meet antisuffragist assertions with counter-
assertions of their own. A few suffragists, however, attempted to place a solid foundation of anthropology and
sociology under their theories.

The only systematic theory linking the demand for
suffrage with the long sweep of history was that of
Charlotte Perkins Gilman, the most influential woman
thinker in the pre-World War I generation in the United
States.[1] Her influence, however, was indirect, for only
here and there did suffragist writings expound her
theories. Her chief task was to make people think, and
in this regard she was a worthy successor to Mrs. Stanton,
intellectual gadfly of the preceding generation. Mrs. Gilman, a descendant of the Beecher family and a lecturer,
novelist, poet, and journalist, undertook to make the
"gynecocentric" theory of Lester Frank Ward compre-
hensible to Americans.[2] But she was not a mere pop-

[1] A convenient summary of Mrs. Gilman's views may be found in
Degler, "Charlotte Perkins Gilman on the Theory and Practice of Feminism," *American Quarterly*, VIII (Spring, 1956), 21–39. Professor
Degler mentions tributes to Mrs. Gilman's importance found in writings of Carrie Chapman Catt, Harriot Stanton Blatch, and others, and
notes her influence on Ashley Montagu. Mrs. Blatch wrote that at
Vassar, Mrs. Gilman's book, *Women and Economics*, was "the Bible
of the student body." T. V. Smith, in *The American Philosophy of
Equality*, p. 298, calls *Women and Economics* "not only one of the
great classics on woman's rights but a rich mine of insight on social
relations in general."

[2] Of Ward's writings, one article of particular importance to Mrs.
Gilman was "Our Better Halves," *Forum*, VI (November, 1888), 266–
75. In her autobiography, she calls it "the greatest single contribution
to the world's thought since Evolution," and writes that it was one
of the two works she read while preparing to write her *Women and
Economics* (see *The Living of Charlotte Perkins Gilman*, pp. 187, 259).
The autobiography and other works of hers are sometimes catalogued
under the name Charlotte Perkins Stetson; Stetson was the name of her

ularizer, for her *Women and Economics*, published in
1898, was an original work that even today provokes
thought and repays study.

Mrs. Gilman argued that in savage society women
who had children necessarily developed the domestic
arts and the capacity for love and service while men
roamed the forests, free, destructive, and irresponsible.
As with other species, the human males competed for
their mates, and the strongest and cleverest perpetuated
their kind. Both men and women obtained their own
food, and the human race evolved much as other species
did, in response to its environment and especially to its
own activities in securing food. But a time came when
it occurred to man that it was easier to enslave one
female once and for all than to compete with other males
again and again. The supremacy of man over woman
began, and woman, being enslaved, could no longer get
her food freely for herself and her young as before. Man,
as the feeder of woman, became the strongest modifying
force in her economic condition.[3]

When man began to feed and defend woman, she ceased
proportionately to feed and defend herself. When he stood
between her and her physical environment, she ceased proportionately to feel the influence of that environment and
respond to it. When he became her immediate and all-important environment, she began proportionately to respond
to this new influence, and to be modified accordingly. . . .
The human female was cut off from the direct action of
natural selection, that mighty force which heretofore had

---

first husband. The theories of Ward's that are relevant here are con-
veniently summarized in Samuel Chugarman, *Lester F. Ward: The
American Aristotle* (Durham, N.C.: Duke University Press, 1939),
chap. XXXI, especially p. 379.

[3] Gilman, *Women and Economics*, pp. 60–61.

acted on male and female alike with inexorable and bene-
ficial effect, developing strength, developing skill, developing endurance, developing courage,—in a word, developing
species. She now met the influence of natural selection acting indirectly through the male, and developing, of course,
the faculties required to secure and obtain a hold on him.
Needless to state that these faculties were those of sex-
attraction, the one power that has made him cheerfully maintain, in what luxury he could, the being in whom he de-
lighted. For many, many centuries she had no other hold, no
other assurance of being fed.

Even in modern times, continued Mrs. Gilman, except
for the increasing numbers of women wage-earners, the
personal profit of women bore but too close a relation to
their power to win and hold the other sex. The open
market of vice caused people to recoil in horror, but
when they saw the same economic relationship made
permanent, established by law, sanctioned and sanctified
by religion, covered with flowers and incense and sentiment, they thought it innocent, lovely, and right. The
transient trade was called evil, the bargain for life good.
But the biological effect was the same; in both cases the
female got her food from the male by virtue of her sex-
relationship to him.[4]

The restricted environment of women, she continued,
had led to restricted knowledge and, more seriously, to
restricted activity. Specialization and organization, the
bases of human progress, were forbidden to women almost absolutely. Each girl inherited her father's large
potentialities for growth, just as each boy inherited his
mother's increasing sex-development. Each woman must
thus suppress anew her impulses toward growth and ful-

[4] *Ibid.*, pp. 60–64; quotation may be found in pp. 61–63.

fillment and to squeeze her talents into the one avenue open to her, marriage. "Is it any wonder that women are over-sexed? But for the constant inheritance from the more human male, we should have been queen bees, indeed, long before this." [5]

Just as most human ills, in Mrs. Gilman's view, resulted from woman's dependence on man, so the restoration of the proper relations between the sexes and the development of the best kind of home would follow from woman's independence. Mrs. Gilman advocated the professionalization of household tasks. The division of household labor, like any division of labor, would lessen the total amount of labor and increase its efficiency. Women would have more time for other activities. She made it clear that she would not abolish the home, but merely the home as it was, perverted from its wonderful function of providing a "common sheath for the budded leaflets of each new branch" by being based upon "the sexuo-economic relation." [6] She looked forward to the time when the home would lose its kitchen as it had already lost its laundry and bakery, when it would be connected with no industry whatever, and remain a place in which to live and love, to rest and play, to be alone and to be together. The sex relation would be made pure by the economic independence of women, and sex-attraction would no longer be a consuming fever. Relationships between people as people would be freer, since with present oversexed people, said Mrs. Gilman, the great obstacle to satisfying deep needs for friendship was the assumption that such needs were sexual. [7] The reason men formed deeper friendships than women was that men

[5] *Ibid.*, p. 72.   [6] *Ibid.*, p. 261.   [7] *Ibid.*, chap. XIV.

worked together. The natural association of common effort conduced to human companionship. Women, on the other hand, worked alone. Women had been trained to personal usefulness, men to social usefulness, each sex reflecting its economic conditions. Humans had thus become psychic hybrids; economic independence of women would harmonize the human soul.[8]

Elizabeth Cady Stanton, like Mrs. Gilman, appealed to anthropology to support her arguments for suffrage. In 1891 she wrote an essay entitled "The Matriarchate" which Susan B. Anthony read before the convention of the National Council of Women.[9] Mrs. Stanton took her theory of the Matriarchate, or Mother-Age, from Lewis Henry Morgan's *Ancient Society* and from a number of other scholarly works to which she acknowledged her debt. With Mrs. Gilman she believed that savage woman had been free and independent and the originator of civilization; care for her children had led to the development of love, altruism, and domesticity. Unlike Mrs. Gilman, however, she did not believe that the long ages of male dominance that followed this Golden Age had caused women to become genetically inferior to men. Woman's present inferiority, she believed, was a cultural inheritance. What to Mrs. Gilman was a product of evolution, to be changed by further, consciously directed evolution, was to Mrs. Stanton a product of education, to be corrected by truer education and by educational devices such as the ballot.

[8] *Ibid.*, chap. XV.
[9] National Council of Women, *Transactions*, 1891, pp. 218–27. The essay was reprinted in the *National Bulletin*, I (February 1891), 1–7. The *Bulletin* was a monthly publication of the *Woman's Tribune*, a suffragist weekly published by Mrs. Stanton's friend Clara Bewick Colby.

Some of the theories that other suffragists developed were wishfully derived in part from anthropology. A few of them postulated a peaceful golden age in which woman had ruled the home and the tribe, replaced by a social organization in which men usurped authority, waged war, and oppressed women. Woman suffrage would help bring back peace and respect for women. Other suffragists postulated a *bellum omnium contra omnes* in the beginning, in which intelligence had not developed far enough to carry much weight in human affairs. In this stage women had necessarily been subordinate owing to their maternal functions and inferior strength and size. The advance of civilization consisted of the gradual replacement of force by reason and hence the inclusion in the electorate of all adults who could reason rather than only those who could fight.

Both Mrs. Gilman and Mrs. Stanton, in acknowledging the present inferiority of American women to American men, opposed the prevailing tone of suffragist propaganda, which implied that millennia of suppression had left women quite as capable of exercising the suffrage wisely here and now as men who had generations of political experience. Occasionally these suffragists had to admit that one of the major obstacles to the victory of their cause was the indifference or hostility of the majority of women. This they ascribed to the effects of suppression. They then asserted that political activity would broaden women's minds and enlarge their consciences. But most of their arguments on this subject, particularly in the period in which the "argument from expediency" dominated suffragist propaganda, emphasized the benefits that would immediately accrue to a society that en-

franchised its women, owing to women's expert knowledge of many of the fields in which modern governments
operated and owing to women's superior morality, so-
briety, and literacy.

Here, then, was a dilemma that lay at the core of all
the suffragists' arguments on the nature of woman. If
centuries of oppression had left women just as capable
of self-rule and political activity as men, the oppression
could not be so severe as the women claimed, and disfranchisement could not be either a symptom or a cause
of the large gap between the status of men and that of
women.[10] On the other hand, if centuries of oppression
had left women inferior to men, even if that inferiority
was cultural rather than genetic, the women who tried
to persuade legislators that woman suffrage would purify
government and advance reform would lose much of
their claim to a respectful hearing.

Suffragists found themselves forced to argue against
antis who explicitly or implicitly based their antisuffragism on woman's inferiority. The exigencies of debate,
as well as of their own need to justify their organizational activities, drove the suffragists to insist on their
essential equality with men. They could acknowledge
present inferiority only occasionally or obliquely. They
admitted the effects of environment only when confronted by antisuffragist taunts that women had never
composed great symphonies or written great poetry, or

[10] Compare Percy Bysshe Shelley's introduction to the long poem,
"The Revolt of Islam." Discussing violence in the French Revolution
that had alienated many well-meaning people, he wrote: "If the Revolution had been in every respect prosperous, then misrule and superstition would lose half their claims to our abhorrence, as fetters which
the captive can unlock with the slightest motion of his fingers, and
which do not eat with poisonous rust into the soul."

by antisuffragist definitions of woman's sphere. It was then that the suffragists discovered the stultifying effects of having been trained solely to be servants and nurse-maids. The principal changes that most suffragists expected their enfranchisement to bring about were not in women but in society and in relations between men and women.[11]

When some suffragists said that women were inferior owing to their long suppression and other suffragists (or the same suffragists at other times) declared that women were at least the equals of their men in the qualities needed for the wise exercise of the vote, they reflected a striking difference between themselves and the great mass of women many of whom must be converted to the cause before it could triumph. The former argument could be thought of as applying to that great mass of indifferent and unemancipated women; the latter argument could be considered a reflection of the suffragists' own superior education and professional accomplishments. Long centuries of oppression could perhaps be blamed for the fact that most women did not particularly desire political equality and hardly thought of issues other than those that immediately touched their own families. The antis insisted that this limited concern for their own families was necessary for women to be good wives and mothers. The suffragists denied that assertion

[11] Note the exception in footnote 8 of chap. III. Some suffragists expected women's participation in government to broaden their minds. They did not conceive of this as a very drastic change, and they expected newly enfranchised women to become politically wise very quickly. Evidence of this may be found in the innumerable suffragist tracts which pointed proudly to the records of the full-suffrage states in the West, the governments of which had allegedly improved soon after their women had received the vote.

with a vehemence perhaps intensified by their knowledge that the success of their cause depended in large part on whether they could convert many of those isolated and apathetic women.

The conflict between the two viewpoints on whether women were inferior to men was seldom expressed openly. Suffragist writers frequently pointed out that traits popularly assumed to be feminine, such as emotionality, appeared in men, as well as in women, or they discussed typically feminine faults in order to show them to be the results of training. The journalist Ida Husted Harper described those faults in her column in the New York *Sun* of August 5, 1900. Discussing a recent editorial in a Rochester paper that deplored women's custom of bringing food and gifts to imprisoned felons, Mrs. Harper explained that that was only what might be expected from women who had as little girls been taught to return a kiss for the blows of their belligerent little brothers. In childhood they were forever rescuing neighborhood dogs and cats from the cruelties of the boys and tearfully binding up the wounds. From the dawn of civilization they had been taught that they had been created for the express purpose of repairing the damages of society, nursing the sick, caring for the dependent, and above all, reclaiming the weak and the wicked.

The belief has by no means died out that it is a woman's sacred duty to marry a dissolute man in order to reform him, although the number of victims sacrificed on this altar is growing somewhat less. So broad, just and progressive a man as Robert Ingersoll used to describe in one of his lectures, with that vivid word painting for which he was famous, the beautiful devotion of the drunkard's wife, who met her husband's curses with sweet words, kissed his bloated lips, bathed his burning face and, staggering under his blows, dragged her bruised limbs about in effort to care for him tenderly until he was able to go out and get drunk again. Then all the men in the audience would applaud, while the women would weep and consecrate themselves anew.

The role of ministering angel was not natural to women, in the opinion of Mrs. Harper and other suffragists who believed that self-respect and self-development were feminine as well as masculine virtues. A frequent theme was that the education of girls to trust in and yield to the dominance of men was one cause of what that era called "the social evil." Ellen Battelle Dietrick, for instance, wrote in the *Woman's Journal* of May 27, 1893, that the world was saturated with the idea that woman was created for man; doctors of divinity taught that she was his in a quite different sense from that in which he was hers. Man was represented as the head of woman, and she was trained to love, to trust, to confide in him, to look forward not to her own self-government and support, but to man's control of her destiny.

As man does not think it modest in her to acquire a knowledge of the realities of life, there is a silent conspiracy to keep the girl in ignorance of everything pertaining to the relations between the sexes. Meanwhile the boy early learns that many of his elders and superiors consider the annual degradation of millions of women in Christendom a "necessary (!) evil." He sees this stated by eminent physicians; he finds it in the writings of Christian moralists . . . ; he will even find it advised by Christian legislators who propose, not to abolish, but, to regulate this, so-called, necessary evil purely with a view to man's protection in indulgence. . . . Trained to emotionality, faith, and confiding trustfulness . . . [a girl] listens to the man . . . who whispers in her ear that "marriages are made in heaven" . . . and that "love is the greatest thing in the universe," and she yields. The king can do no wrong, and to the ignorant girl who "falls," the man she loves has been king.

Mrs. Dietrick continued by describing the subsequent career of the unwed mother who was likely to become either a suicide or a prostitute.[12]

The writers who urged that self-respect and self-development were, or ought to be, feminine virtues emphasized the ways in which women were innately identical to men and often went on record against proposals that would emphasize what they believed to be the nonessential differences between the sexes.[13] Other suffragists refused to speculate as to whether specific traits were innate or the result of training. Alice Stone Blackwell argued that if a trait was inherent it would not be affected by the suffrage,[14] so that the defenders of

[12] Similar opinions may be found in an article by Alice Stone Blackwell in *Woman's Journal*, July 27, 1895.

[13] Mrs. Stanton, for example, criticized the suggestion that cooking and sewing be added to the college curricula of all women students. Why, she asked, ought we to separate the sexes in college when we do not separate them in the home? Further, many women would never have occasion to use the domestic skills which Mrs. Stanton's adversaries, the enemies of coeducation, would teach all women college students. (*Ibid.*, December 29, 1900.) Cf. [Laura Clay] to Sen. James B. McCreary, December 18, 1907, Clay Papers, UK, in which she praised his bill to appropriate money to colleges for instruction in agriculture, manual training, and domestic science. She was happy to learn that domestic science had been raised to the dignity of a department in some colleges, in view of the fact that most women students would become homemakers. The difference in generation and viewpoint between Mrs. Stanton and Miss Clay, significant in suffragist history, is noted on pp. 110–11.

[14] *Woman's Journal*, January 14, 1893, and January 18, 1902.

woman's femininity, of the home, and of marriage need not worry that woman suffrage would produce a nation of sexless, homeless and celibate monstrosities. She also excused women's apparent inability to produce Shakespeares and Beethovens on the ground that they had never had the training that encouraged artistic creativity, as distinguished from the kind of instruction that produced competent performers of others' creations.[15] On the other hand, Miss Blackwell did not fail to call attention to male behavior that implied women's equality or superiority, but in such discussions she did not theorize as to the source of the virtues or faults under consideration. Her columns in the *Woman's Journal* often contained news of rioting in the French Chamber of Deputies [16] fistfights in the House of Commons,[17] a general melee in the Bulgarian Parliament,[18] or beard-pulling in the Nebraska Senate.[19] She entitled these brief notices "Too Emotional to Vote," or something similar. The Rev. Anna Howard Shaw, greatest orator of the suffrage movement, discoursed thus on the same subject:

Women are supposed to be unfit to vote because they are hysterical and emotional. . . . I had heard so much about our emotionalism that I went to the last Democratic National Convention held at Baltimore, to observe the calm repose of the male contingent. I saw some men take a picture of one gentleman whom they wanted elected, and it was so big they had to walk sideways as they carried it forward; they were followed by hundreds of other men scream-

---

[15] *Ibid.*, August 29, 1891.   [16] *Ibid.*, February 12, 1898.
[17] *Ibid.*, January 19, 1895.   [18] *Ibid.*
[19] *Ibid.*, April 27, 1895. Other such incidents are mentioned in the issues of August 22, 1896; June 5, 1897; June 3, 1899; November 12, 1904; and November 26, 1910; and in *Woman Citizen*, July 7, 1917.

ing, yelling, shouting and singing the "Hown Dawg" song; then, when there was a lull, another set of men would start forward under another man's picture, not to be outdone by the "Hown Dawg" melody, screaming, yelling and shouting at their people. I saw men jump upon the seat and throw their hats in the air and shout: "What's the matter with Champ Clark?" Then, when those hats came down, other men would kick them back into the air, shouting at the top of their voices: "He's all right!!!" Then I heard others screaming and shouting and yelling for "Underwood!! Underwood, first, last and all the time!!!" No hysteria about it—just patriotic loyalty, splendid manly devotion to principle. And so they went on and went on until 5 o'clock in the morning—the whole night long. I saw men jump up in their seats, and jump down again, and run around in a ring. . . .

I have been to a lot of women's conventions in my day, but I never saw a woman knock another woman's bonnet off of her head as she shouted: "She's all right!" . . . We are perfectly willing to admit that we are emotional. I have actually seen women stand up and wave their handkerchiefs. I have even seen them take hold of hands and sing, "Blest be the tie that binds."! [20]

[20] Shaw, *Passages from Speeches*, pp. 9–10. Discussing men's emotionality on the subject of woman, Mrs. Harper wrote in her New York *Sun* column on June 10, 1900: "There are very few great editors in the country who have been able to resist the temptation to write a soulful panegyric on the recent Mothers' Congress, indulging in the usual gush over 'wifehood and motherhood.' Men can't help it because they are so emotional; nature made them that way, and, just as the sight of water sends a hydrophobic patient into convulsions so the contemplation of wifehood and motherhood throws these emotional creatures into a fit of hysteria. Imagine every woman in the country who has access to a newspaper using it to glorify husbandhood and fatherhood! . . . There never has been a time since the alphabet was invented when we have not been solemnly assured that mother love is the strongest passion humanity is capable of. From the period of Moses down to June, 1900, we have been told that God and nature, the prophecies, the Ten Commandments, the beatitudes, the revelations, the Church, the Pope, the Bishops, the elders, the editors and the politicians, intended woman to be the mother of the race. She would have found it out herself if nobody had ever told her. . . . Why in the name of common sense are all the small fry in creation

In the 1890s, suffragist propaganda began to admit, then to stress, the differences between men and women, usually ignoring anthropological theories. Especially in the later years suffragist theorists saw woman in two lights. Within her home she was the sex whose chief duty in life was bearing and caring for children, functions that naturally endowed her with capacities for love and service and with peaceful propensities, all of which traits were sorely needed in government.[21] Outside her home she was the half of the population that, whether inherently or by training, was more moral, more temperate, more law-abiding, and (by training only, of course) more literate than the other half.[22] In both roles, then, woman

popping up at this late day and informing her that she has got to be what she always has been? Can it be possible that at this dawn of a new century a free womanhood is about to assert itself and declare that, as man in all the past ages has exercised his individual wish as to whether he will be a husband and father, so woman henceforth will decide for herself whether she shall assume the relations of wife and mother?"

[21] See, for example, Carrie Chapman Catt, "Evolution and Woman's Suffrage," manuscript of speech delivered May 18, 1893, in Catt Collection, NYPL; Alice Stone Blackwell in *Woman's Journal*, January 30, 1904; two clippings in Harriet Burton Laidlaw Scrapbooks, NYHS, setting forth Mrs. Laidlaw's views; Austin and Martin, *Suffrage and Government*, pp. 5, 7; Mabel Vernon to Editor of the *Catholic Herald*, Sacramento, July 9, 1914 (copy), Vernon Collection, UCB; Carrie Chapman Catt, in *Woman's Journal*, January 9, 1915.

[22] See, for example, Lucy Stone in 1892 House *Hearing*, p. 7; Alice Stone Blackwell in *Woman's Journal*, April 30, 1898; Lillie Devereux Blake, *ibid.*, September 3, 1898; a number of articles, *ibid.*, during 1914 after outbreak of war in Europe; Lavinia Dock in *Suffragist*, June 9, 1917; and numerous citations in chap. VI, in discussion of suffragist reactions to the "new immigration." The general impression left on the reader is that women's faults were due to custom and training whereas their virtues were inherent. Jane Addams seems to have sensed the inconsistency when she said in a speech to the Chicago Political Equality League, "I am not one of those who believe—broadly speaking—that women are better than men. We have not wrecked railroads, nor corrupted Legislatures, nor done many unholy things that men have done; but then we must remember that we have

would be a tremendous asset to government if enfranchised. Sometimes the differences between the sexes found imaginative expression that indicated that the antis did not hold a monopoly on poetic talent, although unlike the paeans of the antis, the suffragists' tributes were paid equally to men and women. A common metaphor was that a true harmony in government required the soprano as well as the bass voice.[23] Mrs. Stanton, characteristically, likened husband and wife to centrifugal and centripetal forces, the absence of either of which would produce chaos.[24] The last word on the differences between the sexes as they related to the question of suffrage was spoken, perhaps, by Harriet Burton Laidlaw in 1912 when she covered the subject completely by saying that insofar as women were like men they ought to have the same rights; insofar as they were different they must represent themselves.[25]

A suffragist theory that declared that woman's principal vocation was mothering and at the same time insisted that true womanliness implied strength and inde-

---

not had the chance." (Quoted in *Woman's Journal*, November 20, 1897.) The antis evidently did not believe women's virtues were inherent, when they argued, as they often did, that the suffrage would bring women into contact with dirty politics and corrupt them, a charge that suffragists vehemently rejected. Mrs. Catt declared in 1899: "It is not chiefly because good men fear the influence of bad politics on good women [that women are denied the ballot], but because bad men fear the influence of good women on bad politics." (*Ibid.*, June 2, 1900, quoting Mrs. Catt's remarks at a suffrage meeting at Faneuil Hall, Boston.)

[23] For example, Laura Clay, *ibid.*, June 15, 1901.

[24] Elizabeth Cady Stanton to Ida Husted Harper, September 30, 1902, Harper Collection, HL.

[25] *Twenty-Five Answers to Antis*, pp. 10–11. The pamphlet reprints speeches delivered March 11, 1912, in New York. A copy is in the Ethel E. Dreier Papers, SSC.

pendence [26] clashed head on with the current belief that motherhood meant dependence. It raised sharply the question of the relationship between men and women and therefore also the definition of the home. It challenged antisuffragists' claims that their ideal home was based on the equality of husband and wife, with the husband the head merely insofar as the family was represented in the world.

The home as it was, based on the supremacy of the husband and father, thundered the suffragists, was responsible for prostitution, the double standard of morals, and the increase in divorce. The education of men to rule women, they insisted, led men to justify self-indulgence and the degradation of the sex that had been created for man's convenience. Church, school, and state, all conspired to teach young men that women did not deserve their respect.[27] How then could men be expected to remain faithful to the creatures to whom they were married; how could they be expected to realize that the degradation of a portion of womanhood degraded all? [28]

[26] Other expressions of this description of true womanliness may be found in Anna Howard Shaw, "God's Women," *Woman's Journal*, March 7, 1891; Susan B. Anthony in New York *Sun*, June 23 and July 14, 1901; leaflet published by Michigan Equal Suffrage Association, reprinting an article from the Detroit *Journal* of March 29, 1913, entitled "Four Militant Bible Women," in Clay Papers, UK.

[27] Some expressions of these views may be found in: Ellen Battelle Dietrick, "Awake, Awake, Deborah!" *Woman's Journal*, December 13, 1890; Elizabeth Cady Stanton, *ibid.*, January 19, 1901; Catt, *President's Annual Address* (1902), pp. 5–9 (pamphlet in Catt Collection, NYPL). Suffragists repeatedly distinguished between chivalry and true respect.

[28] When the United States acquired the Philippines and Hawaii the suffragists protested vigorously against the government's efforts to regulate prostitution on the islands. They favored abolition rather than regulation for several reasons: regulation had not protected public health where it had been tried in the United States and elsewhere; regulation implied official tolerance and gave a sort of respectability

Men were generally not taught that chastity was a masculine virtue; quite the contrary. In the same way, women were not taught that courage, strength, and patriotism were feminine virtues. Consequently, a race of people had been bred whose men were brave, patriotic, and promiscuous and whose women were timid, generally unconcerned with the larger interests of society, and very moral. This contrast, implied in many suffragist essays, was made explicitly by Elizabeth Cady Stanton in two discussions of the notorious Parnell case in England. In an essay entitled "Patriotism and Chastity," [29] she criticized Parnell's political opponents for questioning his political fitness on account of his alleged violation of the Seventh Commandment. Webster, Clay, Franklin, and Cleveland had all been imperfect in their private lives, to say nothing of Cleopatra, Queen Elizabeth I, Catherine of Russia, Mary Wollstonecraft, George Sand, Frances Wright, and George Eliot; yet in other ways all these people had benefited society.

If we have a difficult case in court, we inquire for the most successful lawyer; if we have a child at death's door, we seek the most skillful physician; we ask no questions as to

---

to vice; compulsory examination of prostitutes was outrageous because it occasionally caused humiliation of innocent women and also because there was no reason why the men who patronized the prostitutes ought not to have been examined also; and regulation implied approval of the myth that promiscuity was, if not acceptable, at least an ineradicable weakness in men. Suffragist discussions of this issue include: Statement of NAWSA officers, *Woman's Journal,* September 8, 1900; *Proceedings* of the Thirty-Third Annual Convention of the National American Woman Suffrage Association . . . Minneapolis, Minn., May 30 and 31, June 1, 2, 3, 4, and 5, 1901 (Warren, Ohio, n.d.), p. 16; NAWSA, *Proceedings,* 1902, pp. 50, 62–64; NAWSA, *Proceedings,* 1905, p. 91.

[29] *Westminster Review,* CXXXV (January, 1891), 1–5.

social life in either case, but avail ourselves of knowledge and wisdom when we need it.

Mrs. Stanton was in a minority among suffragists here; they sometimes advocated woman suffrage precisely because it would prevent the election of men such as Cleveland. On another occasion she wrote:

As men have not been educated to chastity, why look for it? We might as well require that women, who have never been trained to patriotism, should be public spirited. Let us condemn the system which makes men and women what they are and not crucify the victims of our false standard of morals. The one lesson these social earthquakes teach is to cultivate in woman more self-respect. Instead of hounding men, emancipate women from all forms of bondage. But so long as women are slaves, men will be knaves.[30]

Suffragists never advocated lowering women's moral standards to the level of men's. Victoria Woodhull and her sister, Tennessee Claflin, never for a moment represented suffragist thinking. Mrs. Stanton and Miss Anthony had defended Mrs. Woodhull in the 1870s only out of a sense of sex solidarity, but neither they nor any other suffragists ever espoused her views.[31] The very possibility of even such a temporary association with a Woodhull or Claflin disappeared as soon as the suffrage movement became more than a radical demand by a few individuals. All suffragists believed that the gap between

---

30 Stanton and Blatch, eds., *Elizabeth Cady Stanton*, II, 270.

31 "Mrs. Woodhull, a woman of beauty and wit, championed woman's rights, as well as free love, spiritualism, and quack healing. . . ." (Flexner, *Century of Struggle*, pp. 153–54.) She achieved notoriety, in addition, by publishing, with her sister, *Woodhull's & Claflin's Weekly*, in which she publicized the love affair between the Rev. Henry Ward Beecher and Mrs. Elizabeth Tilton; by making a fortune on the stock market as protégée of Commodore Cornelius Vanderbilt; and by running for President in 1872.

the moral standards of men and women must be closed by raising men's behavior up to the level of women's.[32] Laura Clay, in discussing her plan for a lecture on "The Sanctity of Marriage," declared that a single standard of morals was two-sided, "applying to the uplift of the morals of women in the virtues where men now excel them as well as to the uplift of men in the virtues where women now excel them." [33] One means of effecting this reformation was, of course, the enfranchisement of women. Political equality would broaden women's interests beyond those of the four walls of home, and it would endow them with a greater influence on the education and government of both sexes.

The suffrage, these women believed, would also help to lower the alarming divorce rate. Suffragists differed on the divorce question. Some of them, such as Susan B. Anthony, favored easier divorce, believing that the cohabitation of two people who did not love each other or of a wife with a dissolute husband was immoral.[34] Others, such as Harriot Stanton Blatch, thought divorce merely shifted the underlying problem, the oppression of women, from one home to another.[35] But few suffragists would have quarreled with Mrs. Stanton's statement that states with liberal divorce laws were for oppressed women what Canada had been for

[32] See, for example, the discussion on the admission of a Mormon to Congress, in 1899, in Harper, *Susan B. Anthony*, III, 1150–52, and in NAWSA, *Proceedings*, 1899, p. 15.

[33] [Laura Clay] to the Rev. Samuel Tyler, March 22, 1912, Clay Papers, UK.

[34] "A Summing Up of the Divorce Problem Symposium" (one in a series of articles), New York *American*, December 8, [1902], clipping in Elizabeth Cady Stanton Papers, LC.

[35] "Voluntary Motherhood," in National Council of Women, *Transactions*, 1891, p. 284.

fugitive slaves.[36] Miss Blackwell, in the *Woman's Journal* of January 3, 1891, replied thus to an antisuffragist essay on "The Revolt against Matrimony":

There is no greater mistake than the idea that freedom, education and an acquaintance with public questions are prejudicial to feminine virtue. . . . There is not, and never will be, any general "revolt against matrimony" on the part of women. The revolt is against the unjust and unequal conditions in matrimony which have been established by one-sided legislation. That is a revolt which is growing irresistibly, and in which the best men are fighting side by side with the best women. The sooner and the more completely it succeeds, the better it will be both for the individual and for the race.

Suffragists generally agreed that the number of divorces was rising in that period not because women were taking their marriage vows lightly, but because long-oppressed women were for the first time finding the financial and spiritual resources to dissolve intolerable unions. The antis called the rise of divorce statistics a peril to the nation; the suffragists denounced the conditions that made the divorce statistics rise. Whether they approved or disapproved of easier divorce, suffragists generally agreed that the laws ought to be made uniform from state to state, but they strenuously opposed any such new legislation until women throughout the country had been enfranchised. Women had at least as much interest in such laws as men, they insisted, and must be given the vote to help reform the existing chaos in the laws relating to marriage and divorce.[37]

---

[36] "How Shall We Solve the Divorce Problem?" (one in a series of articles), New York *American*, October 13, 1902, clipping in Stanton Papers, LC.

[37] Among the many discussions of the divorce question are: Stanton, "Divorce Versus Domestic Warfare," *Arena*, V (April, 1890), 560–69;

The divorce problem received attention in the public forum along with another dire threat to American society: "race suicide." As might be expected, the suffragists hotly denied that a woman's chief duty was to rear a large family (although after the turn of the century they frequently said that a woman's chief duty was to be a mother). They declared that the men who, with Theodore Roosevelt, complained about the trend toward smaller families among the Anglo-Saxon part of the population held women in very low esteem. Before the race-suicide question even arose, suffrage ideologists expressed views that forecast the position they were to take on that issue. Alice Stone Blackwell, who devoted many of her columns in the *Woman's Journal* to replies to anti-suffragist articles, asked an anti, in the January 11, 1890, issue, whether matrimony were the chief end of *his* existence. Why then ought it to be considered the chief end of woman's existence? A year later Dr. Shaw, in discussing "God's Women," [38] declared that a woman's highest glory was not motherhood but womanhood. Mrs. Blatch agreed and argued that only voluntary motherhood was sacred.[39] These declarations reflected the insistence by suffragists during the nineteenth century that women must be recognized as human beings first and as women second. But it was as women and as mothers too that they fiercely repudiated the race-suicide theory. Mrs. Harper angrily wrote, in the New York *Sun* of February 22, 1903, that the parents of a large family never felt

---

Susan B. Anthony, "On Marriages That Fail," New York *Sun*, July 14, 1901; Alice Stone Blackwell in *Woman's Journal*, April 22, 1905; Anna Howard Shaw, *ibid.*, July 22, 1905; Anna Howard Shaw to "Dear State President," December 7, 1909, Clay Papers, UK.

[38] *Woman's Journal*, March 7, 1891.

[39] National Council of Women, *Transactions*, 1891, p. 280.

called upon to offer any apology, although their children might have to be supported by charity or might have to begin working at an early age or might inherit some disease or defect. None of these calamities, she wrote, "jars the complacency with which the father of a numerous progeny points to the fruits of his joyful obedience to the alleged divine command, 'Multiply and replenish the earth.'" The mother, however, knows the fearful cost at which their great brood was produced, and prays that her daughters may be spared the experience.

We have only masculine authority that there ever was any such divine command, and it was just as necessary 6,000 years ago as it is to-day that woman should be made to endure excessive childbearing and many other evils, with resignation by means of the faith that she was obeying the direct will of God. It is through the domination of the masculine hierarchy of the Catholic church that its women bear submissively as many children as the Lord sends through willing masculine agency. It is through divine revelation to the masculine heads of the Mormon Church that its women consider no sacrifice too great for the purpose of bringing forth an increase of this religious body. . . .

Unless a man is able to endow his children with perfect physical and moral health and guarantee them at least the necessities of life and a fair start, his greatest anxiety should be *not* to be a father. A woman may be the best of wives and mothers, but unless she can bear healthy children and be sure that they will be properly fed, clothed and educated, and unless she can give them an excellent father, the worst thing she can do for the world is to become a mother.

Senator Albert J. Beveridge incurred the anger of the suffragists also, when at the unveiling of the statue of Frances Willard in Washington in 1905, he said,

The mother of all mothers, the sister of all wives, to every child a lover, Frances E. Willard sacrificed her own life to the happiness of her sisters. For, after all, she knew that, with all her gifts and all the halo of her God-sent mission, the humblest mother was yet greater far than she.

Laura Clay replied that she knew no such thing! In a letter she sent to a large number of papers, Miss Clay wrote:

Why should such an estimate of herself be imputed to Frances Willard? She was above all a Christian, and this is not a Christian idea. When Jesus answered the woman who blessed the mother who bore him he said, "Yea rather, blessed are they that hear the word of God and keep it." . . . Perhaps this extravagant praise of the "humblest mother" was given because the question of "race suicide" is so much discussed. But if there is danger of race suicide at all it is not from a deficiency of that motherhood which is so humble that it aspires to little more than to bring children into the world and takes no thought of the conditions which surround them. Statistics show where the dangers lie when they tell such dreary facts as that half the children die before they attain the age of five years, and that in the city of New York alone 70,000 daily go to school unfed.

The noble understanding of Frances Willard, illumined by her great mother heart, apprehended and taught that the world needs a womanhood sufficiently elevated to be capable of rearing children in health and virtue; and to be possessed of the self-respect to desire their share of political power to enable them to seek out and to secure better conditions in which to rear their children than those that now prevail.[40]

[40] See clippings from more than ten newspapers, in Clay Papers, UK. Others who argued against the race-suicide theory, advocating more attention to the quality rather than quantity of children, and "voluntary motherhood," were Dr. Shaw in *Woman's Journal*, April 22, 1905, and

One most frequently repeated argument concerning the family as it was and as it ought to be rested on the belief that the political status of men and women did not reflect their economic status in the home. According to the vast majority of suffragists, a husband did not support his wife. They could not eat or wear the money he brought home each payday; she must first transform the money into food, clothing, and a comfortable home. Since the final product had resulted from the labors of both husband and wife, neither supported the other. It was only fair that the wife, an equal contributor to the support of the family, should be equal in political status. Here the suffragists clashed once again with Charlotte Perkins Gilman, who demanded the vote, among other things, for women precisely because they *were* supported, and the suffrage would be one step toward economic independence. Her co-workers' insistence that women ought to vote partly because they supported themselves led to a rousing debate in 1909 between Mrs. Gilman and Dr. Shaw, sponsored by the Women's Trade Union League.[41] Just as most suffragists' theory of the nature of woman

Catharine Waugh McCulloch in a 1910 speech quoted in a clipping in McCulloch Papers, RWA.

[41] The New York Evening *Call* of January 7, 1909, devoted more than a page to a full report of the debate. The audience at the end voted overwhelmingly to endorse Dr. Shaw's contention that husbands did not support their wives. This denial appeared regularly in suffragist propaganda. See, for example, Ellen Battelle Dietrick in *Woman's Journal*, January 28, 1893; Mrs. Dietrick at the 1893 NAWSA convention, as reported in Anthony and Harper, eds., *History of Woman Suffrage*, IV, 208–9; Putnam-Jacobi, *"Common Sense" Applied to Woman Suffrage*, pp. 201-2; Harriot Stanton Blatch in *Report of Hearing* before the Committee on Woman Suffrage [Senate]. February 15, 1898 (Washington, D.C., Government Printing Office, 1898), p. 14; *Handbook of the National American Woman Suffrage Association and Proceedings* of the Jubilee Convention (1869-1919), held at St. Louis, Mo., March 24-29, 1919 (New York, n.d.), p. 61, quoting the eleventh resolution.

insisted on her essential present equality with man, so most suffragists' theory of the nature of the home declared that women contributed equally with man to the support of the family. Unlike Mrs. Gilman, therefore, they did not believe any fundamental economic change would be necessary in home relationships for women to achieve equality. Men ought simply to recognize the facts and accord women the suffrage and the respect they merited. The assumption that women were not supported was especially appropriate for middle-class suffragists who did not visualize any essential change in relationships within their own homes other than the acquisition by women of legal powers concomitant with their economic importance. The fact that working-class women attending the Women's Trade Union League debate voted overwhelmingly against Mrs. Gilman's theory indicates, perhaps, the consciousness of these women of their economic importance.

The women who attended the debate voted also, by implication, against the antisuffragist argument that since man was the supporter of the family, he alone should vote. If woman contributed equally there was no reason why the single representative, if there must be one, ought to be the man. On the other hand, there was no reason why the family rather than the individuals in it should be represented in the state if each adult individual had economic value, and by contributing to the family contributed to the state as well.

Both the picture of the ideal woman and that of the ideal home buttressed the suffragists' demands for the ballot. As occasion demanded they could portray the suffrage as conducive to the creation of the strong, intel-

ligent, independent and self-respecting "new woman";
or they could point to woman's contribution to the home
and her other accomplishments to prove that the new
woman had already arrived. In either case and in spite
of lack of unanimity on many related questions, the
suffragists were as one in scorning the relationship of
clinging vine to sturdy oak and the environment that
produced such a relationship. As Dr. Shaw said, "They
who observe more closely the sturdy oak about which
the ivy clings, find it dead at the top." [42]

[42] Shaw, *A Speech*, p. 10. The speech was delivered in Birmingham,
Alabama, on April 16, 1915.

SIX

The "New Immigration" and Labor

Millions of immigrants—Italians, Poles, and Russians, Jews and Catholics—sailed up New York harbor and past the newly erected Statue of Liberty after the mid-1880s. They peopled the cities, worked the mines, created whole new industries—and changed the thinking of those whose ancestors had preceded them to the New World. The antisuffragists, belonging to the latter group, made capital out of the growing ethnic heterogeneity of the American people. Having long harbored doubts as to the stability of a government based on manhood suffrage, they became doubly alarmed at the speed with which the new non-English-speaking immigrants qualified for the vote. The fact that most of the newcomers lived in cities, the increase in strength of urban political machines, the scandal of municipal corruption, the class strife of the 1890s, all seemed to buttress their conviction that non-Anglo-Saxon men were unfit to govern themselves. The frightened antis pleaded with their legislators not to add unfit women to the electorate by giving all women the vote.

When antisuffragists defended the home from woman

suffrage, they were defending the ideal of the white, Anglo-Saxon, Protestant, sober, middle-class home in which the mother was queen of a realm that she never left except to perform good works for the less fortunate. The "new immigration" represented a threat to this ideal home, as well as to the antis' ideal state. The "new immigrants" usually used Sunday for recreation; they did not eschew the use of liquor; their women sometimes worked outside the home; they rarely lived in big houses on tree-lined streets, but rather seemed to prefer overcrowded tenements in which the mother could hardly be a queen or the home a realm. If, as the antis claimed, the family and not the individual was the unit of society, it mattered a great deal what *sort* of family elected the majority of legislators. Surely it would never do to give the unfit families an even greater preponderance than they already had by enfranchising women.

Since the suffragists before this period had based their claim to the vote principally on the inalienable right of every human being to have a voice in making the laws he or she obeyed, they might have been expected to deny the antis' characterization of the new immigrants as unfit for self-government. Although the suffragists' favorite quotations from the Declaration of Independence would seem to apply to all people or none, a change in their rationale took place in reaction to the new immigration, parallel to the change in the antisuffragist argument. Instead of applying the principles of the Declaration of Independence to the newcomers in the same way as they were trying to persuade the voters to apply them to women, the suffragists compromised with "the consent of the governed" principle, and some of them dropped it altogether. The suffragists, after all, belonged more or less to the same social stratum as the antis, and their reaction to the waves of foreigners had essentially nothing to do with the question of suffrage. They soon discovered powerful arguments *for* woman suffrage based on the same antiforeign grounds as the antis' pleas *against* the enfranchisement of women.

At the same time as some white women in the South were beginning to tell their men that they felt humiliated at being ruled by their former slaves, Northern suffragists began saying that having to obey laws made by men from every corner of the earth was an indignity to which descendants of the heroes of 1776 ought not to be subjected. This was one argument that suffragists began using early in the thirty-year period (1890-1920) and continued to repeat until the very last years of the amendment campaign, when they looked for allies among the ethnic groups in the cities. In 1894, Carrie Chapman Catt declared in a speech in Iowa:

This Government is menaced with great danger. . . . That danger lies in the votes possessed by the males in the slums of the cities, and the ignorant foreign vote which was sought to be brought up by each party, to make political success. . . . In the mining districts the danger has already reached this point—miners are supplied with arms, watching with greedy eyes for the moment when they can get in their deadly work of despoiling the wealth of the country. . . . There is but one way to avert the danger—cut off the vote of the slums and give to woman, who is bound to suffer all, and more than man can, of the evils his legislation has brought upon the nation, the power of protecting herself that man has secured for himself—the ballot.[1]

[1] *Woman's Journal*, December 15, 1894. In the 1896 campaign for a suffrage amendment to the California constitution, the xenophobic American Protective Association supported the suffragists (see Harper, *Susan B. Anthony*, II, 868).

Ten years later, Anna Howard Shaw, in a speech in Tennessee, supplied variations on the same theme, indicating the persistence of antiforeignism in the suffragist rationale:

No other country has subjected its women to the humiliating position to which the women of this nation have been subjected by men. . . . In Germany, German women are governed by German men; in France, French women are governed by Frenchmen; and in Great Britain, British women are governed by British men; but in this country, American women are governed by every kind of a man under the light of the sun. There is no race, there is no color, there is no nationality of men who are not the sovereign rulers of American women. . . .[2]

Miss Shaw's feeling that white American women would not have been humiliated if their male rulers had been white American men showed that in one sense the suffragists' rationale had reversed itself completely since the days before the new immigration. Before, they had

[2] *The Handbook of the National American Woman Suffrage Association and Proceedings* of the Forty-Sixth Annual Convention, held at Nashville, Tenn., November 12-17, inclusive, 1914 (New York, n.d.), p. 19. A somewhat different version of the same passage was in an Alabama speech of 1915, printed as *A Speech by Doctor Anna Howard Shaw.* Miss Shaw, of course, was English-born, but the suffragists never included "Anglo-Saxons" among the ethnic groups to which they felt superior. In fact, their American jingoism seemed at times to be merely an expression of Anglo-Saxon "racism." After the Spanish-American War, the suffragists entered the nationwide discussion on the suffrage provisions to be included in the constitutions for the new island possessions. Their main theme was that Hawaiian and Filipino women were no less fitted to vote than their men, and in any case it would be absurd to enfranchise those barbaric men while civilized American women remained voteless. See, for instance, Carrie Chapman Catt, "Our New Responsibilities," *Woman's Journal,* October 1, 1898, and many articles in other issues of that period. See also, Susan B. Anthony's statement quoted in Anthony and Harper, eds., *History of Woman Suffrage,* IV, 296, and Ida Husted Harper's column in the New York *Sun,* January 5, 1899.

claimed the vote because all human beings, men and women, were equal. Now, most suffragists were willing to claim the vote because all human beings, native and foreign born, were *not* equal, and the inferior ought not to rule the superior. When men of no other group than their own were voting in significant numbers, the suffragists' principal argument had to be that men as a sex were not superior to women as a sex. This argument lost some of its force later when suffragists tried to justify their feeling of intense shame at having to obey laws made by men whom they employed in their gardens or to drive their coaches. If men as a sex were really superior there should not have been additional humiliation because of the ethnic heterogeneity of the male lawmakers. If men as a sex were *not* superior, then according to the natural right argument, women ought to desire political equality regardless of the color or place of birth of the present electorate. In either case race or nationality was on principle irrelevant. Hence the principle was compromised.

The elimination of egalitarianism from the suffragist rationale did not happen all at once or without troubled consciences, particularly on the part of women who had been born abroad, such as Miss Shaw, lived abroad, such as Harriot Stanton Blatch, or learned their ideals in the abolitionist movement as had Susan B. Anthony. Miss Anthony, while occasionally expressing disdain for foreign-born or Indian voters,[3] usually added that she op-

---

[3] See, for example, Susan B. Anthony to "Mrs. Olivia B. Bigelow" [the addressee was Olivia B. Hall; the error was the typist's], May 18, 1903, Hall Papers, LC: "There are men enough lying around idle to furnish you and all other women with plenty of help, but these

posed educational or property qualifications for voting and that she was glad they could vote and thus learn American ideals of government. But while they were learning, she admitted, they almost always voted against woman suffrage in state referenda.[4]

Other suffragists also pointed to the election results in state referenda, and concluded that the wards in which the immigrants lived showed majorities against woman suffrage for reasons that no propaganda campaign of their own could change. These reasons were: that foreign-born men had been brought up in a culture in which woman was inferior (here the suffragists forgot earlier arguments and proudly pointed to the respected position of women in their own society); that the ignorance of the foreign born disqualified them from voting wisely; that the new voters generally used alcoholic beverages and feared that woman suffrage would bring prohibition; that foreign-born workers in cities voted as dictated by saloonkeepers, rich employers, or party machines.[5] Most often, however, the reason for the hostility of suffragists to immigrant, Negro, or Indian voters was not mentioned.

Italians come over here with the idea that they must be paid as much as intelligent white men. How long white men will be satisfied to be cowed by these lower classes! As fast as they come here they are a political power; consequently, politicians do not dare to say their souls are their own. But I do not know; white men are hard to understand. They would rather have the most ignorant white wretch at the ballot [sic] box, than intelligent women."

[4] See, for example, *Woman's Journal*, June 2, 1900; Harper, *Susan B. Anthony*, II, 899, 922, 1018-19, quoting statements made in the 1890s.

[5] Catt and Shuler, *Woman Suffrage and Politics*, pp. 113, 116, 130, 195; Harper, *Susan B. Anthony*, II, 887; address of Mrs. Catt reprinted in *Woman's Journal*, February 20, 1904 (see especially p. 61); and many statements that may be culled almost at random from the writings of Mrs. Stanton in this period.

One may assume that the women knew that their intended audience would understand.[6]

Mrs. Stanton obviously knew she was speaking to "her own kind" when she submitted a paper to be read at the hearing of the House Committee on the Judiciary in 1896:

As arguments have thus far proved unavailing, may not appeals to your feelings, to your moral sense, find the response so long withheld by your reason? Allow me, honorable gentlemen, to paint you a picture and bring within the compass of your vision at once the comparative position of the two classes of citizens: The central object is a ballot box guarded by three inspectors of foreign birth. On the right is a multitude of coarse, ignorant beings, designated in our constitution as male citizens—many of them fresh from the steerage of incoming steamers. There, too, are natives of the same type from the slums of our cities. Policemen are respectfully guiding them all to the ballot box. Those who cannot stand, because of their frequent potations, are carefully supported on either side, each in turn depositing his vote, for what purpose he neither knows nor cares, except to get the promised bribe.

On the left side, she continued, stand a group of intelligent, moral, highly cultivated women, descended from fighters for liberty who have made this country all it is. These women are teachers and professors, writers and preachers, lawyers and physicians, and honored mothers, wives, and sisters.

Knowing the needs of humanity subjectively in all the higher walks of life, and objectively in the world of work,

[6] A few examples are: Ida Husted Harper in New York *Sun*, February 10, 1901; *The Suffragist*, March 17, 1917, cartoon entitled "Governed—and Governing"; Putnam-Jacobi, *"Common Sense" Applied to Woman Suffrage*, pp. 74-75.

in the charities, in the asylums and prisons, in the sanitary condition of our streets and public buildings, they are peculiarly fitted to write, speak and vote intelligently on all these questions of such vital, far-reaching consequence to the welfare of society.[7]

Mrs. Stanton here repudiated in two ways the old natural right argument for suffrage. First, her contrast between the degraded men and the cultivated ladies expressed her conviction that the latter only were fit to vote. Second, the last sentence of the quotation shows the educated women were fit to vote for both groups, knowing better than the ignorant men what the latter's interests were. Thus was forgotten the principle she expressed so eloquently in "The Solitude of Self" (see Chapter III), that each human soul was responsible for its own destiny.

In course of time the suffragist rationale came to include two techniques for disposing of the "foreign menace": the use of statistics, and the advocacy of an educational qualification for voting. The former consisted of repeated citation of figures to show that there were more native-born women than foreign-born men and women combined; hence, to give all women the vote was to increase the proportion of native-born to foreign-born voters.[8] Variations on this theme included the argument that women constituted the vast majority of churchgoing persons and a tiny minority of prison inmates, and that they

[7] Harper, ed., *History of Woman Suffrage*, V, 269.
[8] For example, see leaflet put out in August, 1917, by the New York State Woman Suffrage Party, entitled, "Facing Facts": "WOMAN SUFFRAGE WILL MORE THAN DOUBLE THE MAJORITY OF NATIVE-BORN VOTERS IN NEW YORK STATE," citing statistics to back up the statement. A copy is in Suffrage Collection, ssc. See also Mrs. Harper's column in the New York *Sun*, July 8, 1900.

averaged more years in school than men; hence, to en-franchise all women was to increase the proportion of the pious, law-abiding, and educated to the irreligious, vicious, and ignorant voters. They took it for granted that this meant an increase in the ratio of native-born to for-eign-born voters. Occasionally they pointed out that the majority of immigrants were men; woman suffrage would for this additional reason mean an increase in the major-ity of native-born voters.[9] The 1893 convention of the NAWSA passed a resolution that read:

Resolved, that without expressing any opinion on the proper qualifications for voting, we call attention to the significant facts that in every State there are more women who can read and write than all negro voters; more white women who can read and write than all negro voters; more Ameri-can women who can read and write than all foreign voters; so that the enfranchisement of such women would settle the vexed question of rule by illiteracy, whether of home-grown or foreign-born production.[10]

This resolution suggests the second tactic designed to

[9] For example, see leaflet cited in note 8; see another leaflet in the same collection, dated April, 1917, entitled, "WOMAN SUFFRAGE WILL IMPROVE THE ELECTORATE IN NEW YORK STATE." The text argued that woman suffrage would not increase the "undesirable vote" because statistics showed that the increase in the native-born vote would be bigger (the fact that the equation of undesirable with foreign born was unconscious renders it especially significant). Also, Mrs. Harper in New York *Sun,* July 8, 1900; Anthony and Harper, eds., *History of Woman Suffrage,* IV, xxv; Harper, *Susan B. Anthony,* II, 887.

[10] NAWSA, *Proceedings,* 1893, p. 84. See also *Proceedings* of the Forty-Fourth Annual Convention of the National American Woman Suffrage Association held at Philadelphia, Pa., November 21 to 26, inclusive, 1912 (New York, n.d.), pp. 56–57, the report of the Church Work Committee given by Mary E. Craigie, chairman: "Women are recognized as the most religious, the most moral and the most sober portion of the American people. Why deny them a voice in public affairs when we give it for the asking to every ignorant foreigner who comes to our shores?"

exorcise the specter of foreign domination. Perhaps too many in their own social stratum doubted that fit voters would outnumber the unfit even if women voted. The next step that some suffragists took was to suggest eliminating the unfit voters from the electorate altogether. An educational qualification for voting, they suggested, would insure permanent supremacy for the native-born white portion of the population. Presumably those immigrants and Negroes who managed to acquire an education would either be statistically unimportant or, by virtue of their education, vote as the native whites voted. The educational qualification could thus win the support of both those who believed in the innate incapacity of non-Anglo-Saxons and those who defined classes along educational lines rather than by economic or ethnic criteria.

The proposal to bar illiterates from the polls did not easily find a place in the suffragist rationale. This was true especially in a period in which children normally began working at an earlier age than at present, and suffragists found it difficult to assume that a worker's lack of education could always be blamed on his incapacity or indifference. That the advisability of the educational requirement did not slip easily into the catalogue of standard suffragist arguments, despite the almost universal acceptance of the assumptions on which it was based, is indicated by the fact that it became the subject of three heated debates. Two were in the columns of the *Woman's Journal* in 1894 and 1897 and the third in the 1903 convention of the NAWSA.

Mrs. Stanton set off the first debate by a letter to the *Journal* of September 1, 1894, in which she argued that there was a growing feeling among thoughtful people that the thousands of "uneducated foreigners landing every day on our shores" should not be so quickly enfranchised. Despite the legal requirements that they be naturalized and live in the country a certain length of time, many evade the law. "Who keeps the record of their arrival and the prescribed time from the steerage to the polls?" Therefore she advocated a literacy test and a requirement that a voter understand English. This would make Americans a homogeneous people, and as it would take most foreigners at least two years to accomplish it, "we" should be sure they had been in the United States long enough to know something of the spirit of its institutions. Mrs. Stanton then listed her reasons for urging an educational qualification.

1. It would limit the foreign vote.
2. It would decrease the ignorant native vote by stimulating the rising generation to learning. . . .
3. It would dignify the right of suffrage in the eyes of our people to know that some preparation was necessary. . . .

One of the most potent objections to woman suffrage is the added ignorant and depraved vote that would still further corrupt and embarrass the administration of our Government. . . . The intelligent, organized laboring men were hampered in the recent strikes by the violent, unreasoning, ignorant voters, whose folly they could not control.

It is the interest of the educated working-men, as it is of the women, that this ignorant, worthless class of voters should be speedily diminished. With free schools and compulsory education, there is no excuse in this country for ignorance of the elements of learning.

When Mrs. Stanton assumed a connection between the English language and democratic institutions, she reflected the assumption, common at that time, that the "Anglo-Saxon race" had a unique genius for self-government. Presumably, Irish or English immigrants would not have to wait very long to qualify. Mrs. Stanton's mention of "the steerage" was one of at least a dozen instances of her use of that phrase in public statements. If unfamiliarity with American institutions was what she really feared in immigrants, as she supposed, the part of the ship they traveled on should have been irrelevant. In "Universal Suffrage a Pretense," [11] she wrote: "Foreigners are our judges and jurors, our legislators and municipal officials, and decide all questions of interest to us." Inasmuch as judges and legislators were usually literate, it is clear that her objections to immigrant men's voting while native women were disfranchised had really little to do with literacy or the two years she suggested in which a foreigner could learn American institutions.

The 1894 letter from Mrs. Stanton touched off a debate in the *Woman's Journal* that continued for several months. One writer argued that any privileged class, especially a "brain aristocracy," would be dangerous to the nation.[12] William Lloyd Garrison, son of the famous abolitionist, wrote that there was no connection between real intelligence and the ability to read and spell laboriously. If a test ought to be imposed, it should be above the point of bare literacy, but he opposed attempts to convert people to woman suffrage by appealing to prejudice. Garrison believed that it would be better to rely on the principle that governments derived their just powers from the consent of the governed.[13] Later letters and ar-

11 *Woman's Journal,* October 23, 1897.
12 *Ibid.,* October 20, 1894. The writer was Anna Gardner.
13 *Ibid.*

ticles argued that each class must have the right to speak for itself at the polls, that education did not increase one's sense of justice, and that privileged classes always blamed the troubles of society on those with less education.[14] Mrs. Stanton's daughter, Harriot Stanton Blatch, entered the fray with an open letter to her mother, which she sent to the *Journal* from her home in England. Mrs. Blatch wrote that it was a mistake to identify literacy with enlightenment. Many people who could satisfy a board of examiners as to their collegiate accomplishments were lamentably ignorant, whereas many a man without a sign of the three R's about him was gifted with the sterling common sense and abiding honesty which the school of life's experience taught him. But, she added, her mother had gone still further and had assumed that every citizen born in Europe who could not read or write *English* was "an ignorant foreigner," and she reminded Mrs. Stanton that the nations of Europe also had their public school systems. In any case, workers, literate or not, were best qualified to give valuable opinions on the housing of the poor or other such problems.

Let me assure you the spirit of freedom is not a treasure hidden in America, but is everyhere throbbing in the heart of growing Democracy. I do not call the man ignorant or wanting in an understanding of Republican principles who, under the grinding, economic conditions of the Old World, stints himself to lay by, little by little, his passage money across the Atlantic, hoping to find in America a broader freedom for himself, but I do call ignorant, and a real danger to the State, the educated man, born and bred in a Re-

[14] *Ibid.*, October 27, November 3 and 17, December 8, 1894, and later issues.

public, who devotes his highest energies to money getting and neglects his every duty as a citizen.[15]

With the two opposing positions on the educational qualification thus clearly defined, the debate continued intermittently through the years, with more and more of those suffragists who spoke out on the question coming to agree with the views of Mrs. Stanton.[16] The second debate in the *Woman's Journal* took place in 1897, opening with a symposium in the issues of October 2 and October 9. Mrs. Stanton and three others argued for the educational qualification, while Mrs. Blatch and two others wrote against it. The third debate occurred during the NAWSA convention of 1903 in the form of a planned symposium, but this time only Charlotte Perkins Gilman spoke against the proposition. After all the speakers had presented their arguments, the president took an informal vote of the delegates to learn how many favored

[15] *Ibid.*, December 22, 1894.

[16] Her lengthy reply to Mrs. Blatch appeared in the January 5, 1895, issue. She continued to write to the *Woman's Journal*; see, for example, the issues of October 2 and 23, 1897, and February 5, 1898. She sent proposals for resolutions to suffrage conferences; see, for instance, *Report* of the New York State Woman Suffrage Association: Twenty-Sixth Annual Convention, Ithaca, N.Y., November 12-15, 1894 (Rochester, 1895), p. 216. She prepared testimony for legislative hearings; see, for instance, 1898 Senate *Hearing*, p. 21. She also evidently tried unsuccessfully to convert Susan B. Anthony to her point of view (Anthony to Stanton, September 7, 1897, Smith Family Papers, NYPL). Other contributions to the debate may be found in the *Journal* issues already cited and in those of October 9 and 30, 1897, and November 13, 1897, and occasionally thereafter. By the fall of 1898 the question had merged with that of how to deal with the populations of the islands acquired by the United States during and after the Spanish-American War. *Ibid.*, April 12, 1902, in a paper prepared for presentation to the NAWSA convention, Mrs. Stanton argued against excluding illiterate immigrants from the United States. She wrote that the country had plenty of room and work for them; it was their "marching from the steerage to the polls" that she would prevent. The address may also be found in Harper, ed., *History of Woman Suffrage*, V, 32.

the educational requirement, and almost the entire convention stood up. Only five rose to record their opposition. An informal vote was then taken to determine how
many of the delegates were taxpayers. Of about 150
women present, 117 stood.

One feature of the convention was the prominent part
taken by the Southern delegates, who argued that the
interests of Northern and Southern white women were
identical, in that both wished to insure the supremacy
of white Anglo-Saxon Americans against the threatened
domination of Negroes and the foreign born, and that
the best means would be an educational qualification
for voting.[17] The suffrage movement that had begun as
a Northern outgrowth of the abolitionist cause had by
the dawn of the twentieth century become a nationwide
movement. Ironically, one reason for this development
was the common cause made by Northern women who
feared the foreign-born vote with Southern women who
feared the Negro vote. The woman suffrage movement
had ceased to be a campaign to *extend the franchise to*
all adult Americans. Instead, one important part of its
rationale had become the proposal to *take the vote away
from* some Americans—Negroes in the South and naturalized citizens in the North. Although some Northern
suffragists refused to recognize its existence, the alliance
was symbolized by a letter from a Kentucky Democrat
to an Ohio Republican, both national leaders in the
NAWSA, written during the period in which Northern
states were passing literacy tests and Southern states
were amending their constitutions to disfranchise the
Negro:

[17] NAWSA, *Proceedings*, 1903, pp. 60-61; Harper, ed., *History of
Woman Suffrage*, V, 76-78, 82-83.

The National [Association] has always recognized the usefulness of woman suffrage as a counterbalance to the foreign
vote, and as a means of legally preserving white supremacy
in the South. You surely remember Mr. Blackwell's compilation of statistics, showing the preponderance of numbers of
the educated whites in the south.[18] In the campaign in S.
Carolina we distributed that leaflet widely; and never hesi-
tated to show that the white women's vote would give the
supremacy to the white race. And we have also freely used
the same argument in relation to the native born and the
foreign born vote.[19]

While the arguments for woman suffrage based on fear
of the foreign-born vote remained,[20] some suffragists
adopted a new sympathetic approach to the immigrant
shortly after the turn of the century. The two attitudes
continued to live in uneasy coexistence within the suffra-

[18] See chapter VII, p. 168.
[19] Laura Clay to Harriet Taylor Upton, November 19, 1906, Clay
Papers, uk. Ida Husted Harper, in *Susan B. Anthony*, II, 811, wrote
that Mrs. Stanton's paper on "Educated Suffrage" which was read at
the 1895 convention in Atlanta "was especially acceptable to a southern
audience."
[20] See, for instance, Alice Stone Blackwell, "Limited and Unlimited
Suffrage," *Woman's Journal*, February 11, 1911, and an article by
Mary Winsor, president of the Pennsylvania Limited Suffrage League,
in the same issue. At the House Hearing in 1912, Mrs. Harper told the
lawmakers that if suffragists had to campaign for state amendments
they would have to appeal to "the great conglomerate of voters that
we have in this country, such as does not exist in any other," and
asked the congressmen whether they would like to submit their "electoral rights to the voters of New York City, for instance, representing
as they do every nationality in the world." Later Jane Addams respectfully asked to present a point of view different from Mrs. Harper's.
She said that in a recent campaign, in Chicago, some of the greatest
help the suffragists received came from immigrant communities and
added: "The Italian and German women know of the woman's movement in their home countries and often asked why they are not
drawn more quickly into the suffrage movement in America." Later in
the hearing one member of the committee observed that "Mrs. Harper's
statement was one of the worst indictments of the referendum that I
have ever heard." (1912 House *Hearing*, pp. 71-72, 77.)

gist rationale until the very end of the amendment campaign. That they sometimes coexisted within the minds
of individual suffragists was shown in 1906 when Florence Kelley, testifying at a congressional hearing in behalf of a national suffrage amendment, argued that it
was unfair to force the women to work for separate state
amendments because they would then have to campaign
among the voters. She complained that it was "an igno-
minious way to treat us, to send us to the Chinamen in
San Francisco, to the enfranchised Indians of other western States, to the negroes, Italians, Hungarians, Poles,
Bohemians and innumerable Slavic immigrants in Pennsylvania and other mining States to obtain our right of
suffrage." [21] In the very same month, Mrs. Kelley's address to the NAWSA convention berated the suffragists for
their contempt for the immigrant:

I have rarely heard a ringing suffrage speech which did
not refer to the "ignorant and degraded" men, or the "ignorant immigrants" as our masters. This is habitually spoken
with more or less bitterness. But this is what the workingmen are used to hear applied to themselves by their enemies
in times of strike.

Rather should we recognize that, while for the moment
they have power which we need, they have the same interest in the rising generation of citizens, so largely the children of working people.[22]

[21] Harper, ed., *History of Woman Suffrage*, V, 190-91. She expressed
the same sentiments in a speech nine years later, reported in *The
Suffragist*, June 2, 1915.
[22] *Woman's Journal*, March 3, 1906. At the 1909 convention, Mrs.
Kelley asked for the vote for all women in the name of justice and
disapproved of lumping together "the ignorant, illiterate, debased,
foreign women." (*Ibid.*, January 6, 1909.) In 1905 she had written:
"The fear lest the votes of ignorant women may outweigh those of the
intelligent could be met by the imposition of an educational requirement such as is already in force in Massachusetts." (Kelley, *Some*

Suffragists had occasionally argued that one reason they preferred a national amendment to separate state amendments was that once Congress had passed an amendment to the national constitution, the task of the women would then be to persuade state legislators, the picked men of their communities, to ratify it, whereas separate state referenda required them to plead their case before the masses of ignorant voters.[23] In 1916 Mrs. Catt, as president, sent a questionnaire to all state auxiliaries. The twenty-first and twenty-second of the fifty-six questions were: "Have you a considerable foreign population? If so, of what nationality? . . . Is such a population congested in certain sections?" The replies indicated that in most cases little or no effort had yet been made to reach the foreign-born population, and most of those auxiliaries that had made such efforts reported little success.[24]

Realizing that the federal amendment could not be ratified until a large number of states had already passed their own suffrage amendments, some suffragists reconciled themselves to the task of winning the big-city electorate. Distasteful though it was to many of them, they began to speak on street corners in working-class neighborhoods and at labor union meetings and to distribute leaflets and speak in foreign languages, especially in New

Ethical Gains through Legislation, p. 173.) Similar conflicting statements may be found in the writings and speeches of Harriot Stanton Blatch, Carrie Chapman Catt, Anna Howard Shaw, and Ida Husted Harper.

[23] See, for example, speech by Mrs. Catt in 1900, reprinted in Anthony and Harper, eds., *History of Woman Suffrage,* IV, 371-72, and hearing cited in note 20.

[24] The questionnaire and replies are in the Catt Collection, NYPL.

York City.[25] In December, 1915, Mrs. Catt told a Senate committee that working for a state amendment had forced New York suffragists to campaign in twenty-four languages.[26] The advent of World War I added a new dimension to the suffragists' appeals to the foreign born. The task of persuading the latter that American democratic ideals meant extending the right of self-government to women merged with the "Americanization" campaign which the NAWSA undertook. The organization's official organ carried an article stating: "Four things the National American Woman Suffrage Association set out to do in the face of war. I, To protect women workers

[25] Harriet Burton Laidlaw, a wealthy member of New York society, made many such speeches, as evidenced by clippings in Laidlaw Scrapbooks, NYHS. See also Laidlaw, "The Woman's Hour," *Forum*, LVI (November, 1916), 541. And see an article, "Rally in Chinatown," *Woman's Journal*, July 13, 1912, which describes a Woman Suffrage Party meeting at which speakers addressed the street-corner audience in English, Yiddish, Italian and Chinese. That such campaigning was indeed distasteful is suggested in an account in the New York *Times* of February 25, 1916, of a rally in New York under the auspices of the NAWSA and Woman Suffrage Party of New York State. A memorial to Congress, drafted by Mrs. Raymond Brown, Mrs. Catt, and Mrs. Laidlaw, was presented to the assembled suffragists for their approval. It included the usual references to the humiliation suffered by American women at seeing men of all colors and nationalities enfranchised before them. This time, though, some suffragists objected to those references as offensive, while others could see nothing objectionable in them. The memorial was finally approved with a proviso that Mesdames Brown, Catt, and Laidlaw change certain passages. For an interesting discussion of suffragist activities in immigrant and working-class neighborhoods in New York City, see Schaffer, "The New York City Woman Suffrage Party, 1909-1919," *New York History*, XLIII (July, 1962), 271, 274-82.

[26] *Woman Suffrage.* Hearings before the Committee on Woman Suffrage, United States Senate, 64th Cong., 1st Sess., on S. J. Res. 1, a Joint Resolution Proposing an Amendment to the Constitution of the United States Extending the Right of Suffrage to Women, and S. J. Res. 2, a Joint Resolution Proposing an Amendment to the Constitution of the United States Extending the Right of Suffrage to Women (Washington, D.C., Government Printing Office, 1916), p. 21. See also Peck, "Rise of the Woman Suffrage Party," *Life and Labor*, I (June, 1911), 168.

from exploitation. II, To increase food production. III, To help in Red Cross Work. IV, To Americanize the alien." [27] Two rules which the chairman of the Americanization Committee laid down for her members were: "Don't Preach. Don't Patronize." [28]

The one suffragist leader who placed the needs of immigrant women at the foundation of her argument for suffrage was Jane Addams. In this respect she stood alone among the eminent women who held national office in the NAWSA. Some of them, desiring the vote for their own group of middle-class women, sometimes found it advisable in later years to seek allies among immigrants and workers, and others desired sincerely to help immigrant women. Miss Addams, however, was moved by neither expediency nor *noblesse oblige*, but by profound humanitarianism. In many speeches and articles, she reiterated one theme: the modern city performs functions that necessitate the women's vote; a woman cannot care properly for her family if she has no voice in making the laws and electing the officials that determine whether her home has pure water, fresh food, proper sanitation, and adequate police protection; municipal government is housekeeping on a large scale. [29]

She told of Scandinavian women who had voted in

[27] *Woman Citizen*, June 2, 1917.

[28] The chairman was Mrs. Grace Bagley of Boston, who explained in the *Woman Citizen* of June 2, 1917, that she first became interested in the immigrants' problems when she undertook to help the Italians who lived in a tenement in Chicago owned by her husband. The slogan is in the *Woman Citizen* of June 30, 1917.

[29] See, for example, "Jane Addams Declares Ballot for Woman Made Necessary by Changed Conditions," Chicago Sunday *Record-Herald*, April 1, 1906, clipping in Addams Papers, FHL; *Woman's Journal*, June 19, 1909; "Utilization of Women in City Government," Addams, *Centennial Reader*, pp. 113-23. See also chap. III, pp. 68-71.

Europe and found themselves disfranchised in the land of the free. She told of Russian-Jewish housewives who could not understand why in Chicago they must buy their food in dirty, fly-infested markets, whereas in the old country they had shopped in clean, covered markets; they had something to contribute to city government. She told of illiterate Irish women expressing intelligent opinions on various municipal issues. Again and again she insisted not only that these women would vote intelligently but also that they needed the vote in order properly to feed, clothe, and protect their families—the traditional functions of women that in a modern city must be performed in an untraditional way.[30] "The statement is sometimes made," wrote Miss Addams, "that the franchise for women would be valuable only so far as the educated women exercised it. This statement totally disregards the fact that those matters in which woman's judgment is most needed are far too primitive and basic to be largely influenced by what we call education." [31] The egalitarianism that in early suffragist philosophy had grown out of the abolitionists' defense of the Negro now returned to the late suffragist philosophy via a Chicago social worker's defense of the immigrant.

The coexistence within the suffrage rationale of anti-foreignism and a sympathetic attitude toward immigrants coincided with a change in the membership of suffrage organizations. Jane Addams and other social workers who lived in intimate contact with foreign-born

[30] "Miss Addams Gives Examples," *Woman's Journal*, March 28, 1908; "Why Women Should Vote," in Björkman and Porritt, eds., *Woman Suffrage*, pp. 131-50; *The Survey*, October 23, 1915, p. 85; also, items previously cited.

[31] Clipping cited in note 29. The passage also appears in Addams, *The Modern City and the Municipal Franchise for Women*.

groups in the cities constituted a new element among organized suffragists. At the same time immigrant groups were becoming much more receptive to suffragist propaganda, and foreign-born women began joining suffrage clubs here and there.[32] The old suffragist argument that the precincts in which the ethnic groups lived voted consistently against suffrage amendments in state referenda had to be dropped, as analyses of voting patterns proved that, in some referenda, prosuffrage votes were cast mostly during the early morning and late afternoon hours, when the workers went to the polls.[33] In fact, when New York finally passed its state suffrage amendment in 1917, it was New York City, home of a large immigrant population, that made the victory possible, counteracting the unfavorable majorities in native-born, rural, and semirural upstate communities.[34] When some native-born women in the NAWSA could no longer see the immigrant vote as an obstacle to suffrage, part of

[32] New York *Times*, November 7, 1917, Sec. 3, p. 4, notes that strong suffrage clubs had been built among the Negro women of Harlem and also in Chinatown and Italian neighborhoods in New York City. The Suffrage Collection, SSC, has leaflets in Spanish, French, and German that had been used in California, perhaps in the 1911 campaign. See also *Woman's Journal*, April 19, 1913; NAWSA, *Proceedings*, 1912, p. 24; and *Woman's Journal*, February 19, 1910. Also, *The Hand Book of the National American Woman Suffrage Association and Proceedings* of the Forty-Seventh Annual Convention, held at Washington, D.C., December 14-19, inclusive, 1915 (New York, n.d.), p. 92, one of many such statements of new successful efforts to organize ethnic groups.

[33] Kate M. Gordon to "Dear Member of the Business Committee," June 30, 1906, Clay Papers, UK. Miss Gordon was analyzing the recent suffrage defeat in Oregon where workers voted for the amendment. Dr. Shaw in her autobiography cites the same facts and comes to the same conclusions in her discussion of the Oregon election (*Story of a Pioneer*, pp. 292-93).

[34] Park, *Front Door Lobby*, p. 120; Catt and Shuler, *Woman Suffrage and Politics*, p. 298.

their motivation for antiforeignism disappeared. At the same time, the necessity for carrying on a propaganda campaign among the heterogeneous populations in the cities and the closer association with foreign-born women within their own suffrage clubs inevitably helped to dissipate the old prejudices.[35] During this period, also, the city was losing its identification by reformers as the source of all the troubles that afflicted society. Antiforeignism never vanished completely from the suffragist rationale, but toward the end of the long struggle it had to give ground to the immigrant woman's own argument for woman suffrage.

On November 17, 1917, the *Woman Citizen* announced:

One of the things that women seeking the vote have learned is not to be afraid of America's foreign-born population. To the politicians, to the clubman, to the kid-gloved set, to the high-brow, to all people in fact, who are in touch with special superficial processes of life rather than with its mainspring, the foreign-born constitute either a temptation or a fear. To suffragists the foreign-born are a hope and a promise. Seeking the vote, suffragists have come to know what and how much the foreign-born have to offer to America. They have come to know it through coming to know foreign-born women, their habits of thrift, their intensive neighborli-

[35] A discussion in the 1900 convention of the NAWSA was symptomatic of both the old prejudices and their decay. The ladies argued whether suffrage clubs ought to "be exclusive" or "take in all who want to join." Mrs. Merrick of Louisiana, wife of her state's former Chief Justice, said, "I pride myself on being a woman of the people," and urged that "suffrage should be given out just as freely as salvation itself." Mrs. Blake of New York said, "We do not in the least draw society lines in my own club; we have working girls among our members and are glad to have them," but excluded "lunatics" by making a rule that new members had to be accepted and voted in. (*Woman's Journal*, April 7, 1900.)

ness, the pathetic yet inspirational quality of their concern in their children's advancement. For these powerful, first-hand reasons, if for no other, suffragists have always smiled at the fears of the élite who were willing to give Fifth Avenue women a vote, but afraid of the women on Hester Street.

The world *always* in the last sentence was of course inaccurate, but the spirit of this passage signifies that the suffragist movement had ceased to be partly an effort of small-town, middle-class, native-born women to maintain the supremacy of their own group over the residents of the Hester Streets of the big cities.

Perhaps the most important reason of all for the change in suffragists' attitudes toward immigrants had to do less with the immigrants' national origins than with their class. Most suffragists belonged to the native-born middle class; most white workers at that time were fewer than three generations removed from Europe. The changes that took place in the first decade of the new century in suffragist views of the immigrant were paralleled by a new understanding of and sympathy for workers, particularly workingwomen. Jane Addams befriended the immigrant women of Chicago as individuals with special needs, but it was not until suffragists in large numbers began publicly to identify themselves and their cause with workingwomen as workers that labor began to support woman suffrage with more than the formal endorsements that had become traditional at union conventions.[36] This development had to await the unioniza-

[36] For enumeration of AFL conventions that had endorsed woman suffrage, see Gompers, "Labor and Woman Suffrage," *American Federationist*, XXVII (October, 1920), 936-39. See *Proceedings* of NAWSA conventions for the names of the large number of international and local unions endorsing suffrage each year.

tion of women workers in sufficient numbers to produce a group of articulate women leaders who could plead their cause from suffragist platforms, and it had to await the simultaneous appearance among middle-class suffrage leaders of a few women who could show their colleagues that benevolent sympathy for the oppressed shopgirl was not enough. Before that time, the NAWSA annually resolved that suffrage would help women receive equal pay for equal work and that women workers needed the vote for self-protection. These resolutions and the spirit that produced them of course remained in the suffragist rationale until the end, and it is clear that most suffragists continued to use the prolabor argument as one of many ways of attracting sympathy for their primary goal of woman suffrage. A significant number of suffragists, however, continued to consider suffrage a means to a wider goal; to some, that goal was the full development of women's potentialities, to others, the creation of a juster social order. In either case, the interests of working-women as workers would be of primary concern to them, rather than of value chiefly as means to strengthen the suffragist cause.

Elizabeth Cady Stanton, in the 1890s, had defended the needs of workers in the interest of that full development of the human personality that was always her principal aim. She argued vehemently against Sunday blue laws and the proposal to close the 1893 World's Fair on Sundays. As she pointed out, Sunday was the only day workers could attend museums and libraries, enlarge their minds, and widen their horizons.[37] To the vast ma-

---

[37] "Address of Mrs. Stanton," *Woman's Journal,* March 1, 1890; convention report *ibid.,* January 30, 1892; New York *Sun,* April 1, 1900; *Woman's Journal,* May 14, 1898. The last is a letter from Mrs. Stanton, in which she expressed her impatience with the women who

jority of her colleagues, however, workers were merely a sector of the population that drank liquor and opposed woman suffrage. Labor unions in large numbers began passing suffrage resolutions at conventions in the same period in which suffragists asked that the votes of slum dwellers be counteracted by those of women.[38] The distinction between prosuffrage unions and the antisuffrage slum dwellers reflected the division within labor ranks between skilled, native-born, organized workers and unskilled, foreign-born, unorganized laborers. The former could find a basis for cooperation with the suffrage movement; in the early period the latter portion of the population, men and women both, were considered unreachable by suffragist propaganda as well as by unionization.[39] At the 1893 convention of the NAWSA a resolution stating that woman suffrage would solve the problem created by the existence of the illiterate vote accompanied a resolution declaring that workingwomen needed the ballot.[40] The doctrines that equal work should be rewarded by equal pay, that workingwomen could protect their special interests only with the ballot, that women's lack of

---

worked for suffrage and nothing else. She wrote, "We have a higher duty than the demand for suffrage; we must now, at the end of fifty years of faithful service, broaden our platform and consider the next step in progress, to which the signs of the times clearly point—namely, coöperation, a new principle in industrial economics. We see that the right of suffrage avails nothing for the masses, in competition with the wealthy classes and, worse still, with each other."

[38] See Mrs. Catt's speech quoted on p. 125 above.

[39] Union endorsements of woman suffrage are mentioned in Anthony and Harper, eds., *History of Woman Suffrage*, IV, 184 (1891 convention), 359-60 (1900 convention), 446 (1901 convention); Harper, ed., *History of Union Suffrage*, V, 205-6 (1907 convention), 218 (1908 convention), 249 (1909 convention).

[40] Anthony and Harper, eds., *History of Woman Suffrage*, IV, 216; also NAWSA, *Proceedings*, 1893, pp. 84-85.

the vote had weakened their bargaining power, and that women's disfranchisement had dragged down men's wages and weakened men's unions found expression in NAWSA convention resolutions every year thereafter.[41] Of utmost significance was the fact that these resolutions were proposed, discussed, and adopted by middle-class women, motivated by sympathy for workingwomen. In a general way these middle-class suffragists felt that here was one more reason why women should have the right to vote; here was one more wrong that women's votes could eradicate. The belief that woman suffrage was desirable for the good that women could do with the vote (the expediency argument as discussed in Chapter III) in this context implied an assumption that woman suffrage was nevertheless the real goal, and the fulfillment of workingwomen's needs which suffrage would make make possible was a means to that goal. Although improvement of workingwomen's conditions was advanced as the justification, in this instance, of woman suffrage, the possibility of arguing that suffrage would bring that improvement was the real reason the prolabor argument found its way into the suffrage rationale.[42]

A few leading suffragists, such as Jane Addams, Flor-

[41] See *Proceedings* of every NAWSA convention, and issues of *Woman's Journal* shortly after each convention, containing reports of proceedings.

[42] Jane Addams suggested a distinction between the prolabor suffragist argument and the arguments of workers themselves in *The Second Twenty Years at Hull-House*, pp. 88-91. After summarizing the thesis of middle-class women that they needed the vote to help the state fulfill its new responsibilities in inspecting food, reforming delinquents, etc., she observed: "In the midst of these arguments, however, and always in the stirring conventions whether held in Europe or in the United States there remained in my mind the experiences of those simple women who could not do otherwise but make an effort for the franchise because they needed it so bitterly for their children's sake. This provided a sanction quite outside the organized movement."

ence Kelley, and Sophonisba P. Breckinridge, must be excepted from the foregoing generalization. All three were middle-class social workers for whom suffrage was never more than a tool for social regeneration. Mrs. Kelley, especially, became the indefatigable pleader from suffragist platforms for a wider understanding of the horrors of child labor and the exploitation of women in factories.[43] At the Baltimore convention of the NAWSA in 1906, Mrs. Kelley spoke as secretary of the National Consumers' League and chairman of the NAWSA's Committee on Industrial Problems Affecting Women and Children.[44]

Last night, while we slept after our evening meeting, there were in Maryland many hundred boys, only nominally fourteen years old, working all night in the glass-works; and here in Baltimore the smallest messenger boys I have ever seen in any city were perfectly free to work all night. . . . For twenty-five years I have been doing what one person could do to call attention to the unhappy position of the young working children in most of our industrial States. I personally have used the right of petition in every way in which I have been able to use it. At the end of twenty-five years I have to admit that the result is a sorry one compared with the achievements in ten years in Colorado. The conclusion seems to be obvious. We must, of course, work for the immediate enfranchisement of women in every possible way. And while we are doing that, we must in every Suffrage Association have a standing Industrial Committee

[43] See, for example, "Florence Kelley on Working Girls," Woman's Journal, November 7, 1903; a number of issues of that paper in the second half of 1904; "The Young Breadwinners' Need of Women's Enfranchisement," Woman's Journal, July 22, 1905; NAWSA, Proceedings, 1906, pp. 44-48.

[44] The committee had been established at the 1899 convention with Mrs. Clara Bewick Colby of Nebraska as chairman. In 1906, the same year as Mrs. Kelley's address in Baltimore, the Woman's Journal began to bear the union label (see announcement in Woman's Journal, April 7, 1906).

whereby to meet this emergency [the plight of child laborers]. We must do what we can with the powers that we have, feeble as they are, for the children who are here, who will be the voters when we are dead.[45]

Such speeches appeared more frequently as the twentieth century went on, but both speakers and audiences remained middle class, a fact that a few of the more discerning observers commented upon.[46] The chairman of the NAWSA Committee on Industrial Problems Affecting Women and Children, in her report to the 1903 convention, complained of this fact, while the very first sentence of her report gave unconscious evidence of that attitude on the part of suffragists that had helped keep working-class women away from suffrage organizations. Mrs. Clara B. Colby explained her position thus:

As a suffrage society, we cannot swerve from our direct purpose to consider any social wrong or take sides with any cause or class, unless to demonstrate the need of woman's ballot or to aid in securing it. To see if we are justified in such common work, let us look at the matter from its most obvious points of view. . . .

[45] *Woman's Journal*, March 3, 1906. See also her letter to the editor of *The Outlook*, March 17, 1906, p. 622, in which she wrote, "I am convinced that the enfranchisement of women is indispensable to the solution of the child labor problem."

[46] As early as 1901, Mrs. Harper had written that one of the movement's weaknesses had been its failure to recruit working-class women. (See New York *Sun*, May 12, 1901.) At the 1906 convention the secretary of the Women's Trade Union League, Gertrude Barnum, told the assembled suffragists that leisure-class women had preached to workingwomen, "rescued" them, done things *for* them. But they had never come to know them, to work *with* them for the good of their common country. The workingwomen, she went on, would be a great addition to the movement. They needed the vote more than middle-class women. Why, she asked, were women workers not present in this "representative" audience? No one, she said, could speak for them adequately. (Harper, ed., *History of Woman Suffrage*, V, 165-66.)

She proceeded to ask and answer four key questions. First, were there industrial problems especially affecting women? Yes, women were at a disadvantage as women, nonvoting members of the community. Second, would the vote help to remedy bad conditions or to solve these problems? Yes, workingmen had found the vote valuable; further, states in which women became voters immediately passed laws providing for equal pay for equal work regardless of sex. Third, how could suffragists convince workingwomen in large numbers that from their own selfish standpoint, if from no other, they should join suffrage ranks? This, declared Mrs. Colby, was the most important practical question for suffragists to answer. Although talented workingwomen speakers had thrilled suffrage audiences with their oratory, there had been no general rally of workingwomen to secure the ballot for themselves. Fourth, how could suffragists stimulate women at the other end of the economic scale, whose support and influence would be invaluable, to join the cause for selfish reasons if for no other? Her answer to this question explained the common basis on which workingwomen and wealthy women might join together:

We might despair of reaching either the overworked, underpaid, and unresponsive wage-earner, or the indifferent, irresponsible, and almost inaccessible woman of fortune, were it not that all along the social line we are linked by one common possession, our womanhood, which when awakened, is the Divine Motherhood; and it is to this we must appeal.[47]

Mrs. Colby proved a good prophet, for within a few years the suffragist movement enlisted a group of wealthy women, tired of the frivolous diversions of their sisters and moved by more serious concerns, and a contingent of the newly unionized women workers who had learned by experience the need for the ballot and the importance of issues beyond the daily round of their labor. As Mrs. Colby had predicted, moreover, the bond between the two types of woman was their feeling that women of all classes suffered certain injustices in common.[48] In New York City the movement of members of these two groups into suffrage organizations was especially notable. Society leaders such as Mrs. Clarence Mackay and Mrs. Oliver H. P. Belmont vied with one another for suffrage leadership, each organizing her own followers. Mrs. Belmont was not a dilettante; she paid a large part of NAWSA's expenses for several years and later became a leader of the Congressional Union for Woman Suffrage, contributing time and considerable talent as well as money to the cause.

The first test of the devotion of these ladies to the interests of all women came in 1909 when the New York shirtwaist makers went on strike. Mrs. Belmont promptly hired the Hippodrome for a rally to support the striking women and called Anna Howard Shaw, president of the NAWSA, by long distance telephone to ask her to speak.

[48] A letter from Harriet Taylor Upton to the members of the Business Committee, November 13, 1908 (Clay Papers, UK), is symbolic. Mrs. Upton told her fellow NAWSA leaders that Mrs. Ella Reeve Bloor, Socialist, had recently been engaged by Connecticut suffragists to organize workingwomen into suffrage clubs. The rent of the halls in which the organizational meetings were held was being paid by a niece of J. P. Morgan. This information had been sent to Mrs. Upton by the president of the Connecticut affiliate of the NAWSA. Mrs. Upton, as treasurer, was now writing to the Business Committee to secure their consent for the arrangement. As students of the American Socialist movement know, Mrs. Bloor, later a member of the Communist party, came to be known as "Mother Bloor."

The eight thousand in the audience were probably as much impressed by the fact of Dr. Shaw's presence and Mrs. Belmont's initiative as they were by what the speakers said.[49] The *Woman's Journal* wrote a sympathetic account of the mass meeting, at which workers were prominent on the platform as well as in the audience. Sharing the dais with Mrs. Belmont, the Rev. John Howard Melish of Brooklyn's Trinity Church, Dr. Shaw, and others were Rose Schneidermann, Mary McDowell, Clara Lemlich, and other leaders of workingwomen.[50] Later in the year, four months after the *Woman's Journal* had become the official organ of the NAWSA,[51] it reprinted a large cartoon from the Boston *Post*, showing a very fat man with top hat, diamond stickpin, dollar bills stuffed in pants pockets, diamond ring, and a bow tie with a dollar sign on each loop. He was labeled "Special Interests," and the smoke from his cigar formed a dollar sign. He was blowing this smoke into the face of a poor woman with two small children clinging to her skirts. She was holding toward him a market basket bearing a tag: "Prohibitive Prices." In the same issue the *Journal* carried a sympathetic account of the Chicago garment workers' strike and praised the newfound sympathy between the workers and the comfortable women who had come to their support.[52]

[49] See Anna Howard Shaw to members of the Official Board, December 6, 1909, Clay Papers, UK.

[50] *Woman's Journal,* January 22, 1910. See *ibid.,* June 25, 1910, for an account of the suit brought against Mrs. Belmont and other suffragists by a shirtwaist manufacturer for triple damages under the Sherman Act for conspiracy to create an illegal boycott during the strike. Miss Blackwell, who wrote the article, expressed hope that the suit would bring publicity to the cause of justice for the exploited workingwomen.

[51] It became independent again in September, 1912.

[52] *Ibid.,* November 19, 1910.

This newfound sympathy reached its high point on the occasion of the appalling Triangle Fire which took the lives of 146 women garment workers in New York City on March 25, 1911. Shocked suffragists held protest meetings and marched in memorial processions.[53] The tired saying that workingwomen needed the ballot suddenly took on new and fearful meaning, as Mary Ware Dennett, the NAWSA's corresponding secretary, noted in the April 1 issue of the *Woman's Journal:*

Over and over again we suffragists insist that women are citizens and should be equally responsible with men, but a frightful shock like this makes us know it as we never knew it before. It is enough to silence forever the selfish addle-headed drivel of the anti-suffragists who recently said at a legislative hearing that working women can safely trust their welfare to their "natural protectors." We might perhaps be willing to consign such women to the sort of protection, care and chivalry that is indicated by the men who allow 700 women to sit back to back, wedged in such close rows between machines that quick exit is an impossibility; a ten-story building with no outside fire escapes, and only one rickety inside fire escape, with a jump of 25 feet at the bottom of it, and the exits leading to the fire escape shuttered and locked; with iron gates shutting off the staircase, and cigarette-smoking allowed in the midst of inflammable materials.

But we are *not* willing to consign unwilling women or helpless young girls to any such tender mercies. And we claim in no uncertain voice that the time has come when women should have the one efficient tool with which to make for themselves decent and safe working conditions—the ballot.

Perhaps it was the Triangle Fire that gave voice to

[53] *Ibid.,* April 1 and 8, 1911; Flexner, *Century of Struggle*, p. 363.

feelings that the NAWSA's national treasurer, Jessie Ashley, must have been harboring for a long time. In the April 11, 1922 issue of the *Woman's Journal,* Miss Ashley, a wealthy New York attorney and a socialist, berated her fellow suffragists for their patronizing attitude toward the working class:

What are the arguments that the working girl hears when she stops to listen to an impassioned soap-box orator from the suffrage ranks? "Taxation without representation is tyranny." She shrugs—she doesn't know she pays taxes. "The right to vote is the natural, inherent, inalienable right of every adult human being." She turns away. She knows that as a matter of fact she has no right to vote, and she doesn't care. But before she is out of ear-shot comes the plea, "Women must have the ballot in order to protect their homes, to protect their children." She hurries on her way. She has no home nor any children, and she knows she could not do much to protect either on wages of three dollars a week. So the disappointed orator wonders what is wrong.

In reality, Miss Ashley explained, suffragists came to the working class as outsiders. They showed no knowledge of workers' interests. For example, she asked accusingly, had they ever come forward with vigorous support for purely working-class legislation? Had they ever shown themselves ready to back laws that would help workers but at the same time wipe out their own dividends? Had they ever tried to ascertain the workers' point of view and meet it?

Suffragists can reach moneyed interests by middle-class arguments; they can reach professional interests by middle-class arguments; they can even, to a certain extent, reach labor leaders. But the working class as a class will stand aside until they are taught from within and in terms that appeal to them why they should demand the ballot for women. There are already many busy teaching them this, but they are not sent by suffrage organizations.

Miss Ashley expanded her thesis in the *Journal* of June 24, 1911. Describing an article she had read that had compared the handsome ladies in the recent suffrage parade with the working girls crowding into the subway on their way home from work at the same time as the parade, Miss Ashley observed:

Is this not strangely illuminating? The baldness of the contrast between those subway girls and the handsome parading ladies is like a lightning flash clearing for a moment the whole dim subject. For it is those "handsome ladies," and they alone, who have begun to see that women must stand and think and work together, and they, alas, are not the ones whose need to do so is the greatest.

For the most part the handsome ladies are well satisfied with their personal lot, but they want the vote as a matter of justice, while the fluttering, jammed-in subway girls are terribly blind to the whole question of class oppression and of sex oppression. Only the women of the working class are really oppressed, but it is not only the working class woman to whom injustice is done. Women of the leisure class need freedom, too. All women, of whatever class, must become conscious of their position in the world; all must be made to stand erect and become self-reliant, free human beings.

Was there, she asked, a common camp from which all women could march to demand the ballot? Of course, she and other Socialists believed that no common ground existed when the exercise of the ballot was an issue; the workingmen, jammed like the girls into the subway train, should not vote as did the owner of the subway train, nor should the girls vote as did the handsome ladies. Yet, was it not possible for all women to work together to uproot an injustice common to all? Surely, she argued, there must be a way to bring this about.

We must be rid of mere ladylikeness, we must succeed in making the oppressed class of women the most urgent in the demand for what we all must have. When we have brought this about, we women shall be irresistibly strong. But, while we lack enthusiasm and the consecration that can be derived only from the knowledge of great wrongs, we shall continue to show a certain amount of weakness; and great wrongs are not suffered by the handsome ladies as a class, but they are suffered by the working class as a whole. If the working girls ever become really alive to their situation, they will throw themselves into the fight for the ballot in overwhelming numbers, and on that day the suffrage movement will be swept forward by the forces that command progress.[54]

In 1892 Lucy Stone, long hostile to the labor movement, had asked why the Homestead strikers did not

[54] Miss Ashley wrote a few other columns in the *Woman's Journal* along the same lines (see, for example, the August 26, 1911, issue). Although much of what she wrote reflected the new feelings of middleclass suffragists toward workingwomen, she went a good deal farther than they thought proper, and in the January 20, 1912, issue she wrote what she called her "Swan Song," explaining that her earlier articles had elicited protests from suffragists who feared the movement would be identified with socialism. Among her comments was: "I refuse to contemplate the ballot through a magnifying-glass, for suffrage is only a part, though an important one, of the world-wide movement for a real democracy and to give to women their true inheritance." It must be noted that the articles for which she was criticized included explanations of what it meant to workers to be on strike, and a defense of the McNamara brothers. On July 26, 1912, she wrote to Jane Addams, enclosing a draft of an article asking support for Ettor and Giovannitti, leaders of the Lawrence, Massachusetts, textile strike, who had been arrested. She told Miss Addams that she had sent the article to Miss Blackwell, who had thought the *Woman's Journal* ought not to print it, but was willing to let the board decide (Jessie Ashley to Jane Addams, Addams Papers, FHL).

save their earnings to start their own businesses if they were dissatisfied with their jobs.[55] She saw no relation whatever between labor's problems and woman suffrage. In succeeding years suffragists asked for the vote to help counteract the votes of workers. They believed the interests of labor and of middle-class women to be antithetical. At the same time Susan B. Anthony, friend of Eugene V. Debs and of labor, was asking unions to support woman suffrage in their own interest, but remained unwilling to lend her support to any other cause than woman suffrage until such time as she could vote.[56] Shortly after the turn of the century, some suffragists added the need of workingwomen for the vote to their array of arguments, indicating their belief that the interests of workers and of suffragists were compatible, but using the interests of workers primarily to strengthen their own claim to the vote. This remained the chief way in which most suffragists viewed the relationship between labor and woman suffrage. Miss Ashley's position is significant partly in that it shows the extent to which the vast majority of suffragists would not go in identifying the interests of workingwomen with their own. Although a number of Socialists became active suffragists in the years just before World War I and although women factory workers spoke from suffrage platforms,[57] the move-

[55] See K. Anthony, *Susan B. Anthony*, pp. 462-63; Hays, *Morning Star*, pp. 253-54; and *Woman's Journal*, July 23, 1892.

[56] See, for example, "Address of Miss Susan B. Anthony to the Convention, Saturday, January 13," *The Bricklayer and Mason*, II (February, 1900), 19-21.

[57] At the 1913 convention of the NAWSA, the speakers included Rose Winslow, a stocking weaver; Margaret Hinchey, a laundry worker; and Mary Anderson, member of the Executive Board of the National Boot and Shoemakers' Union (Harper, ed., *History of Woman Suffrage*, V, 364-65).

ment remained middle class. Many of the suffragists experienced a new and sincere feeling of solidarity with their working-class sisters, which their activities and organizational forms reflected,[58] and would probably have been perplexed at the privately expressed reaction to their attitude on the part of a leading spokesman of women workers. Writing to a leader of the Women's Trade Union League, the spokesman explained what had recently occurred at a suffrage meeting in New York:

> I feel as if I have butted in wher I was not wanted. Miss Hay gave me a badge was very nice to me but you know they had a school teacher represent the Industrial workers if you ever herd her it was like trying to fill a barrel with water that had no bottom not a word of labor spoken at this convention so far. You would have to be a real politician now to be a Suffrage. this convention is a verry quite serious affair after the hole thing was over some pepole came to me and said I had a right to speak for labor but they kept away until it was over
>
> Lenora they are all old members in this convention all the young people is gone over to the Congressi[on]al Union and there is a big fight but they have taken a vote to standing toghter one to back the other I am not goying to wait for sunday meeting I am goying home satturday.[59]

The New York Woman Suffrage Party, a NAWSA affili-

---

[58] The Congressional Union, the semimilitant wing of the suffrage movement, particularly reflected the change, organizing workingwomen's deputations to the President and public meetings at which workers played leading roles. The NAWSA reflected the new attitude to a lesser degree. *Organizing to Win*, a NAWSA handbook written by leading New York suffragist Harriet Burton Laidlaw in 1914, recommended the organization of Wage-Earners' Leagues, the calling of labor meetings, and participation by suffragists in Labor Day parades and labor demonstrations.

[59] M[argaret] Hinchey to "Lenora" [Leonora O'Reilly], [1913?], O'Reilly Papers, RWA.

ate of which Mary Garrett Hay, mentioned in the above letter, was a leader, published an advertisement in New York City and state papers on October 30 and November 1, 1917, just before the referendum that approved the state suffrage amendment. The advertisement was entitled "Your Mother, Your Wife and Your Daughter" and showed appropriate pictures of three genteel women. The text asked the voter to think of the three when he went to vote on Tuesday:

And remember the first time you ever talked about serious things with your wife? Perhaps you asked her opinion of a man you thought of hiring. Perhaps you were considering a new partnership or an extension of your business. Have you ever checked up on her "woman's intuition"? Has it ever failed you? Haven't you often thought that what is called "woman's intuition" isn't intuition at all—that it is just a quicker, simpler grasp of a situation than you get from many of the men whose opinions you ask? [60]

When the suffragists inserted ads in the foreign-language press or worked in working-class neighborhoods, their arguments were consciously phrased to appeal to workers' interests.[61] But when their propaganda was directed at voters in general and did not call for conscious effort to appeal to specific interests, their assumption that they were middle-class women appealing to middle-class men became apparent.

By the last few years before the Nineteenth Amendment was ratified, many unskilled and semiskilled workers, as well as first- and second-generation Americans,

[60] The advertisement, reproduced as a large poster, is in the Laidlaw Collection, NYHS.

[61] See, for example, leaflet published by Oklahoma Woman Suffrage Association, headed "Vote for the Woman Suffrage Amendment," in Clay Papers, UK, among 1910 material.

became converted to woman suffrage and joined the suffrage organizations. Their recruitment to the cause was undoubtedly due in part to the fact that the suffragists felt more friendly toward them, although the claim that woman suffrage would counteract the foreign-born or worker vote still appeared in suffrage propaganda now and then. Probably the influence was just as great in the other direction; for independent reasons, these groups, and especially women, became interested in suffrage and upon their entrance into the associations came to exert an influence on the middle-class members. The shirt-waist strike and the Triangle Fire provided occasions in which both tendencies came together and reinforced each other. The motives that influenced a native-born middle-class woman to work for suffrage, however, generally remained far different from those that induced a foreign-born or workingwoman to join the same organization and campaign side by side with her for the right to vote.

SEVEN

The "Southern Question"

Since the woman suffrage movement was a demand that democracy be broadened by the participation of one part of the adult population hitherto excluded from its processes, one might assume that the adherents of that movement would support similar claims to the suffrage by other sectors of the population. The very origins of the woman suffrage cause, in the abolitionist crusade, would make such an assumption plausible. Indeed, a few suffragists such as Susan B. Anthony believed in universal suffrage on the theory that women, Negroes, propertyless workers, and naturalized citizens had the same inalienable right to consent to the laws they obeyed as did white, rich, and native-born men. The changing relation of the suffrage movement to the "Southern question," however, shows that women's claim to the ballot could find rationales consistent with a repudiation of the "consent of the governed" and natural right principles.

Three developments mark the change. First, as the woman suffrage movement advanced in popular favor, women who shared their contemporaries' opinions on every other issue joined it, bringing into the movement with them the race-consciousness that by then had become universal in American thought.[1] Whether or not they sympathized with the actions of the Southern constitutional conventions that disfranchised Negroes,[2] they one and all cried out at the injustice of refined white women's being the political inferiors of former slaves. They unanimously believed that the stability of government depended on the rule of the "intelligent" portion of the population, and so they could easily see the consistency of decreasing the political power of "unfit" groups with increasing their own. Second, those abolitionists who survived into the twentieth century largely accepted the new intellectual temper of the times and concluded that the Negro question and woman suffrage were really unrelated; these abolitionists need not advocate Negro suffrage in the South for their own claim to the vote to be consistent. They could even tolerate the use, within their association, of racist arguments for woman suffrage, although they might disagree with those arguments. Some

[1] The universality of racism in the 1890s has been commented on by a number of historians recently. See, for example, Christopher Lasch, "The Anti-Imperialists, the Philippines, and the Inequality of Man," *Journal of Southern History,* XXIV (1958), 319-31, in which the author states that "the atmosphere of the late nineteenth century was so thoroughly permeated with racist thought (reinforced by Darwinism) that few men managed to escape it," and that this universal racism is what gave "the intellectual life of the period its peculiar tone." See also C. Vann Woodward, *Origins of the New South* (Baton Rouge, Louisiana State University Press, 1951), chaps. XII and XIII. The chief suffragist journalist, Ida Husted Harper, commented on the same phenomenon in the New York *Sun,* May 18, 1902.

[2] The Southern constitutional conventions which adopted a variety of mechanisms to deprive Negroes of political power took place between 1890 and 1910. The grandfather clause, one of those mechanisms, was not invalidated until 1915. Thus the period in which Negroes were disfranchised almost exactly coincided with the period in which the woman suffrage cause won its first major victories. This has been commented on by Mowry, *The Era of Theodore Roosevelt, 1900-1910,* p. 81, and Porter, *A History of Suffrage in the United States,* p. 145.

abolitionists discovered that white-supremacist arguments might be used positively to further the women's
cause. They justified their use by appeals to the alleged
long-range interests of Southern Negroes in stable state
governments dominated by the best type of whites,
screened by literacy qualifications for the vote. Third,
Southern white women began building a suffrage movement the principal argument of which was that the enfranchisement of women would insure the permanency
of white supremacy in the South. Although there had
been suffragists in the South since shortly after the Civil
War, the growth of active organizations and recruitment of significant numbers of women had had to wait
until conservative attitudes in their section toward wom-
en's place had begun to soften and until women had begun to work for various reforms. Undoubtedly the
growth of the movement in the South was encouraged
by the spread throughout the rest of the country of the
Southern white viewpoint on the Negro question. When
most Northern suffragists accepted the argument that
woman suffrage in the South could be advocated as a
"solution to the race problem," Southern suffragists could
feel encouraged to join in the nationwide suffrage movement, confident that they were not betraying the ideals
of their class and section.

The official recognition of the new state of affairs
within the NAWSA was the enunciation in the 1903 convention of the principle of "states' rights" as a basis of
the relationship of state suffrage organizations to one
another and to the National.[3] Technically this meant that

---

[3] NAWSA, *Proceedings*, 1903, p. 59: "That this Association, as a
national body, recognizes the principle of State rights, and leaves to

state affiliates would enjoy full power to determine qualifications for membership in their clubs and to use whatever arguments they saw fit for suffrage within their territories. In practice, "states' rights" also meant freedom
for Southern members to express racist views from
NAWSA convention platforms and freedom for Northern
members to announce that the Southerners possessed the
right to do so without being controverted. The development of the woman suffrage organization from a strictly
Northern group of crusaders for the rights of all men
and women to a nationwide association that all but officially sanctioned second-class citizenship for Negroes
may be traced in specific events in the history of the
NAWSA.

The seeds of change from the founders' equal concern for woman and for the Negro sprouted very early—
even before the Civil War—when a few of the women
who had dedicated themselves to the two tasks of winning freedom for the slave and the vote for woman discovered that they sometimes had to choose between
their two causes. They could theorize that in the long
run whatever helped one group of Americans toward full
equality helped the other too, but the choice that circumstances sometimes forced was not easy. In discussions, for instance, of the Fourteenth Amendment prior
to its passage, the Stanton-Anthony wing of the suffrage
movement insisted that the cause of human freedom
would be set back by an amendment that made it easier

---

each State Association to determine the qualification for membership
in the Association, and the terms upon which the extension of suffrage
to women shall be requested of the respective State Legislatures."

for the black man to vote while, by inserting the word *male* in the Constitution for the first time, it made it harder than before for women to get the ballot. The Lucy Stone wing, on the other hand, argued that if efforts to secure the vote for both Negroes and women failed, the women ought to acquiesce in the enfranchisement of Negroes, happy that one group at least had won its rights.[4] Inevitably some suffragists soon began to speculate whether Negroes or women needed the suffrage more. The view of Frederick Douglass, Negro abolitionist who had from the inception of the suffrage movement been one of its most steadfast male champions, was short and full of meaning: To you, he told the women, the vote is desirable; to us it is vital.[5] Many women, however, declared that their rights deserved priority: first, because women were half the population whereas Negroes were only a small minority, and, second, because in their opinion, after the Civil War the Negro man was in many ways better off than any woman, black or white.[6] The latter assertion was buttressed by painstak-

[4] Alice Stone Blackwell explained the two views in *Woman's Journal*, December 31, 1892, and January 14, 1893.

[5] This paraphrase and its implications may be found in Quarles, "Frederick Douglass and the Woman's Rights Movement," *Journal of Negro History*, XXV (January, 1940), 39-41. The statement was made in 1866 and again in 1868 when large-scale violence against Negroes gave their enfranchisement an urgency which it could not have had for white women.

[6] Laura Clay in *Woman's Journal*, January 14, 1899. Only a few years later explicit statements of this opinion were rare; it was no longer necessary to persuade suffragists that their enfranchisement ought to take precedence over that of the Negro. In fact, the widespread view by the last years of the nineteenth century was that Negro suffrage was dangerous and should be nullified by disfranchisement or by counteracting the ballots of Negroes with the more numerous ballots of white women. By then, both arguments mentioned in the text were obsolescent. See also [Laura Clay] to Henry B. Blackwell, October 14, 1907, Clay Papers, UK.

ing researches by women lawyers into the legal disabilities of women.[7]

The stage was now set for the emergence of a suffrage movement of Southern white women, in alliance with a Northern movement that still contained many individuals who had fought for the end of slavery. Some of the latter merely tolerated the alliance, believing that the single most important task was to secure the vote for women even if it meant that other sectors of the population must pay part of the cost. Other old abolitionists actively collaborated with Southern suffragists in developing a new argument for suffrage. Henry B. Blackwell, Massachusetts abolitionist and husband of Lucy Stone, pioneered in this activity. In 1867 he published an essay, *What the South Can Do,* containing statistics that showed that there were more white women in the South than there were Negro men and women combined.[8] Hence, the enfranchisement of women would greatly increase the white majority in the electorate and thus insure white supremacy. This in time became the single most important argument used in the South.[9] Mr. Blackwell and

[7] Catharine Waugh McCulloch of Illinois was an attorney who specialized in this type of research.

[8] This pamphlet is discussed in Quarles, "Frederick Douglass and the Woman's Rights Movement," *Journal of Negro History,* XXV (January, 1940), 40; and Merk, "Massachusetts and the Woman-Suffrage Movement," rev. ed., p. 231.

[9] A few instances of its use in 1890 and after are: Henry B. Blackwell in *Woman's Journal,* September 27, 1890; NAWSA, *Proceedings,* 1893, p. 84, quoting a resolution passed at the convention; Ida Husted Harper, in New York *Sun,* August 25, 1901; speeches by Southern suffragists at the 1903 NAWSA convention, quoted in *Woman's Journal,* April 4 and 25, 1903; speech by Mrs. Desha Breckinridge of Kentucky at the 1911 convention, quoted in *Woman's Journal,* November 4, 1911; statements by two prominent suffragists, Mrs. Guilford Dudley of Tennessee and Miss Maud Younger of California, at the 1918 House *Hearing* (cited in note 38 of chap. II), pp. 19-20, 162. The argument

those suffragists who followed his lead justified their use
of this argument by one or more of the following assertions: that Reconstruction had been a frightful era of
corruption and oppression in the South; that Negro suffrage had proved a failure owing to the unreadiness of
the freedmen for political power; that the events of Reconstruction had caused a reaction throughout the country
against universal suffrage and democracy itself; that the
North, experiencing an influx of "new immigrants," could
now understand what the white South had been saying
for many years; and that the salvation of Anglo-Saxon
civilization in the United States depended on the rule of
the intelligent, which meant native-born whites.[10]

A few old-timers such as Susan B. Anthony could not
go so far as to advocate withdrawal of political power
from Negroes, but by the end of the century the time
had long passed when she believed Negro suffrage and
woman suffrage to be interdependent. In the 1899 convention, she helped put the NAWSA on record as regarding the two causes as completely separate. The turn of
the century, in this as in other respects, opened a new
era for woman suffrage.

In the spring of 1899, the NAWSA held its annual con-

---

paralleled that of the Northern suffragists, who used statistics to show
that there were more native-born women in the United States than
foreign-born men and women combined; therefore woman suffrage
would insure the supremacy of the native born in the North.

[10] A few instances of one or another of these views expressed by
Northern suffragists are: Carrie Chapman Catt's presidential address
to the 1901 NAWSA convention, reprinted in *Woman's Journal*, June 8,
1901; Ida Husted Harper in New York *Sun*, October 4, 1903; Mrs.
Catt's presidential address to the 1904 NAWSA convention, reprinted in
Woman's Journal, February 20, 1904; Alice Stone Blackwell to Laura
Clay, October 6, 1907, Clay Papers, UK.

vention in Grand Rapids, Michigan, a state in which suffrage clubs drew no color line. One Michigan delegate who was a Negro, Mrs. Lottie Wilson Jackson, offered a resolution, "That colored women ought not to be compelled to ride in smoking cars, and that suitable accommodations should be provided for them." The resolution touched off a heated debate described at length in the official *Proceedings*. Mrs. Jackson defended her resolution by explaining that in some parts of the South it was almost impossible for respectable colored women to travel, because of the filthy state of the cars and the insults to which they were exposed from the rough company into which they were thrown. The Pullmans had been their only refuge from such conditions, and it was now proposed to exclude them from these cars. There was great work to be done among the ignorant Negro women in the South, she added, and it was important that educated women of their own race not be prevented from going there to do this work.

Laura Clay of Kentucky objected to the resolution on the ground that it was unfair to Southern delegates, who had come to attend a woman suffrage convention. The resolution, she insisted, was an attack on the Separate Coach Law. She could say from her own knowledge that the conditions complained of did not exist on Kentucky railroads under sanction of law, and she doubted if they existed legally anywhere in the South. Hence the resolution implied that infractions of the law could not be punished in her section and was an insult to the Southern lawmakers and the Southern people.

Mrs. Caroline E. Merrick of Louisiana deplored the renewal of unpleasant feeling between North and South and added that what Miss Clay had said about Kentucky applied to her state as well. Moreover, she said, she had brought a young colored woman with her all the way from Louisiana, and no objection had been made to her presence in the car. Mrs. Mary J. Coggeshall of Iowa remarked that no objection ever had been made to the presence of a colored person traveling with a white person as a servant. Another delegate pointed out that the resolution did not attack the Separate Coach Law and did not express an opinion as to whether Negro women ought to be allowed to travel on the same cars as white women; it merely claimed that decent accommodations should be provided for them.

Alice Stone Blackwell of Massachusetts denied that the resolution insulted the Southern people; it did not claim that these things were done under sanction of law. Rather, it criticized certain railroad companies in a few sections of the South. That the conditions complained of existed in some parts of that section was common knowledge; besides, the convention had Mrs. Jackson's testimony as to her own experiences. Miss Clay replied that public notoriety proved nothing; newspapers often lied or exaggerated. As to Mrs. Jackson's experience, a plaintiff could not be a judge in her own case. Further, it was wrong to spring such a resolution on the Southern delegates. If it was to come up they should have been given advance notice so that they could have collected evidence on the other side. A Missouri delegate then suggested the resolution be amended to omit the word *colored*, since white women frequently received bad treatment also. But Mrs. Jackson asked that the resolution be passed or rejected in its original form.

Susan B. Anthony, in closing the discussion, said in substance that no one would deny that she was true to the colored people, but (in the words of the convention reporter):

We women are a helpless disfranchised class. Our hands are tied. While we are in this condition, it is not for us to go passing resolutions against railroad corporations or anybody else.

Miss Anthony's words evidently swayed many votes, and the resolution was dropped by a large majority.[11]

Miss Anthony, believing that no solution to any national problem could be found until women had won the right to participate in the governing process, evidently felt that her action at the convention was necessary to prevent the association from splitting. Privately, she condemned violations of human rights such as those Mrs. Jackson complained of,[12] but as in 1896 when she tried to prevent the NAWSA from repudiating Mrs. Stanton's anti-Bible opinions,[13] she endeavored to keep all outside issues from suffrage conventions. Her private letters are full of vehement expressions of opinion on not only the Negro question but every issue of the day; but she refused to go on record on those issues until she should have the right to make her views felt at the ballot box and advised all suffragists to follow her example.

The Negro question had before the Civil War been inseparably linked with the cause of woman's equality; now it was merely one of a number of issues the suffra-

---

[11] NAWSA, *Proceedings*, 1899, pp. 59-61.

[12] Jim Crow regulations on railroads are denounced, for example, in Susan B. Anthony to Elizabeth Cady Stanton, December 2, 1898, Anthony Family Collection, HL.

[13] See chap. IV, pp. 83-84.

gists' approach to which had essentially nothing to do with their enfranchisement. Harriet Taylor Upton of Ohio, after having been asked how suffragists ought to approach the Negro question, complained: "It does make me so cross to think they are always quoting the darkey to us. The colored question is no more the question of suffragists than it is the man who already has the right to vote. It isn't half as much." [14]

The final divorce of woman suffrage from abolitionism was accompanied by the rise of a woman suffrage movement in the Southern states. Suffrage associations appeared in one Southern state after another in the early 1890s,[15] and their leaders played more and more active roles in the affairs of the NAWSA as the century drew to a close. Two of these women became influential members of the Official Board; Laura Clay of Kentucky served as an auditor from 1896 to 1910, and Kate M. Gordon of Louisiana was corresponding secretary from 1901 to 1909 and a vice-president in 1910. Several other Southern women held offices on the national level, but for briefer periods; their main energies were devoted to local suffrage affairs.

The differences between Miss Clay and Miss Gordon

[14] Harriet Taylor Upton to Laura Clay, August 31, 1906, Clay Papers, UK.

[15] Accounts of early activities may be found in Allen, "The Woman Suffrage Movement in Alabama, 1910–1920," *Alabama Review*, XI (April, 1958), 83–84; and A. Elizabeth Taylor in many essays, among which are: "The Origin of the Woman Suffrage Movement in Georgia," *Georgia Historical Quarterly*, XXVIII (June, 1944), 63–79; "The Woman Suffrage Movement in Florida," *Florida Historical Quarterly*, XXXVI (July, 1957), 42–44; "The Woman Suffrage Movement in Texas," *Journal of Southern History*, XVII (May, 1951), 194–200; "The Woman Suffrage Movement in Arkansas," *Arkansas Historical Quarterly*, XV (Spring, 1956), 17–52.

perfectly reflected the geographical situation and racial constituency of their respective states. Kentucky, with a small Negro minority, could, according to Miss Clay, afford to give the Negro full security in his voting rights, provided women were enfranchised. Her views on the question of Negro suffrage were moderation itself contrasted to those of Miss Gordon, who lived in a state with a very large Negro population.[16] To her, woman suffrage should, if possible, be accompanied by a "whites only" clause, and she showed considerable ingenuity in her endeavors to make such a clause constitutional. The activities of this New Orleans reformer have been ignored in the historiography of the woman suffrage movement because they deviated from the main line of suffrage campaigns and propaganda. But they merit attention because they lay bare, as extreme positions sometimes do, the implicit logic of the majority viewpoint; because they show the impact of various events of the day in the South on the ideas of the suffragists; and because they incited differences of opinion within the NAWSA that elucidate the thinking of the leaders of the organization on those events.

Kate M. Gordon became corresponding secretary of the NAWSA in 1901, replacing a Pennsylvania woman. Susan B. Anthony had resigned the presidency the year before, the last of the pre-Civil War abolitionists to have

[16] See U. S. Department of Commerce, Bureau of the Census, *Negroes in the United States, 1920–32* (Washington, D.C., Government Printing Office, 1935), pp. 9, 10, 15. In 1890 Louisiana had 559,193 Negroes and 558,395 whites. In 1900 the respective numbers were 650,804 and 729,612; in 1910, 713,874 and 939,789. Percentage of Negroes in the total population of the state dropped from 50.0 in 1890 to 47.1 in 1900 to 43.1 in 1910. Only Mississippi had a Negro majority in those years, but Miss Gordon and many others assumed Louisiana did also.

exercised national leadership. Two of the seven members of the Official Board were now Southerners. Wishing that Southern women "could make this race question the power to enfranchise the white women of the South," [17] Miss Gordon proposed first that the Southern states pass laws explicitly conferring the suffrage on white women. Of course, their constitutionality would be challenged, since the Fifteenth Amendment prohibited denial or abridgment of the "right of the citizens of the United States to vote" on account of race, color, or previous condition of servitude. However, reasoned Miss Gordon, the Supreme Court's interpretation of the suffrage provision of the Fourteenth Amendment in the case of *Minor v. Happersett* (1875)[18] had made it possible to reconcile white-woman suffrage laws with the Fifteenth Amendment. In the *Minor* case, the court had declared that the amendment had not created any new voters, but simply furnished an additional guarantee for those privileges and immunities already possessed by citizens. The suffrage was not one of them. Therefore the fact that Mrs. Minor, who had brought the suit, was incontestably a citizen did not imply that she had the right to vote under the Fourteenth Amendment. Instead of pressing for a reversal of the *Minor* decision, as suffragists had been doing for a generation, Miss Gordon advised accepting it as a tremendous asset to the cause of white woman suffrage. Since, according to the *Minor* decision, no Federal amendment had conferred the vote, directly

[17] Kate M. Gordon to Laura Clay, March 30, 1907, Clay Papers, UK.

[18] Mrs. Virginia Minor was a Missouri suffragist who sued for her right to vote, arguing that the wording of the Fourteenth Amendment implied that the suffrage was included in the definition of citizenship.

or indirectly, on any woman, a state could give the ballot to white women without contravening the Constitution. Negro women could not protest that their right to vote had been denied thereby, because according to the court they had never possessed that right.[19] Miss Gordon readily admitted that this argument was "specious," [20] but so was the *Minor* decision, she declared. She hoped to reopen the question of the interpretation of the Fourteenth Amendment, making it a vehicle for the enfranchisement of the white women of the South. Apparently, however, the argument was a bit too specious, for more than one lawyer advised her that her plan was unfeasible.[21]

By the end of 1908 Miss Gordon had devised the strategy that was to determine her activities from that time on—a strategy for forcing Southern lawmakers to pass woman suffrage amendments to their state constitutions. First and last she opposed a national amendment, believing that it would give the federal government, occasionally controlled by the Republican party, power over Southern elections.[22] Her first step was to write to

[19] This line of thought is developed in Kate M. Gordon to Laura Clay, August 2, 1907, Clay Papers, UK; and in an undated and unaddressed letter in the same collection, evidently written by Miss Gordon in 1907.

[20] In the second letter cited in footnote 19.

[21] Florence Loeber (New Orleans attorney) to Kate M. Gordon, February 25, 1908, Clay Papers, UK; Laura Clay to Catharine Waugh McCulloch, April 16, 1908, McCulloch Papers, RWA. However, Miss Gordon continued to believe in her plan, as is shown by her letter to President Taft (see note 23), although the lawyers evidently persuaded her that the constitutional reinterpretation could not be secured through the courts. Hence she attempted to secure this reinterpretation through bipartisan understanding.

[22] This and her other reasons for opposing the amendment are given in a statement at the end of her report as corresponding secretary at the 1908 convention. See *Proceedings* of the Fortieth Annual Convention of the National American Woman Suffrage Association, held at Buffalo, N.Y., October 15 to 21, inclusive, 1908 (Warren, Ohio, n.d.), pp. 30–

President Taft informing him that his wish to divide the solid South could be fulfilled any time he chose, if the Republican party could assure the South that the Fifteenth Amendment did not apply to women. "The Democratic South," she wrote, "is nothing else but a concise way of expressing anti-nigger." Once Southern Democrats believed that woman suffrage would not bring Negro woman suffrage, white women would be enfranchised, and the white voters could divide on party issues without fear that such division would usher in an era of Negro rule.[23]

In 1909 Miss Gordon resigned her position on the

31. See also [Kate M. Gordon] to Anna Howard Shaw (carbon copy of typed letter), February 12, 1909, and Kate M. Gordon to Business Committee, April 26, 1909 (her resignation as corresponding secretary), both in Clay Papers, UK.

[23] Kate M. Gordon to Laura Clay, December 8, 1908, and Kate M. Gordon to President William Howard Taft (copy sent to Miss Clay), May 11, 1909, both in Clay Papers, UK. In the latter document, she wrote "that if the solid south is ever to be broken, the first essential is to secure to every section of the south a safe white majority. This is as desirable to southern republicans as it is to southern democrats. That the Fifteenth Amendment has led to wholesale fraud, and created a condition that is intolerable to all but a few interested politicians, is likewise beyond contradiction. . . . The actual mention of the word 'male' in the Fourteenth Amend[ment] clearly seems to preclude any other interpretation, than that it was designed to protect colored males and they [sic] alone in their right to vote. . . . The negro woman's position would be no worse than that now accorded her equally with white women. There can certainly be no *abridgement* of rights never enjoyed, in the extension of citizens rights by any state to the white women of that state."

It must be recalled that Northern suffragists undertook the struggle for a woman suffrage amendment to the federal Constitution only after it had become clear that the Supreme Court did not believe the Civil War amendments applied to women. They would have much preferred, of course, the long struggle to have been unnecessary, which would have been the case if the court in the *Minor* decision had declared the suffrage provisions of the Fourteenth and Fifteenth amendments to apply to women. Here Miss Gordon was basing her entire strategy in this period on her insistence that the war amendments did *not* apply to women.

National Board to devote her energies to securing a
Louisiana state law enfranchising white women, to build
a specifically Southern suffrage movement, and to avoid
acquiescing any longer in the NAWSA's advocacy of a
federal amendment.[24] Although she served as a vice-president of the NAWSA in 1910, she concentrated her efforts
on the South. In 1913 her preparatory work was done,
and the Southern States Woman Suffrage Conference
(SSWSC) was organized.[25] Miss Gordon explained its purposes thus:

A strategic position is held by southern suffragists. With
the concentration of effort for a Nationbl [*sic*] Amendment
the point of resistance will be the south. In the south the
Democratic Party alone determines political policies, and
the crux of the whole situation consists in making the Party
live up to its traditions on States Rights and under which
cloak it is hiding in its opposition to a National Amendment.

[24] Kate M. Gordon to Business Committee, April 26, 1909, Clay Papers, UK. Later she wrote that as long as the agitation for the amendment had been a formality, she could acquiesce, since such agitation
had propaganda value—and besides, the amendment stood no chance of
passage without Southern votes (see Kate M. Gordon to Laura Clay,
January 21, 1918; to Southern States Woman Suffrage Conference,
May 11, 1915; and to Southern Suffragists, May 31, 1915, all in Clay
Papers, UK).

[25] Miss Gordon's plans for such an organization and its intended
purposes are described in [Kate M. Gordon] to Laura Clay, September
30, 1913, and Kate M. Gordon to Laura Clay, November 6, 1913, both
in Clay Papers, UK. The founding of the association is noted in [Laura
Clay] to Catharine Waugh McCulloch, November 14, 1913, in the
same collection, which also contains a copy of *The New Citizen*, Vol.
III (December, 1913), a magazine published by Miss Gordon's Era
Club in New Orleans. This issue contains an account of the conference
in New Orleans that established the new organization and elected officers. Miss Gordon, of course, was president, and Miss Clay vice-president. The foundation of the SSWSC was noted also in *Woman's Journal*,
November 22, 1913. It must not be assumed that the leaders of the
NAWSA opposed this movement. In fact, Anna Howard Shaw, national
president of the NAWSA through 1915, was among the prominent Northern suffragists listed on the SSWSC letterhead.

This means that a tremendous whirlwind campaign must be carried on in the south in the next two years to educate National, State and Local leaders of democratic opinion, that the democrats of the South cannot straddle the question of woman suffrage in the next National Platform. If we force the issue we have the party at bay on a fundamental principle—state rights—and upon which position the democrats of the enfranchised states can make a vulnerable [*sic*] attack for the preservation of party integrity.

By virtue of the race issue which is involved, the movement must by the very nature of things be under the guidance of southern women. Southern women must throw the gauntlet that declares, that if southern democrats do not preserve woman suffrage as a state right, we women who believe as unalterably as do the men in the expediency of a state defining its own electorate, will be forced to appeal to the men of other sections to secure for us our inalienable and greatest of all rights, the birthright of citizenship through a coercive National Amendment.[26]

How was the Democratic party to be thus forced to grant woman suffrage in Southern states? Miss Gordon described the strategy thus: Southern states have recently resorted to dubious expedients to evade the Fourteenth and Fifteenth amendments. The rest of the country has consented to these dubious expedients not because it believes them constitutional but because it recognizes the injustice of those amendments, in their interference with what the Democratic party declares is the right of each state to define its electorate without federal dictation. If the Southern white men, benefiting from this Northern acquiescence, will not extend its advantages to the women of their own race, the women will be forced to inaugurate a campaign to publicize the unconstitutionality

[26] Kate M. Gordon to "My Dear Fellow-Suffragist" (printed circular letter dated "1914" on sswsc stationery), Clay Papers, UK.

of the Southern electoral laws and the hypocrisy of the Democratic party which has full power to determine policy in Southern governments. The women will also be forced to appeal for their enfranchisement to the men of other sections, to pass a federal amendment, and the consequent disgrace will rest upon the Southern Democratic party which thus will have betrayed its own principles.[27]

Part of this grand strategy was to put the Democratic party definitely on record for woman suffrage. Miss Gordon pointed out that Democrats in Congress and the Democratic President had been using the slogan of states' rights to avoid doing anything at all for woman suffrage, but once an endorsement of suffrage became part of the party platform, Democratic legislators would be bound by duty and consistency to apply the principle at home and not just in Congress. Failing to do this, the party would be assuming the responsibility for forcing Southern white women to appeal to men of other sections and parties for their enfranchisement—precisely those other men whose leniency toward the Southern constitutions had permitted Southern men to ignore the Civil War amendments. Accordingly, Miss Gordon set the SSWSC the task of working for a woman suffrage plank in the Democratic platform of 1916.[28]

Miss Gordon evidently believed her strategy of threatening the Democratic party succeeded, for, in June of

[27] Kate M. Gordon, "Southern Suffragists Begin Big Campaign," *Woman's Journal,* May 16, 1914; Kate M. Gordon, "The Southern States Woman Suffrage Conference," in Clarke, compiler, *Suffrage in the Southern States,* pp. 95–96; Kate M. Gordon, "Southern States Woman Suffrage Conference," (a "Press Bulletin" reprinting Miss Gordon's address at Chattanooga on November 10, 1914), Clay Papers, UK.
[28] Press Bulletin referred to in footnote 27.

1915 when the Supreme Court voided the grandfather clauses in the Louisiana and Oklahoma constitutions, she took credit for the decision: "I claim for the Southern Conference, that its open and avowed declaration that, 'if the Democratic Party did not go on record in favor of votes for women,' we would attack the illegal Constitutions of the South, as the real reason for the sudden decision." If the NAWSA, she continued, would agree to keep hands off the South and leave all suffrage work in that section to Southern women, to prevent Southern antis from identifying suffragism with Republicanism, she proposed to turn the Supreme Court's action into a victory for suffrage. Louisiana was one of the states whose grandfather clause had been invalidated; Miss Gordon believed that her state could now lead the South for woman suffrage in the coming election. "If we do not succeed," she added, "it then justifies an organized effort to make equally unconstitutional the literacy and understanding clause amendment." [29] Accordingly, she sent copies of the understanding clauses in the Mississippi and Virginia constitutions to her lawyer friend Mrs. McCulloch and asked for an analysis of all the points at which the clauses might conflict with the national Constitution. Of course, Mrs. McCulloch was an Illinoisan, and it was only fair to warn her of the real purpose of this strategy. Miss Gordon wrote:

Now do not misunderstand me; if Louisiana employs an understanding clause to preserve white supremacy and will grant woman suffrage, then I will not have a word to say

[29] Kate M. Gordon to members of the Official Board, National American Woman Suffrage Association, June 23, 1915, Clay Papers, UK (a copy is also in Suffrage Archives, LC).

against it. White supremacy is going to be maintained in the South by fair or foul means. The only ammunition I want is to strike at the unconstitutional points in any subterfuge that will not include white women in its protection. I want to make it clear, that the fighting of these subterfuges will not be left to defenseless negroes but that the white women of the South will fight them in order that they may be raised to the status of the negro men in the United States.[30]

That Northern leaders of the NAWSA also saw the relevance of the decision (*Guinn v. U.S.*) to their cause is shown by a statement written by Ethel M. Smith in behalf of Mrs. Medill McCormick, chairman of the NAWSA's Congressional Committee.[31] Miss Smith wrote that the frequent statements of Chief Justice Clark of the North Carolina Supreme Court, that woman suffrage would insure white supremacy in the South, had become especially timely since the United States Supreme Court's invalidation of the grandfather clauses. She quoted his statistics to the effect that in every Southern state except Mississippi and Louisiana whites outnumbered Negroes and that the white women's votes could be relied on to form a bloc against any measure or man threatening

[30] Kate M. Gordon to Catharine Waugh McCulloch, August 19, 1915, McCulloch Papers, RWA. Back in 1901, Ida Husted Harper (native of Indiana) had written in the New York *Sun*, August 25, about "the opera bouffe in Alabama, otherwise called a Constitutional convention," which was in session. She quoted a member of the convention to the effect that "as the provisions of the new Constitution would doubtless eliminate the Negro as a voter, the giving of this right [of suffrage] to women would not be necessary in order to preserve white supremacy in the State." This is another proof that Miss Gordon's proposed fight against the state constitutions disfranchising Negroes was aimed at forcing the legislatures to grant the vote to women not to save face with the rest of the country but to "save white supremacy" at home.

[31] The letter enclosing the statement is Ethel M. Smith to Mrs. Henry Wade Rogers, June 26, 1915, Suffrage Archives, LC.

Anglo-Saxon supremacy. As for the two states supposedly having Negro majorities, woman suffrage would not change existing voting ratios. Miss Smith's statement, with Mrs. McCormick's endorsement, was written two days after Miss Gordon's request that National stay out of Southern work (the letter in which it was enclosed was dated a day after that). Miss Gordon accused Mrs. McCormick of trying to take over Southern work and of intending to pay the expenses incurred in this enterprise. Miss Gordon was not too worried, however, since, as she wrote, all she had to do was leak to the papers that Mark Hanna's daughter (Ruth Hanna McCormick) wanted to dictate Southern policies. "You know," she remarked, "in this neck of the woods, Mark Hanna's name is not one to conjure with." [32]

For many years, the NAWSA's work for the federal amendment had been perfunctory. But now, for a number of reasons, [33] the giant organization began to mobilize its forces for a final push to secure the passage and ratification of what became the Nineteenth Amendment. When the Democratic convention in 1916 adopted a plank endorsing woman suffrage by state legislation, Miss Gordon felt that one purpose of the SSWSC had been achieved, while Mrs. Catt, in behalf of the NAWSA, was sorely dis-

[32] Kate M. Gordon to Catharine Waugh McCulloch, August 3, 1915, McCulloch Papers, RWA.
[33] See chap. VIII for discussion of the development of new types of suffragist activity that by 1916 made it possible for Mrs. Catt to mobilize the entire association for its final drive. See also chap. VI (pp. 138-46), for discussion of ideological changes within the NAWSA that helped to win a number of state amendments; these victories in turn convinced Mrs. Catt that if an amendment could be pushed through Congress, enough states would ratify it to make it part of the Constitution.

appointed [34] and immediately began laying plans for the historic 1916 convention of the NAWSA that inaugurated the final and victorious campaign. Miss Gordon, on the other hand, concluded that Mrs. Catt's disappointment at the Democratic plank was but one more evidence that the National was becoming more and more a tool of the Republican party.[35] Mrs. Catt, she believed, feared successful campaigns by Southern suffragists for state amendments because they would make the federal amendment superfluous, they would deprive the Republican party of the glory of having enfranchised American women, and they would prevent the North and West from reopening the Negro question.[36]

Events had left Miss Gordon behind; by the time she expressed these views, the national amendment bandwagon had acquired enough new passengers, North and South, to carry it to victory, and some of those passengers were fellow Louisianians.[37] Although the SSWSC apparently went out of existence in 1917,[38] Miss Gordon con-

[34] Kate M. Gordon to Laura Clay, June 26, 1916, and Carrie Chapman Catt to "Dear Madam President" (addressed to all state presidents), June 27, 1916, both in Clay Papers, UK; Harper, ed. *History of Woman Suffrage*, V, 673; New York *Times*, August 4, 1916; [Kate M. Gordon] to governors of Southern states (carbon of typed letter), December 13, 1916, McCulloch Papers, RWA.

[35] Kate M. Gordon to officers of the Southern States Woman Suffrage Conference, July 7, 1916, Clay Papers, UK. Other accusations of the NAWSA's alleged Republican partisanship may be found in her criticisms of Mrs. McCormick, cited in note 31; Kate M. Gordon to Laura Clay, December 21, 1916, and January 21, 1918, both in Clay Papers, UK.

[36] Kate M. Gordon to Laura Clay, January 21, 1918, Clay Papers, UK.

[37] See, for example, Senate *Hearings* cited in footnote 26 of chap. VI. The hearing took place in December, 1915. On pp. 37-38 is a colloquy between a senator and a suffragist on the subject of Miss Gordon's influence. Mrs. Roach pointed out that other Louisiana suffragists favored the amendment, and Miss Martin of Nevada added that sentiment for a federal amendment was growing among Southern women and statesmen because of "our tremendous national problems."

[38] Harper, ed., *History of Woman Suffrage*, V, 673.

tinued to lead her Era Club of New Orleans. In 1918 the NAWSA's permissive attitude finally ended, and its recording secretary wrote to Miss Gordon's sister Jean, advising her that opposition to the NAWSA's federal campaign was not consistent with membership in the NAWSA.[39] A suffrage club had been formed earlier in New Orleans to work for the federal amendment, and the NAWSA, over Miss Gordon's protests, promptly accepted it as an affiliate equal to the old Era Club.[40] It must not be inferred that the suffragists' who favored the national amendment necessarily disagreed with Miss Gordon's racial views. In the South, both types of suffragist, and the antis also, generally agreed on the Negro question. The principal defense offered for each of the three positions was that it would insure white supremacy. The differences were solely tactical.

If Kate M. Gordon represented the extreme Southern position that remained acceptable to the NAWSA until late in the campaign, Laura Clay of Kentucky stood for a moderate Southern point of view that at a still later date also found itself beyond the limits of suffragist orthodoxy. Miss Clay's differences with Miss Gordon were more those of temperament and of geography than of principle. A native of a border state and a woman of generally acknowledged common sense and moderation, Miss Clay sought the middle ground between Mrs. Catt's unqualified endorsement of the federal amendment and

[39] See Mrs. Halsey Wilson to Jean Gordon (copy), April 29, 1918; Kate M. Gordon to Mrs. Wilson (copy), May 7, 1918; Justina L. (Mrs. Halsey) Wilson to members of the Official Board, May 20, 1918, all in Harriet Burton Laidlaw Papers, RWA.

[40] [Kate M. Gordon] to Mary Ware Dennett, July 12, 1913, Clay Papers, UK.

Miss Gordon's equally categorical rejection of any federal legislation. Although approving Miss Gordon's plan, she never quite accepted its legitimacy and very early found the golden mean in the United States Elections Bill which both the NAWSA and the SSWSC formally but tepidly endorsed.

Like Miss Gordon she saw the South as the key to nationwide suffrage, and early and late she urged NAWSA leaders to accept this theory. Since the South, according to Miss Clay, must be won if the women of the United States were to be enfranchised, the NAWSA had to learn the proper way to bring the suffrage gospel to that area. Especially necessary, she insisted, was that suffrage propaganda not be linked with propaganda for any other reform:

When we go through the South advocating woman suffrage, without attaching it to dress reform, or bicycling, or anything else, but asking the simple question why the principles of our forefathers should not be applied to women, we shall win. The South is ready for woman suffrage, but it must be woman suffrage and nothing else.[41]

Miss Clay made this appeal at about the time Northern suffragists were beginning to link woman suffrage with reforms a bit more ominous than the shorter skirt. Advocacy of child-labor legislation, factory regulation, and so on—reforms for which the South was allegedly not

[41] This passage appears in Miss Clay's report as chairman of the Southern Committee, in NAWSA, *Proceedings*, 1896, p. 76. Dress reform had recently been attracting attention among reformers. The bicycle, of course, was a related issue, since it was impossible to pedal while wearing the voluminous skirts of that day. In an interview with Nellie Bly, Susan B. Anthony endorsed sensible clothing as conducive to self-reliance and useful activity and expressed enthusiastic approval of women bicyclists. ("Champion of Her Sex," New York *World*, February 2, 1896.)

ready—had become a standard part of the Northern suffragist rationale.[42] Miss Clay advised suffragists to restrict
their propaganda in the South to precisely those arguments on justice and natural right which were then beginning to take second place in the Northern suffragists'
creed. The suffrage movement in the South arose a generation later than that in the North, and it possessed the
characteristics of the earlier stages of the Northern movement, the concentration on the justice argument and the
reliance on quotations from the Declaration of Independence, the minimum demands and abstract arguments
appropriate to a movement whose victory was far away.
Yet these had a strange ring in the special context in
which Southern suffrage agitation was carried on. In
1915, for instance, a leading suffragist reported that the
women had canvassed Louisiana, "speaking . . . to every
white man and woman we met," and that the speeches
they had made had referred to governments "deriving
'their just powers from the consent of the governed' and
similar principles." [43]

Miss Clay believed that, if suffragists carried on an intensive educational drive in the South along the lines
she suggested, they could break the solidity of the South
on the question of votes for women. Once that had been
done, victory all over the nation would be imminent, for
the South was the strategic area, and after the West the

[42] See chap. III. Miss Clay was willing to make an exception of
temperance, however.
[43] Jean M. Gordon in NAWSA, *Proceedings,* 1915, p. 115. Northern
suffragists doubtless overlooked the contradiction between campaigning among whites for white woman suffrage, and the "consent of the
governed" principle, because *they* were asking for the vote partly to
counteract the votes of unfit ethnic groups constituting the new immigration.

most promising section. "The next great political movement in this country," she explained at the beginning of
1896,

will probably be a coalition between the South and West.
The West is ready to put woman suffrage into its program
if it is not hindered by fear of the Solid South; but no political party will antagonize the solid South for the sake of
woman suffrage. What we must do is to break the solid
South on this question.[44]

After Bryan's defeat that November, she amplified her
views:

The West has long viewed woman suffrage favorably, while
the South is at least popularly supposed to be radically opposed to it. Any one who has followed the discussions on
woman suffrage in the conventions of Prohibitionists and
Populists must have observed that the supposed opposition
of the Southern States has weighed heavily against party
declarations in favor of woman suffrage. This indicates how
it will work in the new political alliance between the West
and the South, unless something is done to prevent it.[45]

Miss Clay believed that the race issue ought not to stand
in the way of intersectional cooperation for woman suffrage, for woman suffrage would settle the race issue in
the South peacefully and honorably. She urged that all
women in the South be given the vote, provided they
passed an educational test. Once Negro votes were so
far outnumbered that they could not affect the outcome
of any election, the race problem would have been solved
in such a way as "would insure the most dignified position for the negro voters; because it would be a guarantee

[44] *Woman's Journal*, February 22, 1896.
[45] *Ibid.*, April 3, 1897.

that their votes would be as untrammelled as those of any other voters." [46]

It was not long, however, before Miss Clay began to waver from her willingness to give the vote to all literate women. By August 1907 she was writing to Miss Gordon that she fully sympathized with the latter's strategy, but feared the constitutional obstacles were insuperable. [47] A month later those obstacles appeared a bit smaller owing to the "recent manipulations of the suffrage" to disfranchise Negroes, and she now thought Miss Gordon's plans for white woman suffrage more promising. [48] By October she was arguing for "white women only" suffrage laws: because Southern whites would never consent to any voting laws which enlarged the Negro electorate while they had no assurance that white women would vote in large enough numbers to counteract the Negro vote; because white women needed the ballot more than Negro men; because if white women voted, laws for both races would be improved; because white woman suffrage would

[46] [Laura Clay] to "Editor of the Oklahoma Post" (carbon of typed letter), January 10, 1907, Clay Papers, UK. Similar views are expressed in [Laura Clay] to Laura R. White, May 7, 1907, Clay Papers, UK. In the latter letter, Miss Clay discussed the "statistical argument" noted on page 168 and attributed its development to "Mr. Blackwell, of Boston, a very warm friend of the negro race; and he thinks, as I do, that it places the negro voter in the only dignified position the race opposition to his voting will allow him to hold,—, namely, a minority vote, where his vote is not feared, and therefore not fraudulently cast out." She went on to explain that this outnumbering of Negro voters was what had solved "the Race Problem in Ky." where the Negro vote was "as free and unhindered as that of any other ignorant and venal class. In the states where are many more negroes this is not the case, and probably will not be in our lifetime; but it is hampered by the 'doubtful expedients' referred to."

[47] [Laura Clay] to Kate M. Gordon, August 6, 1907, Clay Papers, UK.

[48] [Laura Clay] to Henry B. Blackwell, September 22, 1907, Clay Papers, UK.

hasten the day when Negroes could vote, since white people would no longer dread their ballots; and, most important of all, because "if white women may have the right extended to them constitutionally, suffragists would have something to offer politicians which will make them willing to take up our cause." [49] Miss Clay had gradually come to agree with Miss Gordon's strategy of working for suffrage for white women, although unlike Miss Gordon she argued that such a reform would benefit the Negro in the long run. Like Miss Gordon, she continued to harbor doubts as to its ability to withstand the scrutiny of the Supreme Court; therefore, she advised the NAWSA not to endorse any campaign for a voting law with the word *white* for a qualification but to allow individual Southern states to make the experiment. [50] By the end of 1907 she had become an ardent champion of Miss Gordon's crusade for white woman suffrage. Nevertheless, she continued to favor NAWSA's public sponsorship of the federal amendment, for although she believed in states' rights and felt that passage of the federal amendment would be a misfortune, she wrote that she would rather obtain her ballot in that way than not at all. [51]

[49] [Laura Clay] to Henry B. Blackwell, October 14, 1907, Clay Papers, UK.

[50] [Laura Clay] to Anna Howard Shaw, October 30, 1907, Clay Papers, UK. The advice was unnecessary; the NAWSA would not have considered any such endorsement. There are a number of letters from Miss Shaw stressing the policy of the National not to sanction officially any plan for limited suffrage. See, for example, Miss Shaw to Belle Kearney, November 15, 1906; to Laura Clay, November 15, 1906; and to Hon. R. S. Vessey, governor of South Dakota, February 8, 1909, all in Clay Papers, UK; also, Anna Howard Shaw to Caroline Katzenstein, May 31, 1914, quoted in Katzenstein, *Lifting the Curtain*, p. 59.

[51] One of many Official Board votes that were solicited and cast by mail, when members were scattered around the country, shows Miss Clay favoring the introduction of the bill for the amendment and Miss

Miss Clay found the middle ground in the United States Elections Bill, which was introduced in the Sixty-Fourth Congress in 1916 as S. 4257. It provided that women citizens who possessed the qualifications requisite for men to be electors of the more numerous branch of the state legislature would be eligible to vote in all elections for senators and congressman.[52] Both the NAWSA and the SSWSC had endorsed the Elections Bill, and Miss Clay lobbied for it in Washington as a representative of the latter organization.[53] She was puzzled at the widespread indifference she met in both associations to what she believed to be the ideal compromise between federal and state suffrage legislation.[54]

By 1916 Miss Clay had come to oppose the national amendment; although she felt it could never pass, she

---

Gordon opposed. The vote was taken in March, 1911; a copy of it is in Clay Papers, UK. Miss Clay's opinions on the amendment may be found in [Laura Clay] to Catharine Waugh McCulloch, November 14, 1913, Clay Papers, UK.

[52] A copy of the bill is in McCulloch Papers, RWA, near a letter from Laura Clay to Catharine Waugh McCulloch, May 21, 1916, in which she discussed its difference from a similar bill introduced by Mrs. Clara B. Colby, pointing out that Mrs. Colby's bill assumed that Congress had the right to determine the qualifications for voting for congressmen. Implied in this analysis is Miss Clay's belief that S. 4257 could permit white woman suffrage in the South, by leaving all qualifications for the states to determine, provided that sex not be one of them. Miss Clay had supported the Elections Bill since the 1880s (see Harper, ed., *History of Woman Suffrage*, V, 659–60), but her advocacy of it naturally acquired its greatest significance for the NAWSA at the time the states' rights argument was gaining ground; for Miss Clay herself, it acquired its greatest significance when she was on the verge of repudiating the national amendment.

[53] [Laura Clay] to Nellie N. Somerville, November 24, 1915, Clay Papers, UK.

[54] Laura Clay to Catharine Waugh McCulloch, January 2, 1915, and October 2, 1915, both in McCulloch Papers, RWA; [Laura Clay] to Kate M. Gordon, October 28, 1915, and to Nellie N. Somerville, November 24, 1915, Clay Papers, UK.

believed that the NAWSA's endorsement of it lessened the chances for state-legislated woman suffrage in the South. In her opinion, Southerners who favored votes for women but opposed federal regulation of the suffrage might assume that every state that gave its women the vote would bring the national amendment nearer. Such people, thought Miss Clay, would refuse to vote for state suffrage amendments.[55] Accordingly, she joined Miss Gordon in taking the antifederal-amendment side in a NAWSA debate in 1916.[56] But the NAWSA continued to support the national amendment in spite of what Miss Clay believed to be the certainty that thirteen southern states would prevent its ratification. Even more disturbing to her was that at the very convention at which the debate took place, the organization accepted Mrs. Catt's plans for an all out campaign for that same national amendment. Mrs. Catt herself advised suffragists in the states to avoid separate state amendment campaigns that were not part of the over-all plan, because they required tremendous amounts of money and work, and more often than not the suffragists were "counted out" by open fraud.[57] Miss Clay reacted by moving even closer to the position of Miss Gordon. After the NAWSA convention,

[55] *Ibid.*

[56] Harper, ed., *History of Woman Suffrage*, Vol. V, chap. XVI; NAWSA, *The Hand Book of the National American Woman Suffrage Association and Proceedings* of the Forty-Eighth Annual Convention, held at Atlantic City, N.J., September 4–10, inclusive, 1916 (New York, n.d.), pp. 26–27; *Woman's Journal*, September 16, 1916.

[57] See many letters in the Clay Papers, UK, written by Miss Clay in the latter part of 1916, expressing her belief that the amendment could never pass. Mrs. Catt's views are expressed in Carrie Chapman Catt to Laura Clay, November 27, 1916, in the same collection, which also contains Miss Clay's reaction to that letter, in [Laura Clay] to Catharine Waugh McCulloch, November 30, 1916.

she wrote fretfully to her friend: "I feel that in many respects the Southern Conference is of more importance than even it has been before. It seems that the present policy of the National, either designedly or otherwise, is distinctly for the advantage of the Republican party." [58] For one fleeting moment, Miss Clay wavered in her now adamant opposition to the federal amendment. That moment came in January 1918 when President Wilson finally urged Congress to pass the measure,[59] but the intransigence of the NAWSA leaders and her fear of helping the Republican party caused her to revert quickly.[60] A few months later at a rally in Lexington, Miss Clay cast the sole vote against a resolution asking Kentucky's senators to vote for the amendment.[61] Four months later she even questioned President Wilson's sincerity in endorsing the federal amendment, since if he had really wished to enfranchise women as a war measure, as he claimed in his Senate message in September, "all the franchise women need is the Federal suffrage, as it is only the National Congress and President who have any voice in the questions of peace and war." Therefore, he ought to have asked Congress to pass the United States Elections Bill.[62]

By the end of the year, her opposition had become bitter and permanent. In a letter to a local paper, she wrote:

[58] [Laura Clay] to Kate M. Gordon, December 19, 1916, Clay Papers, UK.

[59] [Laura Clay] to "My Dear Sallie" [Sallie Clay Bennett], January 14, 1918, Clay Papers, UK. See also a letter to Mrs. Catt on the same subject, quoted in Goodman, *Bitter Harvest*, p. 59.

[60] Laura Clay to "My Dear Sallie," January 30, 1918, and [Laura Clay] to Kate M. Gordon, March 30, 1918, both in Clay Papers, UK.

[61] [Laura Clay] to Kate M. Gordon, June 4, 1918, Clay Papers, UK.

[62] These views are expressed in Laura Clay to Kate M. Gordon, October 2, 1918, Clay Papers, UK.

Woman suffrage in the Anthony amendment is its minor proposition. It is true that its first section provides for woman suffrage; but when fifteen States have full suffrage already and twenty-five have partial suffrage by State action; when women can vote for 336 out of the 531 presidential electors and every political party of 1916 declared for woman suffrage, a Federal amendment is too late to be [of] prime importance for woman suffrage, whatever it may have been in 1878 when it was first proposed.

The major proposition of the Anthony amendment is in its second section, providing for Federal legislation on State elections in all of the States, and it is cumulative in effect to the second section of the Fifteenth amendment.[63]

A few months later, Miss Clay resigned from the Kentucky Equal Rights Association and organized a group of women to work for the vote by state action alone.[64]

The path that Miss Gordon and then Miss Clay took isolated them not only from the National Association but also from the majority of Southern suffragists. By the last year of the federal amendment campaign every Southern state suffrage association was working for the national amendment.[65] The reason why the majority of

[63] Letter to the editor of the [Lexington (Kentucky) *Herald*, February 16, 1919], clipping in Clay Papers, UK.

[64] See open letter from Miss Clay and three other women, entitled "Citizens' Committee for State Suffrage Amendment" in Lexington [Kentucky] *Leader*, June 2, 1919 (clipping in Clay Papers, UK), which states that the withdrawal from the ERA and the formation of the new club took place "recently." Goodman, in *Bitter Harvest*, pp. 60–61, 64, cites the ERA convention *Minutes* of 1919 to indicate that the resignation took place in March and adds: "The new organization, headed by Laura, waged energetic war against the federal amendment. . . . The federal amendment passed Congress on June 6, 1919 as the nineteenth amendment, but Laura still hoped that it would not be ratified by the states. . . . Victory for the women at the expense of the states remained for her ever a bitter pill. 'Nothing but my religion has enabled me to stand it.'"

[65] Ida Husted Harper to Elizabeth C. Carter, March 18, 1919, Mary Church Terrell Papers, LC. This letter is quoted at length on pp. 214–15.

Southern suffragists remained loyal to the National Association and its agitation for the federal amendment may be inferred from remarks by the most prominent Alabama leader, Mrs. Pattie Ruffner Jacobs, at a Senate hearing in 1915. Mrs. Jacobs said that women of Alabama had wanted to give their own state a chance to act for woman suffrage, but, when the legislature refused to pass the amendment which would then have gone to the electorate for final approval, the lawmakers had said in effect that the men of Alabama had no right to decide the question; the legislature had arrogated to itself the right to decide for them. Therefore, continued Mrs. Jacobs, since women were the logical sex, the Alabama women decided that *all* legislatures ought to have the same right to decide, after Congress voted that they might do so. The federal amendment was thus no infringement on states' rights.

If this amendment is adopted it in nowise regulates or interferes with any existing qualification (except sex) which the various State constitutions now exact. It leaves all other qualifications of the voter to be determined by the various States through their constitutional agencies. It does not inject any new problem into the franchise problems of the States; it does not complicate any existing problem. It is a fallacy to contend that the prohibition of discrimination on account of sex would involve the race problem or any other complication. Both sexes will be obliged to meet all requirements of citizenship imposed by the State and each State

---

See also *Proceedings* of the NAWSA conventions; each volume includes reports from the respective state affiliates, and reports from the South are among them. The activities of these Southern auxiliaries are recounted in the articles of Lee Allen and A. Elizabeth Taylor (cited in footnote 15) and in other essays by Prof. Taylor.

can still protect the exercise of the franchise to the fullests [sic] extent of its power.

The actual working out or application of the principle would be, in the South, to enfranchise a very large number of white women and the same sort of negro women as there are now negro men permitted to exercise the privilege.

Later, Mrs. Jacobs added that in areas of Negro majority, there was no reason to assume that the Negro women would be able to meet the tests imposed any more than the Negro men.[66]

Although these Southern suffragists repeatedly demonstrated that woman suffrage would not jeopardize white supremacy in their section,[67] the legislators from their states remained unconvinced by the statistics offered in evidence. Apparently, the suffragists and their lawmakers were really arguing about different issues. When those same Southern lawmakers supported the Prohibition amendment without fear that States' rights would be endangered by its ratification they emboldened

[66] Mrs. Jacobs' remarks are in *Hearings* cited in note 26 of chap. VI. See also Mary Beard to Alice Paul, October 30, [1914], National Woman's Party Collection, Box 152, LC. Speaking of NAWSA leaders who were overly fearful of antagonizing Southern Democrats, Mrs. Beard wrote: "So many of these women never think of the south for whom the pressure of a federal amendment is the driving force or who may never get the suffrage except through a federal amendment." Mrs. Harper also pointed out that Southern women would be "dead a long time" before all their states had passed suffrage amendments (Ida Husted Harper to Laura Clay, February 7, 1917, Cay Papers, UK).

[67] See, for example, the testimony of Mrs. Guilford Dudley of Nashville, at the 1918 House *Hearing* cited in footnote 38 of chap. II. On pp. 19–21, Mrs. Dudley is quoted as reminding the congressmen that under the Democratic administration the Constitution had recently been twice amended. The child-labor and eight-hour bills, though not amendments, were open to the states' rights objection, but Southern Democrats, in one House or both, had proposed both. She concluded that the theory of states' rights was invoked only when women pleaded for their rights. Later she gave the usual figures to show that woman suffrage would not endanger white supremacy.

the suffragists to contend that their states' rights objection to the suffrage amendment was insincere. Some suffragists declared that Southern men feared women's votes against child labor in Southern factories. But many also very likely opposed woman suffrage on any terms,[68] the federal amendment merely representing the immediate target of a general conservatism as to woman's place in society. The women thus had additional reason for believing that their choice was not between federally guaranteed and state guaranteed suffrage but rather between federally guaranteed suffrage and none at all.

A significant step in the direction of a new attitude of Northern suffragists toward the South and the Negro had been taken by Mrs. Catt in her presidential address to the 1901 convention. Speaking at great length on the impediments to women's enfranchisement, she suggested that three obstacles loomed largest: militarism, less powerful than in earlier centuries but still influential; prostitution, which affected the esteem in which all women were held; and

the inertia in the growth of Democracy which has come as a reaction following the aggressive movements that, with possibly ill-advised haste, enfranchised the foreigner, the negro, and the Indian. Perilous conditions, seeming to follow from the introduction into the body politic of vast numbers of irresponsible citizens, have made the nation timid. . . .[69]

[68] There were, of course, Southern legislators who favored woman suffrage. See, for example, copy of John Sharp Williams to Kate M. Gordon, October 28, 1915, Clay Papers, UK, in which the Mississippi senator wrote, "I think you are going about the business in the right way."

[69] Note that "the nation" here logically means only native-born white Americans. Surely the Negro, foreign-born, and Indian voters were not dissatisfied with the results of their own enfranchisement.

Democracy has been the boast of our country for a hundred years, but at present there is little enthusiasm over it. Men believe in the theory, but do not like its apparent results. In consequence, there is a hesitancy to extend the suffrage to any class, no matter how well qualified.[70]

At the 1904 convention, Mrs. Catt again discoursed at length on the same subject. After mentioning the foreign-born vote in the North, she turned her gaze Southward:

The Negro vote has proved another powerful factor in producing the reactionary spirit. Several States in the South have made successful efforts to disfranchise the Negroes, and although there is good reason to suppose some of the methods employed are unconstitutional, there has been none of the vigor of protest from the North which would have been the inevitable result twenty years ago. It was the North which enfranchised the Negro, and it was the North which a few years ago opposed the shot-gun policy of intimidation with the shot-gun policy of defense. Northern party platforms were eloquent for many years with determination to defend the Negro against any infringement of his voting rights. Why has the North now become so strangely silent and indifferent? . . . The cause is not difficult to find. The North thinks it has discovered that the Negro vote is largely a purchasable vote. . . . Surely, the statement that every Negro vote is purchasable must be an exaggeration, but the currency of such rumors has its effect upon the general opinion that prevails among those who have come in most direct political contact with the Negro, that a very large per cent. of the vote is pur-

---

Hence, the opposition to woman suffrage of those groups, of which suffragists often complained, must have had other grounds than the prevalent skepticism about democracy. One ground was suggested by Dr. W. E. B. DuBois, in the April, 1915, issue of *The Crisis*, when he said that "the reactionary attitude of most white women toward our problems" had caused many Negroes to oppose woman suffrage. DuBois himself was a suffragist and the author of a pamphlet published by the NAWSA. A copy of it is in Box 7 of the Laidlaw Papers, RWA.

[70] *Woman's Journal*, June 8, 1901.

chasable in all those States where party pressure has led to the corruption of the suffrage at the polls.

Mrs. Catt noted that with the recent migration of Negroes to Northern cities, where they allegedly had become a purchasable balance of power in some centers, the race question had become nationwide. Northerners could now learn firsthand of the problems faced by Southern whites after the Civil War, and she observed, "It is little wonder that the North is beginning to question the wisdom of the indiscriminate enfranchisement of the Negro in 1868." After a similar discussion of the new immigrants Mrs. Catt turned to proposals for reform, among which she strongly advocated a literacy test and suggested careful consideration of plans for the adoption of a small property requirement.[71]

With the door thus opened, it was not surprising that Southern suffragists marched in, confident that they could build their own associations in their own section with the sympathetic help of National. They may even have seen the unusual 1903 convention as something of a test of how far the present NAWSA leaders had receded from Mrs. Stanton's 1894 assertion that

our mistake in the South, when we had the power, was not in securing to the blacks their natural rights, but in not holding those States as territories until the whites understood the principles of republican government and the blessings of individual freedom for others as well as themselves.[72]

If the 1899 convention of the NAWSA shattered the old alliance between Negro freedom and woman suf-

---

[71] *Ibid.*, February 20, 1904.
[72] E. Stanton, *Suffrage a Natural Right*, p. 5.

frage, the 1903 convention sealed the new pact between woman suffrage and white supremacy. The convention took place in New Orleans in March, just after a newspaper of that city attacked the organization for its supposedly unacceptable attitude on the race question. The officers replied in a letter to the editor, explaining that as a nationwide body, the NAWSA included individuals of all sections who held the views customary in their respective areas; that the association as such held no view at all on race; that the association recognized the doctrine of states' rights as governing the relation of local clubs to the National; that the NAWSA deplored attempts by antisuffragists to arouse sectional feeling against the Association; and that the race question was irrelevant to the purposes of the NAWSA.[73]

One major speech at the convention was made by Belle Kearney of Mississippi, who recounted the history of slavery in the United States, emphasizing the complicity of the "Puritan of the North" as well as that of the "Cavalier of the South." In her section on Reconstruction, Miss Kearney intoned,

The world is scarcely beginning to realize the enormity of the situation that faces the South in its grapple with the race question which was thrust upon it at the close of the Civil War, when 4,500,000 ex-slaves, illiterate and semi-barbarous, were enfranchised. Such a situation has no parallel in history. . . . The South has struggled under its death-weight for nearly forty years, bravely and magnanimously.

[73] "The Race Question at New Orleans," *Woman's Journal*, March 28, 1903. The newspaper was the *Times-Democrat*, and the officers' letter that appeared in the March 19 issue was signed by Susan B. Anthony, Carrie Chapman Catt, Alice Stone Blackwell, Laura Clay, Kate M. Gordon, Harriet Taylor Upton, and Anna Howard Shaw.

Coming up to the present, Miss Kearney explained the meaning of the Southern constitutional conventions:

The Southern States are making a desperate effort to maintain the political supremacy of Anglo-Saxons by amendments to their constitutions limiting the right to vote by a property and educational qualification. . . . The present suffrage laws in the different Southern States can be only temporary measures for protection. Those who are wise enough to look beneath the surface will be compelled to realize the fact that they act as a stimulus to the black man to acquire both education and property, but no incentive is given to the poor whites; for it is understood in a general way, that any man whose skin is fair enough to let the blue veins show through, may be allowed the right of franchise.

The industrial education that the negro is receiving at Tuskegee and other schools is only fitting him for power, and when the black man becomes necessary to a community by reason of his skill and acquired wealth, and the poor white man, embittered by his poverty and humiliated by his inferiority, finds no place for himself or his children, then will come the grapple between the races.

Miss Kearney demanded the enfranchisement of women coupled with educational and property qualifications to apply to men and women voters of both races. The poor white would thus be spurred to improve himself, and civilization would be saved. Miss Kearney bid for the sympathetic understanding of the Northerners present when she remarked that the civilization of the North, too, was threatened: "by the influx of foreigners with their imported customs; by the greed of monopolistic wealth, and the unrest among the working classes; by the strength of the liquor traffic, and by encroachment upon religious belief." Then she explicitly proffered the alliance:

Some day the North will be compelled to look to the South for redemption from these evils, on account of the purity of its Anglo-Saxon blood, the simplicity of its social and economic structure, the great advance in prohibitory law, and the maintenance of the sanctity of its faith, which has been kept inviolate. Just as surely as the North will be forced to turn to the South for the nation's salvation, just so surely will the South be compelled to look to its Anglo-Saxon women as the medium through which to retain the supremacy of the white race over the African. . . . Anglo-Saxonism is the standard of the ages to come. It is, above all else, the granite foundation of the South. Upon that its civilization will mount; upon that it will stand unshaken.[74]

Later during the convention, Mrs. Catt commented on Miss Kearney's address and noted the transiency of the dominance of any race. Once upon a time, she said gently, the Anglo-Saxons were considered so low that the Romans refused to have them for slaves. Things may change again: "The race that will be dominant through the ages will be the one that proves itself the most worthy." Mrs. Catt then reiterated that the woman question had nothing to do with the Negro question and that the NAWSA recognized the states' rights principle.[75]

One result of the convention was that Kate M. Gordon's Era Club in New Orleans doubled in membership in the next two months.[76] Other results were not so pleasing. Although no Northern suffragist interpreted the states' rights principle as permitting her to defend racial equality from the same platform from which Southern suffragists called for the salvation of Anglo-Saxon civili-

[74] *Woman's Journal*, April 4, 1903. During the debate on the educational qualification (discussed in chap. VI), Mrs. Hala Hammond Butt, prominent Mississippi suffragist, expressed similar views.
[75] *Ibid.*, April 25, 1903.   [76] *Ibid.*, June 13, 1903.

zation, consciences pricked. William Lloyd Garrison, Jr., for one, assailed the convention and all its works. In a letter to the *Woman's Journal* he insisted that there was a logical connection between Northern suffragists' approval of Negro disfranchisement in the South and their silence in New Orleans. "One looks in vain among the speeches," he remonstrated,

for a clear statement of the principles upon which suffrage rests, or any protest against their unblushing violation in Louisiana and the other ex-slaveholding States. Under the circumstances, to borrow Whittier's words, "silence is crime." To purchase woman suffrage at the expense of the negro's rights is to pay a shameful price.[77]

Alice Stone Blackwell replied with a long editorial, revealing her own conflicts in the difficult situation in which Northerners had found themselves at the convention, but strongly denying that their silence at New Orleans implied acceptance of the wisdom of Negro disfranchisement. Although she did not approve of all the steps taken to deprive the Negro of political power, she believed that some measures were required to restore government to the intelligent portion of the Southern population. As for Northerners' silence at New Orleans, she justified it to some degree by repeating the formula that the NAWSA existed to fight solely for the end of disfranchisement on account of sex and that whatever other qualifications ought to be imposed on voters was a question irrelevant to the association's purposes. She did admit that Northerners had been disturbed when some Southern members dragged the irrelevant subject into the discussion:

[77] *Ibid.*, May 21, 1903.

Some of the Southern delegates were so full of the race question, so boiling over on the subject, that it seemed impossible for them to keep off it. Several of them branched off from the woman question and discussed the race question at considerable length, and from the extreme Southern point of view. It is a fair question, when they did that, whether some of the delegates from the North or West should not have got up and given an equally vigorous statement of it from the point of view of the rest of the civilized world.

While Miss Blackwell admitted that much might be said to support Garrison's contention that they should have done so, she felt that a suffrage convention was not the place to wander off into such discussions. Yet, she acknowledged, there had of late been "so many pusillanimous concessions to the spirit of race prejudice," that some delegates would have welcomed an earnest protest even though it might have been out of place. She was one who kept silent with great pain and difficulty. On the other hand, she insisted that Garrison's remark about purchasing woman suffrage at the expense of the Negro's rights was altogether unjustified. If Southern women won the vote on the terms on which Southern white women asked for it, she said, no Negro voter would be deprived of his ballot. On the contrary, Negroes would benefit.

I do not myself believe in a property qualification for suffrage, yet I should be glad to see Massachusetts give a vote to women who pay taxes, because it would help to break down the arbitrary distinction of sex which now debars all women from the ballot. Just so it would be a benefit to the Negro to substitute an educational and property qualification, impartially applied, for a general and indiscriminate exclusion of colored people, on account of race.[78]

[78] *Ibid.*

The Northerners' insistence that the Negro question and woman suffrage were unrelated could be interpreted in two ways. It could be used to excuse silence in the face of challenges such as the New Orleans convention represented. When Northern women felt less on the defensive, the principle that the two questions were not related could be used as a way of denying positively that they *were* related in the manner in which the Southern suffragists connected them. The time had long gone when the woman suffrage movement had consisted solely of Northern women who assumed to one degree or another that the interests of the Negro and of women were linked. A second period had also passed, in which all suffragists had agreed that the two causes were unrelated—a period in which Laura Clay had urged that the suffrage gospel be propagated in the South without linking it to any other question. Now a third epoch had arrived, in which Southern suffragists resurrected the intimate connection, though of a different nature, between the interests of women and of Negroes, whereas the Northerners, fearing to split the association, continued to insist there was no relation between them. An individual Northerner's decision whether unity was worth the price would depend on whose votes, in her opinion, American democracy needed more: those of Negro men or those of white women.

Eleven years later the problem still existed, although in a different form. Some leading suffragists feared that the states' rights objection to the federal amendment had convinced so many people that the NAWSA must meet it somehow. They managed to secure the NAWSA's approval of a substitute amendment at the 1914 convention. The substitute, named after its congressional sponsors, Senator John F. Shafroth of Colorado and Representative A. Mitchell Palmer of Pennsylvania, both Democrats, provided that if more than 8 percent of the legal voters in a state petitioned for a referendum and if in the referendum a majority voting on the question voted favorably, then the women of that state would be enfranchised, notwithstanding any contrary provisions in the state constitution. In their effort to conciliate the states' righters, the advocates of the Shafroth-Palmer resolution almost split the NAWSA. The association experienced one of its more turbulent conventions, as the defenders of the old Susan B. Anthony amendment [79] fought in vain against what Senator Joseph L. Bristow of Kansas described as "more of a national initiative and referendum amendment than a woman suffrage amendment." [80] The National Board had previously voted unanimously, at the request of Mrs. Medill McCormick of Illinois, chairman of the NAWSA's Congressional Committee, to endorse the compromise measure, and the delegates finally acquiesced. The leaders of the Congressional Committee defended the Shafroth-Palmer resolution on a number of grounds. First, it shifted responsibility for enfranchising women from con-

[79] This was the measure, first introduced in Congress in 1878, that ultimately became the Nineteenth Amendment: "The right of citizens of the United States to vote shall not be denied or abridged by the United States or by any State on account of sex. Congress shall have power to enforce this article by appropriate legislation."

[80] Quoted in Blatch and Lutz, *Challenging Years*, p. 246. Senator Bristow, along with Representative Frank Mondell of Wyoming, had for a long time acted as sponsor for the Susan B. Anthony amendment. Criticisms of the Shafroth-Palmer resolution on the part of the young women of the Congressional Union may be found in Box 152 of the National Woman's Party Collection, LC.

gressmen to the people in the states, so that politicians, always willing to evade responsibility, would be more likely to vote for this amendment in Washington, especially since they could claim that they were upholding the principle of local democracy. Second, Shafroth-Palmer could be expected to please Northern congressmen who felt they owed atonement to the South for the Fifteenth Amendment and Southerners who feared dictation from Washington on the question of defining their states' electorates. Third, Shafroth-Palmer could expect a friendly response from Democrats, whose party had gone on record for the initiative and referendum, but not yet for woman suffrage. Fourth, the Shafroth-Palmer amendment, if ratified, would overcome the almost insuperable constitutional obstacles that existed in some states to passing woman suffrage amendments, would thereby enable suffragists to increase the number of full-suffrage states, and would thus improve the prospects of eventually passing the Susan B. Anthony amendment.[81]

Opponents of the Shafroth-Palmer resolution pointed out that suffragists who for a generation had engaged in one costly and heartbreaking state campaign after another, most of which had been unsuccessful, now were being asked to undertake thirty-nine separate state initiative and referendum campaigns. Harriot Stanton Blatch wrote in her memoirs that

this Amendment smacked strongly of having been suggested

---

[81] These arguments may be found in NAWSA, *Proceedings*, 1914, pp. 82–88. Arguments pro and con the Shafroth-Palmer resolution appeared in *Woman's Journal*, April 11, 1914, and other issues about that time.

by Congressmen who wished to give women some political crocheting to occupy their hands and relieve Congress of their disconcerting attentions. It might well have had for its short title, "A bill to encourage tatting for women." [82]

One year with the Shafroth-Palmer resolution was enough. The association suffered from dissension and apathy. The rival Congressional Union for Woman Suffrage grew, made headlines, and showed vigor and originality in its all out offensive in behalf of the Susan B. Anthony amendment. [83] What was most disconcerting of all was that the states' righters did not seem to be appeased. Suffragists began to say publicly that the states' rights argument was a mere cover for other objections to the amendment—the real objections being fear of women voting in the South against child labor in cotton mills or objections to democracy itself or opposition to woman suffrage on any terms. [84] After the debates in Congress over the proposed amendment for nationwide prohibition began, it became even more difficult to take the states' rights objection to the suffrage amendment seriously, for many Southern congressmen arose in Congress to deliver exceedingly quotable tirades against the states' rights objection to prohibition. Each voted against the suffrage

[82] Blatch and Lutz, *Challenging Years,* p. 246. Other arguments against the resolution may be found in *Suffragist,* official organ of the Congressional Union, February 13, 1915; March 13, 1915; and other nearby issues. See also Ida Husted Harper to Laura Clay, March 8, 1914, Clay Papers, UK.

[83] The Congressional Union is discussed at length in the next chapter. Its members generally shared the views of NAWSA members on the Southern question, but from the day of its founding in 1912 (it seceded from the NAWSA in 1914) it never compromised with the states' rights objection to the national amendment.

[84] The *Suffragist* all through 1915 ran many articles purporting to show the insincerity of the states' rights argument. See also pp. 47–48 of the *Hearings* cited in note 37.

amendment soon afterward, as the *Suffragist* carefully informed its readers.[85] The congressional apostles of states' rights helped to number the days of the Shafroth-Palmer resolution in still another way. A survey revealed that with but one exception every man who voted against the national child-labor bill was an antisuffragist and that the same men who filibustered against the child-labor bill, using the states' rights argument, forgot that argument when the convict-labor bill, involving the same principles, was under consideration. At its convention in December 1915 the NAWSA decided that henceforth the Susan B. Anthony amendment would receive its undivided support.[86]

More than one impatient suffragist had suspected that the NAWSA's lukewarm support of the Susan B. Anthony amendment, even before the temporary endorsement of the Shafroth-Palmer substitute, had been due partly to fear of the South. At least one of them reasoned that President Wilson's stubborn refusal to endorse the amendment before 1918 [87] had been motivated by his desire to protect the Southern Democrats in Congress. Sue Shelton White of Tennessee wrote:

During the time that the suffrage amendment was pending

[85] January 23, 1915, issue. Many other articles on the same subject may be found by random leafing through the issues of that period. The *Woman's Journal* also ran articles showing the insincerity of the Southern Democrats in Congress. See, for instance, the issue of January 2, 1915; and Catt and Shuler, *Woman Suffrage and Politics,* p. 317. However, see one answer to the assumption that the prohibition and suffrage amendments were comparable, on p. 39.

[86] The child-labor argument is in NAWSA, *Proceedings,* 1915, pp. 76–77. The reaffirmation of support for the old amendment is in *ibid.,* pp. 12, 43. See also Blatch and Lutz, *Challenging Years,* p. 247.

[87] The President endorsed the amendment January 9, 1918. On September 30, 1918, he appeared before the Senate in person to ask its passage as a war measure.

in the 65th Congress, both houses of which were controlled by the Democrats, there were two things which, apparently, the President was trying to do. It would seem that he was trying to protect the southern members in their opposition, and at the same time to keep the suffragists satisfied, so that the western senators from suffrage states would not have to pay the penalty for their party's delay, caused by the opposition of their southern colleagues. . . . Then, when the general election of November was approaching and Democratic candidates were meeting opposition from Republicans in western suffrage states, the President, on September 30th, five weeks before the election, & six weeks before the signing of the armistice, did what suffragists had been demanding for months. He made his speech to the Senate asking for the passage of the amendment as a war measure. It was a great speech, and for a time, suffragists took it in good faith, but the southern members of the Senate by their votes showed that they did not count it quite so serious as they might have done, had the same speech been forthcoming on the eve of their own elections,[88] and when the outcome of the war was still in doubt.[89]

It must be emphasized, however, that other causes ex-

[88] Southern primaries, equivalent to election, had been held in the summer.

[89] Manuscript article in White Papers, rwa, apparently by Miss White, but untitled and unsigned. It should be noted that Miss White was not typical of suffragists. She had switched from the nawsa to the semimilitant Woman's Party by 1918 (her reasons are discussed in the next chapter). The majority of suffragists believed that President Wilson's Senate speech resulted from a true conversion to the justice of the women's cause; the conversion was supposed to have happened at the 1916 nawsa convention. Unlike the Woman's Party which contended that Wilson aided the cause only when and to the extent that he was·compelled to, the nawsa women regarded him as their most faithful ally. As an evidence of this see *A Tribute to Woodrow Wilson* (New York, National American Woman Suffrage Association, 1919), a copy of which is in the Rare Book Room, nypl. This finely wrought volume consists of warm letters of gratitude to the President from each of the state auxiliaries of the nawsa. See also J. P. Louis, "Sue Shelton White and the Woman Suffrage Movement, 1913–20," *Tennessee Historical Quarterly*, XXII (June, 1963), 170–90.

isted for the NAWSA's relative inactivity and its failure to work vigorously for the amendment before 1916. Between 1896 and 1910 no new states adopted woman suffrage, and each unsuccessful referendum further dampened the spirits of the faithful campaigners. The NAWSA's president, the Rev. Anna Howard Shaw, though a great orator, was a poor organizer, and the size and dispersion of the membership contributed to the disorganization of the association. Personality conflicts among the leaders prevented united work for the common goal.[90] One observer, probing more deeply, wrote:

Financial depression, industrial disturbances, the Spanish War, with its resulting colonial expansion, the rise of gigantic combinations in the world of trade and finance, with the struggle of the people to control them, the appearance of a new social consciousness in many lines of reform—all these vast and vital issues for a time obscured the fundamental issue of democracy as it affected half the nation.[91]

One result of this state of affairs was that legislative hearings and lobbying activities had become mere formalities, exciting the interest of neither the legislators nor the suffragists.[92] Awareness of their lack of influence may have made the NAWSA leaders especially anxious to conciliate the Southerners in Congress. Their extreme prudence in advocating their cause in turn may have made it easier for the President and other statesmen to brush their pleas aside.

[90] See Flexner, *Century of Struggle*, chap. XIX. The McCulloch Papers, RWA, and Clay Papers, UK, are full of evidences of bitter personal antagonisms, especially between 1910 and 1915.

[91] Peck, "Rise of the Woman Suffrage Party," *Life and Labor*, I (June, 1911), 166.

[92] Flexner, *Century of Struggle*, chap. XX; Blatch and Lutz, *Challenging Years*, p. 195.

At the end of 1915 the NAWSA underwent a drastic change in leadership. Dr. Shaw retired from the presidency. In 1916, owing to the leadership and organizing genius of Mrs. Catt, it became a united army fighting for national suffrage according to a carefully devised plan in which each state played its assigned role. No longer could the NAWSA tolerate antiamendment activities within its ranks; in 1919 Laura Clay followed Kate M. Gordon out of the association. It must be emphasized, however, that the NAWSA's new unity did not signify complete agreement on the southern question, the issue that lay at the root of Miss Gordon's and Miss Clay's split with the NAWSA. It did signify, among other things, general agreement as to the relationship of that question to woman suffrage. Until the end of the amendment campaign, suffragists North and South repeatedly resorted to the two principal arguments involving the Negro: that white women ought not to be the political inferiors of Negro men and that woman suffrage would insure or at least not threaten white supremacy in the South.[93]

Two incidents will suffice to show the persistence of white supremacy as an issue within the suffrage movement until its final victory in 1920. The first occurred in the same year that Kate M. Gordon founded the SSWSC. In 1913 both wings of the suffrage movement (the NAWSA and the Congressional Union, which had not yet

---

[93] A few examples of these arguments appearing in the last few years of the campaign are: Mimeographed "Press Release," put out by the Washington Branch Press Bureau, January 3, [1918], containing statement by Mrs. Guilford Dudley of Nashville, Laidlaw Scrapbooks, NYHS; account of large suffrage meeting in New York City, reported in New York *Times,* February 26, 1916, p. 6; The *Suffragist,* August 5, 1916, and November 24, 1917.

seceded to become an independent association) cooperated in staging the spectacular suffrage parade in Washington on the day before Wilson's inauguration. The
shocking treatment accorded the marching suffragists by
the sidewalk mob almost completely crowded another
significant incident from the newspapers. Before the parade, NAWSA leaders had asked Mrs. Ida B. Wells-Bar-
nett, eminent Chicagoan and president of a suffrage club
of Negro women, not to march with the Chicago delegation, since certain unnamed Southern women had said
they would not march in a parade with racially mixed
contingents. The request was made publicly during the
rehearsal of the Illinois contingent, and while Mrs. Barnett glanced about the room, looking for support, the
ladies debated the question of principle versus expediency, most of them evidently feeling that they must not
prejudice Southerners against suffrage. Eventually Mrs.
Barnett was banished to the Negro women's contingent.
She replied that she would march with Illinois or not
at all. When the parade began she was nowhere to be
seen, but later she quietly stepped out from the crowd
of spectators and joined the Illinois ranks. Two white
Illinois women then took their places on either side of
her, and the rank composed of these three women fin-
ished the parade without further incident.[94]

The other incident occurred at the very end of the
amendment campaign. In 1919 the Northeastern Federation of Women's Clubs, a Negro organization, applied
for cooperative membership in the NAWSA. Although ad-

[94] The episode is described in folder No. 152 of McCulloch Papers,
RWA, which includes both private correspondence and a full page
from the Chicago *Daily Tribune*, March 4, 1913.

mitting that the federation was eligible to membership, the association begged it to postpone its application temporarily, until the amendment had been passed and ratified. Writing in behalf of Mrs. Catt, Ida Husted Harper explained to the federation's president:

The situation in regard to the Federal Amendment has now reached its climax, and without that amendment there will not be universal woman suffrage in your lifetime. Until within a few years the Southern members of Congress have stood like a solid wall against it and have been sustained by the women of their States. Through reason, argument, logic and diplomacy every Southern State Suffrage Association now supports the Federal Amendment. With this backing 56 Southern Representatives voted for it when it was carried in the Lower House, Jan. 10, 1917. In March, 1914, three Democratic Senators voted for it; in October, 1918, 12; in February, 1919, 13. These figures show the remarkable progress in Southern sentiment.

Mrs. Harper went on to explain that the amendment was now a question of cold, hard politics. The Republicans in Congress did not control two-thirds of the votes; some Democratic votes were necessary, and most of those must come from the South. Once the amendment passed Congress, it must be ratified by at least some Southern state legislatures.

Such is the situation. Many of the Southern members are now willing to surrender their beloved doctrine of State's rights, and their only obstacle is fear of "the colored woman's vote" in the States where it is likely to equal or exceed the white women's vote. . . . The opponents [of the amendment] are not leaving a stone unturned to defeat it and if the news is flashed throughout the Southern States at this most critical moment that the National American Association has just admitted an organization of 6,000 colored women, the enemies can cease from further effort—the defeat of the amendment will be assured.[95]

Mrs. Harper asked the federation to postpone its application until the crisis had passed, although it is not clear why she believed the federation would want to join *after* the NAWSA's purpose had been fulfilled.

Most of the Northern suffragists who endeavored to secure the necessary Southern support evidently never suspected that their compromises might not appear perfectly reasonable to Negro women as well. Mrs. Harper's letter quoted above included among its arguments the statement that once the amendment had been ratified, Negro as well as white women would be enfranchised and that therefore the federation ought to withdraw its application and do anything else necessary to bolster the amendment's chances of passage. One is irresistibly reminded of Laura Clay's argument that once Negro votes were decisively outnumbered by those of white women, Negroes could vote freely and with dignity. In both cases, Negroes were being offered the form of political equality on terms that threatened its substance.

Although in the last few years of the campaign Negroes joined Northern suffrage clubs or formed their own groups and although the NAWSA as such never endorsed any plan for limited suffrage, the practical policy followed by the association was determined by its leaders' apparent assumption that the success of woman suffrage required the support of at least some Southern white-

[95] Ida Husted Harper to Elizabeth C. Carter, March 18, 1919, Mary Church Terrell Papers, LC. See also Ida Husted Harper to Mary Church Terrell, March 18, 1919, and Emma Winner Rogers to Mary Church Terrell, January 20, 1920, both in the Terrell Papers, LC.

supremacist legislators. While Northern suffragist leaders accepted white supremacy to different degrees, none of them announced from a NAWSA platform that Negroes as well as white women were entitled to vote, and none refused to support suffragist tactics characterized publicly as ways of reducing Negro political power. The amount of white supremacy that suffragist leaders felt they could "live with" in the NAWSA implies their attitude toward the relationship of woman suffrage to Negro suffrage. They were perfectly content to secure the vote without enfranchising any Negroes at the same time, or on terms that disfranchised Negroes, if that proved necessary or feasible. They parted company with Misses Gordon and Clay not on the desirability of white supremacy in the South but on the relation of white supremacy to woman suffrage. Unlike Miss Gordon and Miss Clay, these leaders and the majority of suffragists believed that the amendment did not conflict with Southern traditions. They thought that Negroes and white supremacists should both support the Susan B. Anthony amendment, the former because the amendment enfranchised Negro women in Northern states that could not secure state suffrage amendments,[96] and the latter because the amendment would render Southern Negro votes meaningless.

[96] A more succinct analysis of majority suffragist attitudes toward this question appeared in a private letter from one Negro leader to another: "Just as you say, all of them are mortally afraid of the South and if they could get the Suffrage Amendment through without enfranchising colored women, they would do it in a moment." (Walter F. White to Mary Church Terrell, March 4, 1919, Terrell Papers, LC.) Note that this was written years after the NAWSA rejected the Shafroth-Palmer attempt to conciliate the South. The NAWSA took the path it took because it had no choice if it was to survive and not because it no longer feared the South.

Misses Clay and Gordon devised their strategy on the ground that the South was a special region with a special problem; woman suffrage must be brought to that region by making the special problem the key element in suffragist strategy. The majority of Southern and Northern suffragists, on the other hand, felt that the special problem; woman suffrage must be brought to that re- the woman question (one expression of which was the famed "Southern chivalry") meant that woman suffrage could be brought to the South only from outside, that is, through a federal amendment. Regarded from another angle, the differences between the Clay-Gordon viewpoint and that of the other suffragists North and South involved their respective opinions of the sincerity of the states' rights objection to the federal amendment. The majority of suffragists found the desirability of white supremacy and the federal amendment to be perfectly compatible; they themselves accepted both. Why then must Southern congressmen insist they were mutually exclusive? Obviously, thought the women, there was a hidden reason that the politicians could ill afford to admit: either they feared women's reform votes in their own localities or they believed women were inferior and had no business in government. When the majority of suffragists rejected the states' rights argument they were not necessarily rejecting states' rights; they were denying that the amendment would endanger states' rights or white supremacy. Misses Clay and Gordon, on the contrary, saw a necessary connection between the maintenance of white supremacy in the South and the continued right of Southern legislatures to exercise complete power over local elections. Acceptance of the Clay-Gordon thesis, the other suffragists felt, would destroy suffrage as a national movement. Acceptance of the majority suffragist thesis, Miss Clay and Miss Gordon believed, would shake the very foundations of Southern society.

EIGHT

Political Parties and Suffragist Tactics

One of the oldest arguments for woman's right to vote was the indifference with which legislators heard vote-less women's petitions contrasted with the respect accorded the requests of enfranchised men of every type. Anna Howard Shaw, addressing the NAWSA convention in 1891, bitterly complained of this difference in treatment. She told how during the South Dakota amendment campaign of the previous year,

Indians in blankets and moccasins were received in the State convention with the greatest courtesy and Susan B. Anthony and other eminent women were barely tolerated; how, while these Indians were engaged in their ghost dances, the white women were going up and down the State pleading for the rights of citizens.[1]

Men had the political power to turn inattentive listeners out of office; women had no such power and could be ignored.

This argument not only constituted a basis for the claim to the vote but also posed a puzzling problem for

[1] Anthony and Harper, eds., *History of Woman Suffrage,* IV, 182. See also NAWSA, *Proceedings,* 1916, pp. 59–60.

the suffragists: how a group without political power could obtain such power from those who already had it. Suffragists always believed in supporting their friends and opposing their enemies, but why should politicians value the support or fear the opposition of voteless citizens?

At every political convention all matters of right, of justice, of the eternal verities themselves, are swallowed up in the one all-important question, "Will it bring party success?" And to this a voteless constituency cannot contribute in the smallest degree, even though it represent the Ten Commandments, the Sermon on the Mount, the Golden Rule, the Magna Charta and the Declaration of Independence.[2]

If the lawmakers ignored the petitions and delegations of women asking for reform legislation, how could they be expected to heed the petitions and delegations of the same women asking for the vote? In the early days of suffragist agitation the problem could not be solved. The women had no choice but to embark on a relentless educational campaign and to rely on their ability to persuade as many voters as possible to vote for state suffrage amendments.

Eventually a time came when millions of women voted on equal terms with men. It was then that the question could arise whether suffragists ought to continue their campaign of persuasion or whether they might use the votes of enfranchised women as a weapon with which to secure political equality for all women. In either case, suffragists would find it necessary to define their proper relationship to the parties. The NAWSA never considered using the votes of enfranchised women as a weapon. It

[2] Anthony and Harper, eds., *History of Woman Suffrage*, IV, 444–45.

continued to depend on that same "indirect influence" that suffragists had always identified with helplessness and ineffectiveness. What the more militant suffragists might have called a contradiction between one of the arguments for suffrage and the method of working for it did not become explicit until the last six years of the federal amendment campaign. But suffragist organizations occasionally debated the corollary problem of what their relationship to political parties ought to be.[3] This problem grew gradually in importance and urgency as the prospect of success for the amendment grew brighter. Suddenly, in 1914, it ripped the NAWSA apart. Although the reasons for the insurgents' revolt were new, the resistance of the majority of organized suffragists to basic change in their approach to the parties can be understood only in the light of the history of the association.

The Stanton-Anthony wing of the suffrage movement was born in 1869 out of the demand for a woman suffrage amendment and the bitter disillusionment with the Republican party, which the women had trusted to support that demand. When, as the women thought, the post-Civil War Republican leaders betrayed their trust by arguing that that was "the Negro's hour" and that the women must wait still longer, that group of suffragists acquired a lasting suspicion of parties and politicians that found expression and new justifications repeatedly during the next fifty years. The faction led by Lucy Stone and her husband Henry B. Blackwell, which spoke through the *Woman's Journal*, believed that the

[3] For example, see *ibid.*, pp. 280–82, for an account of a debate at the 1897 convention of the NAWSA.

Republican leaders had not betrayed the suffragists. This group contended that woman suffrage probably could not have been won in any case in that early day, while Negro suffrage was a practical possibility. They believed, too, that if the drafters of the Fourteenth and Fifteenth amendments had linked woman suffrage with Negro suffrage, the latter would have been lost; half a loaf was better than none.[4] This Boston group of suffragists, while generally supporting the NAWSA's policy of nonpartisanship, was somewhat friendlier toward the Republican party thereafter than the Stanton-Anthony, or New York, group which invoked a plague on both political houses.

The suffragists adopted a policy of asking each party at each election for a plank in its platform endorsing woman suffrage. From 1868 on, suffragist speakers made the rounds of the political conventions presenting petitions and testifying at hearings of resolutions or platform committees.[5] Their prospects for success during state party conventions usually depended on a number of factors wholly outside the women's sphere of influence. The fate of the suffrage planks often became tangled up with intrastate politics and interparty power struggles, with the Prohibition issue and Negro suffrage, with the possibility of alienating this interest or the advisability of conciliating that group of reformers. Popular votes on propositions for suffrage amendments to state constitutions frequently fell victim to the same tugs of war.[6] A Kansas suffragist told the delegates to the 1895

[4] This position was carefully explained by Alice Stone Blackwell in the *Woman's Journal*, December 21, 1892.

[5] Anthony and Harper, eds., *History of Woman Suffrage*, Vol. IV, chap. XXII, gives details on how they fared at each such convention in the early days.

[6] Laura Clay to Ida Husted Harper, April 3, 1902; Kate M. Gordon

NAWSA convention that the suffrage referendum in her state the previous year had failed because it had become caught in the struggle between the Republicans and the Populists. The Republicans, fighting to regain control of Kansas, had felt that endorsement of suffrage would cost them votes. After the election, in which the Republican party had triumphed, Populists informed her that since the Republicans had refused to permit the Populist administration to gain the prestige of enfranchising women, the Populists would not allow the incoming Republican administration the glory of giving women the vote.[7]

It was small wonder that suffragists came to take pride in their exemption from the cynicism supposedly implied by affiliation with a political party.[8] Their nonpartisanship, however, had a deeper cause than disillusionment

to "Dear Member of the Business Committee," February 6, 1909; and a composite of reports of state organizers to the NAWSA Official Board in 1910, all in Laura Clay Papers, UK; Susan B. Anthony to Elizabeth Cady Stanton, July 19, 1894, Smith Family Papers, NYPL; Susan B. Anthony to "The Kansas Woman Suffrage Amendment Campaign Committee . . . ," March 11, 1894, in Harper, *Susan B. Anthony*, II, 782; Bowman, "A Short History of Woman Suffrage in California," p. 25 (copy in NYPL).

[7] *Proceedings* of the Twenty-Seventh Annual Convention of the National American Woman Suffrage Association held in Atlanta, Ga., January 31 to February 5, 1895 (Warren, Ohio, n.d.), pp. 31–38.

[8] Susan B. Anthony reiterated her strong belief that, as long as women could not vote, any partisanship on their part would not only impede the progress of the movement but also degrade those women who would thus be "Spaniels & lick the hand that smites us—" (typed copy of Susan B. Anthony to Clara B. Colby, July 6, 1894, Colby Papers, HL). On the other hand, she was not averse, for tactical reasons, to helping a party that endorsed woman suffrage. In 1894 she raised a storm in suffragist circles by publicly thanking the Populists in Kansas for their endorsement. Her action was interpreted as partisanship, although she said nothing publicly about any other issue dividing the parties (see Anthony to Clara B. Colby, Aug. 1, 1894, Colby Papers, HL; Anthony Diaries, Anthony Papers, LC; Harper, *Susan B. Anthony*, Vol. II, chap. XLIII).

caused by the rebuffs they received. They shared the hostility toward political parties characteristic of most of the reformers of that day. The Genteel Reformers of the late nineteenth century tended to identify the city and its political rings with most of the evils that they saw destroying their society. The suffragists of the same period commonly listed Big Business, Commercialized Vice, and the Liquor Interests as the core of the antisuffragist coalition. All three monsters, of course, were city-bred and depended for their control of government and for their very existence on the urban political machines. A large number of suffragists condemned and contemned the votes of immigrants who, they said, cast the ballots that kept those machines in power. While Genteel Reformers did not always favor woman suffrage, political parties became anathema to both the good government forces and the suffragists. When the chairman of the NAWSA's Committee on Education said in 1909 that "the same forces which have brought about the growth of democratic ideals and non-partisan politics are also responsible for the advancement of women," [9] she was expressing the deep-rooted conviction of most suffragists that "democratic ideals" and "non-partisan politics" were almost interchangeable terms and that the advancement of women was causally related to both.[10]

Antisuffragists were fond of arguing that if women secured the franchise, they would lose that nonpartisan-

[9] Pauline Steinem of Toledo, Ohio, speaking at the convention reported in NAWSA, *Proceedings*, 1909, p. 62.

[10] NAWSA conventions sometimes passed resolutions for the initiative and referendum "as a potent factor in the progress of true democracy" (1905) and to "make it easier to win success for many reforms, including woman suffrage" (1906). See chap. III, footnote 23.

ship which assured legislators of their disinterestedness when they petitioned for reforms. Once women voted, the antis contended, they would inevitably be suspected of working for some party and their petitions would be treated as just so many political issues. Suffragists sometimes admitted that enfranchised women would probably divide on the main issues in the same proportion as men. But they usually took it for granted that women would remain as aloof from party warfare as they had been before they obtained the vote and that their new political power would be exerted to support moral men and righteous measures regardless of party affiliation or endorsement.[11] Before the turn of the century the suffragists claimed the vote principally on the basis of their contention that men and women were identical in their humanness, whereas the antis emphasized the "divinely ordained" differences. On this one point, however, the antis claimed that enfranchised women would melt into the partly-ruled electorate, whereas the suffragists insisted that the differences between men and women were so profound that having the vote would not affect women's nonpartisanship. The antis declared that suffrage would make women partisan and unwomanly; the suffragists maintained that it would enable their unchangeable womanliness to undo the evil that men had wrought

[11] See, for example, Anthony and Harper, eds., *History of Woman Suffrage,* IV, xix, one of a number of instances of the argument that immoral candidates who were acceptable to male voters on partisan grounds would be rejected by women voters regardless of party. See also NAWSA, *Proceedings,* 1894, p. 141, where a Kansas suffragist said that woman suffrage in Kansas cities had caused the character of the candidates to become more politically significant than before and that "the new constituency has acted as a check upon the evils of partisanship." See also Shaw, *Story of a Pioneer,* p. 272; and NAWSA, *Proceedings,* 1914, p. 93.

through their sordid parties. If their claim had been valid, perhaps Big Business, Commercialized Vice, the Liquor Interests, and the undesirable urban machine voters would have had good reason to fear the feminine ballot.

The relation of suffragists to the existing parties could not become a major issue within the association until enough men had become converted to the cause to force the suffragists to consider practical ways and means of achieving their goal. The first decade of the twentieth century saw the flourishing of novel forms of organization within the National Association, in response to this new need and this new opportunity. Prior to that time, even those suffragists who worked hardest to secure party endorsements consoled themselves for their failures by reasoning that such activities had primarily educational ends.[12] In fact, the old association and all its affiliated clubs were virtually educational bodies. The women held meetings, published manifestoes, testified at legislative hearings, edited newspapers, and distributed leaflets— all aimed at persuading men that woman suffrage was simple justice or that it would benefit society. But at about the time that male advocates of the initiative, recall, referendum, and other reforms began forming their own parties, the suffragists, too, began to sense the need to adopt a more political type of activity and form of organization.[13]

[12] When in Kansas in 1894 the Republicans decided to remain silent on woman suffrage and the Democrats declared against it, Miss Anthony wrote that "the good that will come— will be the discussion— and that is what we are after—" (Susan B. Anthony to Elizabeth Cady Stanton, July 19, 1894, Smith Family Papers, NYPL).

[13] Some of the suffragists went all the way and supported the Progressive party in 1912, the most notable being Jane Addams, first

Carrie Chapman Catt prepared the way for this development as early as 1895 when, as chairman of the Committee on Plan of Work, she told the NAWSA convention that although in some states suffrage sentiment was great enough to carry an amendment, that sentiment must be organized to be made effective.[14] The following year Mrs. Catt renewed her call for strenuous organizational activities and recommended that suffrage clubs be organized along political boundary lines to influence more effectively legislators and local party organizations.[15] At about that time, California suffragists seem to have developed this type of club independently.[16] In 1907 Harriot Stanton Blatch organized the Political Equality League of Self-Supporting Women, in New York, and inaugurated exciting new methods of

vice-president of the NAWSA, who seconded Theodore Roosevelt's nomination at the Chicago convention. Her action caused an explosion in the NAWSA, with some members publicly accusing her of betraying the suffrage cause by deviating from its nonpartisan rule. Her defenders pointed out that Miss Addams joined the Progressive party as an individual, not as an officer of the NAWSA, and that suffrage organizations had never imposed nonpartisanship on individual members acting as such. Her critics retorted that actions of prominent members would inevitably be identified by the public with the organization. See *Woman's Journal*, August 17 and 24, 1912; Anna Howard Shaw to Jane Addams, August 16, 1912, Addams Papers, FHL; "Jane Addams Points to the Progressive Party as Hope for Woman Suffrage," *Indianapolis Star*, October 27, 1912, clipping in Addams Papers, FHL; "Woman and the Ballot: What Shall I Do with the Parties?" *Chicago Sunday Record-Herald*, October 6, 1912, clipping in Addams Papers, FHL; Harper, ed., *History of Woman Suffrage*, V, 342. Ida Husted Harper, who wrote the account in the *History*, was Miss Addams's most vehement critic. She set forth her views in a letter to the New York *Times*, August 10, 1912. A rejoinder to Mrs. Harper's attack may be found in an undated and untitled manuscript article by Catharine Waugh McCulloch, in McCulloch Papers, RWA.

[14] NAWSA, *Proceedings*, 1895, pp. 21–22.
[15] *Ibid.*, 1896, pp. 39–51, 62.
[16] Peck, "Rise of the Woman Suffrage Party," *Life and Labor*, I (June, 1911), 166.

bringing the suffrage gospel before the public. Soon the fresh, imaginative forms of work merged with the new political-precinct basis of club organization, and woman suffrage parties came into being, first in New York, later in other big cities, and became part of the network of organizations federated in the NAWSA.[17] The new precinct clubs, like the older suffrage groups, which continued in existence, were educational societies. However, instead of aiming their propaganda primarily at the lawmakers, they deliberately set out to convert the masses of voters, who were then expected to create a grass-roots demand on their legislators for woman suffrage amendments in the states. By such means, it was hoped, enough states would pass suffrage amendments to create a large bloc of congressmen and senators in Washington half of whose constituents would be women. In other states prosuffrage men would be sent to Congress, and thus the federal amendment could at last become a reality.

This strategy was explained in a handbook for working suffragists written in 1914 by a New York suffrage leader. Although the purpose of the pamphlet was to instruct suffragists working for state amendments rather than for

[17] See Blatch and Lutz, *Challenging Years,* especially pp. 91–134; Schaffer, "The New York City Woman Suffrage Party, 1909-1919," *New York History,* XLIII (July, 1962), 269–73, 279, 284; Flexner, *Century of Struggle,* chap. XIX; C. Catt, "The New York Party," *Woman's Journal,* September 24, 1910. See also [Laura Clay] to Mary Ware Dennett, June 18, 1910; Jessie Ashley and Mary Ware Dennett to members of the Official Board, December 1, 1910; Harriet Burton Laidlaw, Jessie Ashley and Mary Ware Dennett to members of the Official Board, January 26, 1911, all in Clay Papers, UK. The letters to the Official Board members are also in the papers of another member of that board, Catharine Waugh McCulloch, RWA. Also, see Peck, "Rise of the Woman Suffrage Party," *Life and Labor,* I (June, 1911), 166–69.

the federal amendment, the emphasis on conversion of the electorate and lawmakers was present also in the NAWSA's campaign for the amendment to the national Constitution. The author urged that

At every political meeting, and in every political committee, the *Woman Suffrage Party's* voice must be heard in undeviating demand for *the submission of the woman suffrage amendment to the voters.*

It must be impressed upon the minds of all citizens in political life that the members of the Woman Suffrage Party intend to pursue an unswerving course side by side with the men of the dominant parties from whom their enfranchisement in any State must come. Wherever the men are meeting, making platforms, considering candidates for the State Legislature, passing resolutions, or holding primaries or conventions, the Woman Suffrage Party officers and members should be with the insistent and persistent demand that they express themselves in some way upon the submission question, that they shall send men to the State Legislature who are pledged to *submit the suffrage amendment to the voters* of the State, whether the Legislator believes in suffrage or not.[18]

Clearly, the two old suffragist principles remained, even after suffrage clubs were organized on the precinct basis. The organization still eschewed coercion of any kind, relying on the desire for reforms or the sense of justice of the men who could be reached by suffragist propaganda; and it retained the strict nonpartisanship as defined by the NAWSA. The NAWSA believed that any deviation from these policies would antagonize enough voters and lawmakers to defeat the legislation.

The assumption that enfranchised women would re-

[18] Laidlaw, compiler, *Organizing to Win*, p. 4.

main, if not nonpartisan, at least aloof from party politics had a certain plausibility in the years before many
women could vote and gain political experience. The
NAWSA's annual resolutions reaffirming its nonpartisan
policy [19] expressed the antipartisanship in that period of
the naïve reformers who set out to purify governments by
appealing to the higher instincts of the moral part of
the electorate. At later conventions, the NAWSA continued
to pass resolutions asserting its nonpartisanship, at a time
when many women had won the vote and learned the
facts of political life and when male reformers, too, had
seen the need to fight party with party. After the turn of
the century, when endorsements of long-sought reforms
had begun to appear in party platforms, the NAWSA's
nonpartisan policy expressed the fact that its membership
included women who on most issues were Republicans,
Democrats, Socialists, Prohibitionists, or Progressives as
well as women who sympathized with no party. The
NAWSA's nonpartisan policy represented in the first period antipartisanship and in the later period multipartisanship. Nonetheless, the second variety of nonpartisanship meant a continuation of the emphasis on persuasion
and conversion that, some suffragists were now coming
to believe, had been more appropriate in the days when
the women had had no other tactic at their disposal. The
early antipartisanship had forbidden suffragists to *sup-*

[19] See, for example, NAWSA, *Proceedings*, 1893, p. 84; *Proceedings*
of the Twenty-Ninth Annual Convention of the National American
Woman Suffrage Association . . . , Des Moines, Iowa, January 26–29,
1897 (Philadelphia, n.d.), p. 51. The 1893 resolution read: "That the
National American Woman Suffrage Association is non-partisan, and
appeals to the enlightened men of all parties to do justice to women
citizens as a plain matter of fidelity to the principles upon which our
National Government is professedly founded."

port any party; the later multipartisanship forbade them to *oppose* any party. NAWSA members usually interpreted this to mean that they must not hold any party responsible for the position of any of its members on the suffrage issue or any man responsible for his party's stand on suffrage. This interpretation planted the seeds of revolt within the NAWSA.

The rebels who founded the Congressional Union for Woman Suffrage, the semimilitant organization that later, as the Woman's Party, picketed the White House, felt that the suffrage movement could not triumph within a reasonable time as long as it adhered to its old principles. Between 1896 and 1910 no new states passed suffrage amendments, but by the beginning of 1914 five states (and Alaska) had enfranchised their women, raising the total to nine.[20] In addition, the crucial state of Illinois in 1913 had given its women the presidential ballot. Alice Paul, a New Jersey Quaker still in her twenties, and a group of her followers felt that the time had come when women could cease begging for their rights. With ninety-one votes to be cast in the Electoral College by states in which women had full or presidential suffrage, the women could now rely on their own votes to enfranchise all the women in the United States.[21] It

[20] The full suffrage states were now Wyoming, Colorado, Utah, Idaho, Washington, California, Oregon, Arizona, and Kansas. In 1914, Nevada and Montana brought the total up to eleven.

[21] An indication of how foreign this way of thinking was to most suffragists was the complaint that every state that won full suffrage meant a drop in NAWSA membership because women in full-suffrage states no longer needed to convert their men. The NAWSA had little else for them to do, even after it embarked on its intensive campaign for the federal amendment after 1916, since congressmen from full-suffrage states could usually be depended upon, without pressure from

ought to be possible, she reasoned, to influence enough
of the four million women's votes in such a way as to
affect the outcome of the next presidential election. This
was "coercion." If the suffragists could use this balance
of power to spell victory or defeat for one party, they
could then force the two major parties to compete for
those ballots and thus induce one of them in its own
interest to force the amendment through Congress. The
tactics that the Congressional Union adopted to carry out
this strategy led the NAWSA to accuse it of "partisanship."
The Congressional Unionists were impatient with NAWSA
strategy because they felt that that strategy, though political in form, was in content as nonpolitical as the traditional NAWSA activities had been before the development
of precinct clubs.[22] The conservative suffragists—as the
young insurgents called them—had organized their new
clubs along precinct lines in order more effectively to
ask men to give women the vote. But as long as the

constituents, to support the amendment. See *Proceedings* of the Thir-
tieth Annual Convention of the National American Woman Suffrage
Association and the Celebration of the Fiftieth Anniversary of the
First Woman's Rights Convention . . . , February 13–19, 1898 (Philadelphia, n.d.), pp. 14-15; *Proceedings* of the Forty-Fifth Annual
Convention of the National American Woman Suffrage Association
held at Washington, D.C., November 29 to December 5, inclusive, 1913
(New York, n.d.), p. 14. The official organ of the Woman's Party explained that if the suffragists worked to defeat every anti in Congress
they would most likely help maintain the present party balance and thus
accomplish nothing. It added, "All the candidates for office in the enfranchised States are Suffragists. Is it suggested that we be inactive in
the only places where we possess real political power?" (Reprinted in
Irwin, *The Story of the Woman's Party*, p. 50.)

[22] Mary Beard, in a letter to Alice Paul, October 11, [1914], in Box
152, National Woman's Party Collection, LC, referred scornfully to
"those older women whose sole task has been educational." The occasion of her comment was a letter in the October 8, 1914, New York
Times, in which Mrs. Catt repudiated both the CU and its tactical
theories.

women remained in the position of supplicants, asserted the cu, the men could continue to play political football with the demand for suffrage.

Miss Paul had participated in the militant campaign in England, where the "suffragettes" held the party in power responsible for the fate of suffrage legislation, and she believed that that policy could be adapted to American conditions. Miss Paul and her followers contended that the majority party in the United States had charge of all legislation in Congress, and after Wilson's inauguration they called attention to his use of party discipline to force bills through Congress even against the will of Democratic legislators. An article entitled "Government by Parties," in the *Suffragist* of February 20, 1915, quoted a Democratic senator from the *Congressional Record* as saying, "This has been from the first a government of political parties. I say without qualification that it is my opinion that when it ceases to be a government by political parties the liberties of the American people will be well-nigh at an end." The article also cited Wilson's demand for the ship-purchase bill, and it quoted various senators to the effect that the President could get what he wanted from Congress. It quoted Wilson himself in a recent speech as asserting that if any

group of men should dare break the solidarity of the Democratic team *for any purpose or from any motive* theirs will be a most unenviable notoriety and a responsibility which will bring deep bitterness to them. The only party that is serviceable to a nation is a party that can hold absolutely together and march with the discipline and the zest of a conquering host. . . . If a man will not play in the team then he does not belong in the team.

If the President failed to exert the same pressure on his fellow Democrats to pass the suffrage amendment, Miss Paul argued, it could only mean that he chose not to. The task of the CU, then, would be to make the party in power see that its continuance in office depended on its favorable response to the women's demand for the vote.[23] Accordingly, the CU worked during the 1914 congressional elections to defeat Democratic candidates in the equal-suffrage states. Each of those nine states, except Utah, explained Miss Paul, had in the past voted for first one party and then the other and was now doubtful. A small number of women who put suffrage above party loyalty or any other issue could swing the election away from the Democratic party.

Suppose the Party saw votes falling away all over the country because of their attitude on Trust legislation—they would change their attitude on Trust legislation. If they see them falling away because of their attitude on Suffrage they will change their attitude on Suffrage. When we have once affected the result in a national election, no Party will trifle with Suffrage any longer.[24]

Not all observers agreed with those NAWSA spokesmen

[23] The best source of information on CU policies and actions from its own point of view is its weekly paper, the *Suffragist*. An excellent secondary source for a sympathetic analysis is Stevens, *Jailed for Freedom*. See also Irwin, *The Story of the Woman's Party*; Part II of Katzenstein, *Lifting the Curtain*; and chap. XXVI of Dorr, *Susan B. Anthony*.

[24] This speech is reprinted in Irwin, *The Story of the Woman's Party*, pp. 75–77. On a later occasion (February 2, 1916) the *Suffragist* pointed out that a Nevada Senator had recently been elected by a forty-vote plurality, that many elections in Western states hung on a handful of votes, that the CU could certainly influence that number of women, and that it could thereby induce Democratic legislators to press their party for a strong stand on suffrage. See also [Alice Paul] to Mary Beard, September 5, 1914, Box 152, National Woman's Party Collection, LC.

who dismissed cu tactics as foolish and futile. The New York *Times* of June 17, 1916, in describing the Democratic National Convention, reported in detail the discussion on the suffrage plank and noted that this was the first time that the question of votes for women had been the star feature of a national convention of any party. The change was startling from the days when the women had pleaded to be heard. Senator Walsh of Montana, remarked the reporter, wasted no words on sentiment; he did not mention the hand that rocks the cradle; he made no appeal for equal justice for the two sexes. He told the convention to adopt the suffrage plank or give up the electoral votes of the states where women had the ballot. He declared that the Woman's Party had the votes to beat the Democrats and to give the presidency and the Senate to the Republicans.

The leaders of the Democratic party, however, although adopting a compromise plank, remained unconvinced of the party's own self-interest in forcing the amendment through Congress. The cu planned its next step: to campaign actively against all Democratic candidates for national office, including Wilson himself, in 1916.[25] Miss Paul explained the policy thus:

It seems to me that it does not make much difference, as far as our amendment is concerned, whether Mr. Wilson or Mr. Hughes is elected in November, but it does make a great

---

[25] It should be noted that the cu carried on other activities, such as circulating petitions, organizing an automobile cavalcade across the country, and sending delegations to statesmen. Here, I am discussing only those major actions which implied differences in philosophy between the two suffragist organizations. That the cu considered its 1914 campaign to have succeeded in worrying Democratic members of Congress is clear from the analysis of a hearing before the House Judiciary Committee in the *Suffragist* of December 25, 1915.

deal of difference whether the women voters have supported Mr. Wilson or have registered a protest vote against him. If, after the way he has persistently opposed the national enfranchisement of women, voting women flock to his support it would make it exceedingly difficult in the next Congress to secure respectful treatment for the suffrage amendment from any party. It would be considered that the national suffrage amendment was not an issue which excited the interest of women voters and that it could be brushed aside with impunity, as far as they were concerned. The situation is the same as it would be if the laboring population of the country should, at election time, support men who had steadfastly opposed the interests of [working] men, which of course would encourage disregard of the welfare of labor by future Congresses. A protest vote on the part of labor, even though it did not succeed in turning the party which was responsible for hostility to labor out of office, would induce a wholesome respect on the part of all parties toward labor.[26]

When the NAWSA remonstrated that a policy of opposing Democrats because they were members of the party in power would mean working to defeat loyal suffragists from the West, the CU replied that in those states both Republicans and Democrats were suffragists since their constituents included women.[27] The replacement in Congress of a suffragist Democrat by a suffragist Republican would not change the number of sympathetic congress-

[26] [Alice Paul] to Mrs. Robert Stevenson, September 20, 1916, Anne Martin Papers, UCB. Another CU leader discussed Hughes's endorsement of the amendment, giving some credit to his sense of justice, but attributing the decisive influence to party expediency (see Anne Martin to Alice Paul, August 1, 1916, and the statement pinned to it, which Miss Martin had issued to local papers, Box 152, National Woman's Party Collection, LC). Later in the same statement she attributed Wilson's intransigence to his "allowing himself to be dominated by the reactionary southern wing of his party for fear of losing the south, which he could not lose."

[27] Stevens, *Jailed for Freedom*, pp. 33–34.

men, but it *would* prove that suffragism was a political asset to a party. When accused of partisanship, the CU, now the Woman's Party, explained that it was not pro-Republican or anti-Democrat; it was simply prosuffrage. If the Republicans had had the power to pass the amendment but refused to use it, the WP would have fought them.[28]

It is difficult to assess the effect the WP campaign had on the results of the 1916 election, which was fought on other issues, particularly the questions of peace and preparedness. But the women felt that they had demonstrated their strength [29] and that their next task was to drive home the lesson by means of public acts even more spectacular than the parades and demonstrations with which these young women had for four years publicized their cause. Consequently, in January 1917 they began to picket the White House, to call attention to the key role the President played in determining Democratic voting in Congress and to what they considered his record of duplicity and evasion of responsibility on the

---

[28] Lucy Burns in the New York *Times*, January 25, 1914, sec. 3, p. 4. The WP'ers were accused of more than partisanship. At various times, members and leaders of the NAWSA called them un-American, agents of the Republican party or of the antisuffragists, and numerous more personal epithets. During the war hysteria later, Laura Clay thought they might be unwitting tools of German agents. NAWSA leaders repeatedly pleaded with the public and with congressmen not to confuse the older organization with the "militants." In 1917 and 1918, when even antisuffragists were shocked by the brutal prison treatment received by "militants" who had picketed the White House, most NAWSA leaders remained silent, so fearful were they of being identified with tactics they deplored.

[29] *Suffragist*, November 11 and 25, 1916. One of the slogans they had used in the West to answer the argument that Wilson "kept us out of war" was that he "kept us out of suffrage." See Irwin, *The Story of the Woman's Party*, p. 175.

suffrage issue.[30] One proof, from the WP point of view, of this duplicity was Wilson's strong pressure on Congress to accord, as a war measure, greater self-government to Puerto Ricans, to insure their loyalty. The women asked, "Why not ask for a suffrage amendment on the same grounds?" The WP's poet laureate expressed this puzzlement in a "Washington Patter Song":

Yes, ladies, my endorsement of the suffrage cause is hearty,
But a President is nothing but a servant of his party.
All bossism and leadership, of course, I must keep clear of it,
Though no one's more astonished than the Democrats to hear of it.
My principles and honor I should undermine and vitiate
If any legislation I should urge or should initiate.
I hope you will excuse me for I'm very, very busy now,
The duties of my office are enough to make one dizzy now;
And I must urge the passage of the Porto Rican bill,
Which Congress thinks it will not pass, but which I think it will.[31]

[30] The January 2, 1915, issue of the *Suffragist* had carried an article describing a number of meetings with President Wilson, quoting his excuses for inaction on each occasion. When he explained that he was limited by party policy, they recalled that he had forced through a position on the Panama Canal tolls issue contrary to a plank in his party's platform. During the eighth delegation's meeting with him, he said that suffrage was a matter for the states to decide for themselves. The WP, believing that the states' rights excuse was the last resort of antisuffragists, hoped that the President would soon abandon that as he had abandoned previous excuses for failing to act as strongly on the suffrage amendment as he had on other issues. See also Stevens, *Jailed for Freedom*, chap. III; also, [Alice Paul] to Mary Beard, June 16, 1914, Box 152, National Woman's Party Collection, LC, in which Miss Paul wrote that now that Wilson had induced Congress to pass the Panama Canal tolls repeal bill, which he had initiated and which contradicted the Democratic platform, he could no longer use his inability to take the initiative as an excuse for inaction on the suffrage amendment. Therefore she proposed another deputation to the President.
[31] Alice Duer Miller in the New York *Sunday Tribune*, February 25, 1917, reprinted in the *Suffragist*, March 3, 1917.

After the United States entered the war, the pickets carried banners calling attention to the lack of congruence between American democratic war aims and American undemocratic practice in denying self-government to half its citizens. When accused of embarrassing the United States abroad, the WP replied that the Democratic party and its leader were to blame because of their refusal to use the power they possessed to swing sufficient Democratic votes to pass the amendment.[32] Although repeatedly called "militant," the members of the Woman's Party never resorted to the tactics of the militant suffragettes of Great Britain from whom the epithet was borrowed. They threw no rocks and broke no windows, but merely stood still by the White House gates with their banners or walked silently along the curb and occasionally interrupted the speeches of government officials with pointed questions. Later, after Wilson had gone abroad, they lettered excerpts from his European speeches on large sheets of paper and publicly dropped them into a large urn, symbolically burning his impassioned declarations

[32] Accounts of the picketing episode; the WP's burning of a cardboard effigy of Wilson; the notorious "Kaiser Wilson" sign some of them carried; the mob attacks on the pickets; the arrests of many women for "obstructing traffic"; their experiences in prison; the hunger strikes of several of their leaders who demanded to be treated as political prisoners; the resignation of Dudley Field Malone, collector of the Port of New York and friend of President Wilson, in protest against Wilson's apparent condoning of the brutal treatment of the prisoners; other related events; and the tremendous nationwide interest aroused by these occurrences may be found in the *Suffragist*, the *Woman's Journal*, the *Woman Citizen*, and other periodicals of that period, as well as in the Stevens, Irwin, and Katzenstein books. The abundance of news items and editorials on the subject in newspapers and magazines during 1917 and 1918 suggests that it was a much more important issue at the time than one would infer from most secondary works dealing with that period. However, a detailed account of these events is beyond the scope of this study.

on democracy which, they said, he refused to apply to American women. The fact that they broke no laws was indicated by the contrived charges on which they were arrested and by the fact that the flimsiness of those charges induced a congressman to introduce a bill to outlaw picketing in wartime. In this manner, the questions of freedom of speech and freedom to picket became involved in the suffrage issue. A leading Tennessee suffragist found herself gradually becoming more sympathetic toward the Woman's Party because it had become identified with the cause of freedom of speech, and she noted that a labor journal that had formerly favored the NAWSA affiliate in Tennessee had severely criticized an official of that group because of the way it had treated the pickets.[33]

Mrs. Oliver H. P. Belmont, wealthy society matron and an officer of the Woman's Party, defended her or-

[33] Sue Shelton White to Carrie Chapman Catt, April 27, 1918, White Papers, RWA. Rose Schneidermann was one of two women at the Saratoga Conference of the New York State Woman Suffrage Party on August 30, 1917, who voted against a resolution condemning the pickets. She explained that as a member of a trade union she could not vote for a condemnation of picketing (New York *Times*, August 31, 1917, p. 18). The bill to outlaw picketing was quoted in the New York *Times* of August 19, 1917. Although pointed at the suffragists, it spread a wider net. It would have forbidden anyone during wartime to hold, wave, or possess a flag, sash, or other device containing any reference to the President, Vice President, the Constitution, "the suffrage right of citizenship," any government official, any proposed amendment to the Constitution, or any proposed law, that might tend to cause confusion, excitement, or obstruction of the sidewalk or street. At the time the bill was being offered, six Woman's Party pickets were being sent to the notorious Occoquan Workhouse, having been convicted of obstructing traffic. The proposed bill must be viewed not only as an admission that the women's actions were really not unlawful but also in the light of other suppressive wartime legislation. See also J. P. Louis, "Sue Shelton White and the Woman Suffrage Movement, 1913–20," *Tennessee Historical Quarterly*, XXII (June, 1963), 170–90.

ganization's policies in a long letter to the antisuffragist New York *Times* of July 9, 1917:

American women have been imprisoned for holding at the gates of the White House banners demanding democracy at the hands of a Democratic Administration. They have committed no violence, but have stood there quietly, peacefully, lawfully, and gloriously. In return they have been attacked by the metropolitan police and their property destroyed. One of the banners they were arrested for holding bore a quotation from President Wilson's book, "The New Freedom."

She quoted the President's democratic phrases and asked whether, if democracy was noble, an ideal worth dying for, it was not an extraordinary attitude on the part of the President and Congress which allowed women no right even to appeal for justice, let alone receive it. If women were sitting in Congress, they would not have to use the humiliating method of printing their appeals on banners, the only recourse left to them.

And shall we not protest when men not only continue to refuse to give us our liberty but decide the manner in which we shall demand our liberty? . . . "Militant?" Why all this tenderness and delicacy about "militancy" in the form of banner-bearing when the Governments of all nations are conscripting their men, including our own nation, to be militant? . . . The sentimental ladies and gentlemen who are so afraid lest we fatigue the President are urged to remember that we ourselves are very, very tired, and perhaps the sentimentalists will confer some pity on the faithful women who have struggled for three-quarters of a century for democracy in their own nation.

The key word in WP thinking was *power*. As one leader explained:

We are told that we should adopt the plan followed by suffragists in the past, and apparently to be followed by them throughout long years to come, of opposing anti-suffragist Congressmen and supporting those who are suffragists. The difficulty of this plan is that you are not working at the source of power. The individual Congressman is a very frail fighting force. If he is absolutely honest, he can vote for you, but not until your measure has passed many Congressional obstacles in which the party, and not he, is master of the situation. If he is at all subject to pressure, he will find many reasons for believing that a postponement of your question is wise. If he is a henchman of a party which is opposed to suffrage, he will fight you under cover. To seek action from a Congressman and at the same time ignore his party affiliation, is to ignore the most important influence that affects his conduct.[34]

The simplest objection the NAWSA made to WP policy was that it could not work. Spokesmen for the older organization denied that the campaign of 1914 had caused the defeat of any candidate for Congress in the suffrage states or that the WP had hurt the Democratic party in 1916. Enfranchised women, they declared, could not be made to vote as a bloc. This belief stemmed di-

[34] Lucy Burns, vice-chairman of the CU, in *Woman's Journal*, February 21, 1914. The *Suffragist* noted the amazement of congressmen at the women's exercise of power in the CU campaign of 1914: "Is it to be wondered at that politicians were puzzled at first by this new development in the suffrage question, that after years upon years of pleas politely phrased, they doubted their senses and lost their tempers when they found themselves face to face with a protest couched in words of political power? All other mysteries of woman faded before this last one, that she should stop asking her 'friends' to give, and attempt, herself, to get. In the most modern of her activities, politics, the old-fashioned woman has persisted longest. No one now looks for the appealing creature of the '80's in the drawing room, or for the helpless amateur needing a lift over fences in the field of sports; but in the political arena there is evidently a certain shock in finding us able to take care of ourselves." (December 25, 1915, issue.) See also Abby Scott Baker in the New York *Times*, July 20, 1917, p. 7.

rectly from the view that women voters would remain aloof from party struggles. Alice Stone Blackwell wrote:

Ever since women began voting in the West, now nearly half a century ago, their most conspicuous trait as voters has been that they pay more attention to a candidate's character and record than to his party label. This is their inveterate tendency; and it is through this tendency that they are considered to have rendered their greatest service to the enfranchised States. We 'do not believe that it will be possible to get any large number of the enfranchised women to vote against a thoroughly worthy condidate—perhaps an old and tried friend of the women's cause—on account of sins of his party for which he was not to blame.[35]

A second reason why WP policy would not work, according to the NAWSA, was that the tactic of fighting Democrats antagonized sympathizers and legislators who belonged to that party. The suffrage cause would lose the votes of men who resented attacks on the party which they supported on issues that they considered more important than woman suffrage.[36] WP behavior alienated people not only on partisan grounds but also

[35] *Woman's Journal*, June 19, 1915. See also Alice Stone Blackwell in *ibid.*, August 19, 1916; and [Laura Clay] to Catharine Waugh McCulloch, November 30, 1916, Clay Papers, UK. A large amount of material dealing with the NAWSA-CU dispute, mostly from the NAWSA standpoint, may be found in Boxes 234, 235, and 236, Suffrage Archives, LC.

[36] Anna Howard Shaw wrote that during the 1914 campaign in the West, Democratic men had asked NAWSA speakers, "Why should Democrats vote for suffrage, when suffragists are trying to defeat Democrats?" (Anna Howard Shaw to Catharine Waugh McCulloch, August 13, 1913, McCulloch Papers, RWA.) See also Ida Husted Harper to Anne Martin, March 28, 1919, Martin Papers, UCB; Park, *Front Door Lobby*, p. 23; Anna Howard Shaw to Lucy E. Anthony, typed copies of many letters during 1914, Shaw Papers, RWA; Catt and Shuler, *Woman Suffrage and Politics*, p. 248; and "*Dr. Shaw's Outline of Her Position on the Different Policies of the National Association and the Congressional Union.* July 27, 1916," Box 236, Suffrage Archives, LC.

because of the widespread feeling, shared by many suffragists, that it was not seemly for women to resort to force, even in the form of political pressure. Anna Howard Shaw was evidently pleased when one Senator in 1918 referred to her as the "ex-president of the ladylike" suffragists.[37] In 1914, along with a letter to Mrs. McCormick, she enclosed a copy of a letter she had written to President Wilson, which appeared in many papers and which stated:

The officers of the National Woman Suffrage Association desire on its behalf to state that when you granted an audience to its representatives, who sought your aid in securing favorable Congressional action last November, to whom you stated your position as President of the United States, and as the highest representative of the political party which elected you, we accepted your statement, looking forward to the time when the political situation would presage a more favorable response, and your great influence might be given to aid in extending the principles of "The New Freedom" to women.

To this end . . . we have sought to secure favorable Congressional action; but at no time has any delegation from the National Suffrage Association endeavored to secure an audience with you upon this subject since November, 1913.

We greatly deplore any act in the name of woman suffrage which mars the record of dignity, lawfulness, and patriotism which has marked the conduct of the campaigns to obtain political justice for women in the United States.[38]

A third reason why WP policy could not work, reasoned

[37] Anna Howard Shaw to Lucy E. Anthony, September 28, 1918, typed copy in Shaw Papers, RWA. See also [Anna Howard Shaw] to Dr. Esther Pohl-Lovejoy, March 12, 1914, typed copy in Shaw Papers, RWA.

[38] Anna Howard Shaw to [Mrs. Medill] McCormick, July 8, 1914, Box 196, Suffrage Archives, LC.

the NAWSA, was that there was really no "party in power" in the United States. Since an amendment to the Constitution required a two-thirds vote in Congress, the "party in power" theory might have been valid at that time only if the Democratic party controlled two-thirds of the seats in the Senate and in the House of Representatives. Since this was far from being the case, continued the NAWSA analysis, the passage of the amendment depended on the suffragists' obtaining as many votes as possible among members of both parties.[39] Hence, the NAWSA believed that President Wilson had no such power as the Woman's Party attributed to him, but it was up to the suffragists to try respectfully to convert him to their cause so that he might use what influence he had over the Congress.

But the NAWSA's objections to the Woman's Party policies went deeper than the mere conviction that those policies could not work. The larger organization opposed them on principle. Although the theory on which this opposition rested was nowhere worked out systematically, the NAWSA leaders apparently felt that the suffrage cause would be debased by tying its success to party expediency. Whether seen as a matter of justice or as the response to the new need of government to utilize woman's special talents, the cause of woman suffrage was regarded as inconsistent with the kind of party politics implied in the strategy adopted by the Woman's Party. Believing woman suffrage to be the inevitable by-product of the slow evolution of democracy, of the replacement of force by reason as the basis of government, and

[39] See, for example, Harper, ed., *History of Woman Suffrage*, V, 455.

of the social and economic changes that caused many women to earn their livings, the NAWSA relied on persuasion and on the skillful organization of existing pro-suffrage sentiment to achieve the inevitable victory. It pitted its "positive" program against the WP's "negative" policy. Accordingly, the NAWSA insisted on regarding legislators as individuals who favored or opposed woman suffrage; it deliberately ignored their party affiliations. In Washington, Democratic NAWSA members tried to persuade Democratic congressmen to influence colleagues of their own party, and Republican NAWSA members worked to exert the same influence on Republicans.[40] Even a rock eventually gives way under the constant dripping of water, said Mrs. Catt,[41] and the opposition to woman suffrage had gradually disintegrated before the growing strength of the suffrage movement. Presumably a continuation of the activities that had worked in the past, but made more effective by organization, would be all that was necessary. "Our policy in regard to Congress," explained a national NAWSA leader in 1914, "is to be one of education and argument in order to pass the amendment. We appreciate the support we are being given by many Democrats, as well as Republicans and

[40] Lobbying techniques and experiences are fully described in Park, *Front Door Lobby*. A typical NAWSA statement of its policy of regarding legislators as individuals was a resolution passed at the 1914 convention: "That the N.A.W.S.A. is absolutely opposed to holding any political party responsible for the opinions and acts of its individual members, or holding any individual public official or candidate responsible for the action of his party majority—on the question of Woman Suffrage." (NAWSA, *Proceedings*, 1914, p. 11.) On NAWSA's appeal to history and democracy as sanction for its policy, see "A Bourgeois Movement," *Woman Citizen*, July 7, 1917, and Carrie Chapman Catt, "The Crisis," NAWSA, *Proceedings*, 1916, pp. 48–68, especially pp. 52–57.

[41] *Ibid.*, p. 53. The speech, including this figure of speech, may be found in manuscript in the Catt Collection, NYPL.

Progressives throughout the country, and intend to maintain a perfectly non-partisan attitude." [42]

The fact that political parties acted according to expediency thus gave rise to two opposite policies: the WP sought to use party interests to the advantage of the suffrage cause while the NAWSA largely ignored parties and preferred to convert individuals who might respond to principle.[43] Carrie Chapman Catt admitted that this method "may have delayed the coming of woman suffrage." But, she added, "when it comes, women will be absolutely free to choose parties, candidates, and causes, without obligation to any." [44]

The NAWSA's distaste for using party mechanisms to its own advantage may have resulted from its traditional conception of women's political role as that of a pressure group working for humanitarian reforms and ignoring or cutting across party lines. It may also have resulted from the suffragists' heritage of contempt for political ma-

[42] Mrs. Medill McCormick, daughter of Mark Hanna and chairman of the NAWSA's Congressional Committee, in *Woman's Journal*, January 31, 1914.

[43] See, for instance, Anna Howard Shaw, "The Nonpartisan View," in Chicago Sunday *Record-Herald*, October 6, 1912, clipping in Jane Addams Papers, FHL. Miss Shaw discussed the various candidates for President in 1912 and refused to see much difference between them on the suffrage question because, as she believed, Roosevelt had endorsed woman suffrage only to capture the votes of Western women, whereas Wilson and Taft had refused their endorsement only to avoid losing votes in other sections. In all three cases, political advantage had dictated their positions, and for that reason she thought suffragists ought to make no distinction among them. The WP, on the other hand, did not care what Hughes's motives in 1916 were and was quite as prepared to accept his help on the basis of expediency as it would have been if his endorsement had been all that Miss Shaw desired. It should be pointed out, incidentally, that the NAWSA believed in working to defeat certain members of Congress whom it considered incorrigible antis.

[44] "The Suffrage Platform," *Woman's Journal*, June 12, 1915.

chines, those who bossed them, and those who followed them. Although by this time most suffragists supported one party or another on ordinary issues, they could hardly be expected now to recognize the legitimacy of party government by adopting a policy that acknowledged the ability of the party in power to accomplish what they, as supraparty humanitarians, could not accomplish. Although the WP, in its propaganda, continued to demand the franchise on two grounds—the right to self-government of all citizens and the good that women could do with the vote—its activity implied a conviction that argument of any kind had actually become obsolete. Whichever kind of argument women used to persuade men to give them the ballot, they would still be asking, not taking. They would still be using that indirect influence the inadequacy of which had always been a cardinal tenet in suffragist philosophy. Whereas Jane Addams and many other suffragists tried to persuade right-thinking men by argument that woman suffrage was socially expedient, Alice Paul and her followers attempted to convince the parties by experience that woman suffrage was politically expedient. Thus did each group present its evidence to those who, it believed, held the power to enfranchise women.

NINE

Woman Suffrage in Perspective

The "argument from justice" and the "argument from expediency" [1] as used by the suffragists shared an important characteristic: they both expressed, in different ways, the suffragists' conception of democracy. Democracy, they contended, was incompatible with the rule of force. Justice was the rule of reason, the antithesis of force; a government concerned with legislating reforms, and consequently one that needed women's votes, could not possibly be based on force. Only a government whose electorate included all fit adults could be considered democratic. [2]

It followed that governments that excluded women from their electorates not only violated the democratic principle that demanded that they be based on the con-

[1] See chap. III.
[2] An item in "Editorial Notes," *Woman's Journal*, June 13, 1891; Alice Stone Blackwell in *ibid.*, May 25, 1895; NAWSA, *Proceedings*, 1893, p. 84, quoting the first resolution passed at the convention; Putnam-Jacobi, *"Common Sense" Applied to Woman Suffrage*, p. 187; E. Stanton, *Suffrage a Natural Right*; NAWSA, *Proceedings*, 1907, pp. 41-43, and 1910, p. 70, quoting reports of Committee on Peace and Arbitration; Jane Addams in "Women in Public Life," *Annals* of the American Academy of Political and Social Science, LVI (November, 1914), 1-4; Shaw, *Passages from Speeches*, pp. 12-13.

sent of the governed but also relied on force instead of consent. Suffragists' belief that force and consent were incompatible, along with their assumption that the reform they demanded would be realized in the future, provided the rationale for a theory of history that placed "government by force" at an early stage of history and "government by consent" at a later stage. Historical progress consisted partly in the replacement of the former by the latter.[3] The suffragists believed that they stood somewhere in the transition period.

This theory contrasts sharply with one argument frequently found in antisuffragist polemics. In Helen Kendrick Johnson's *Woman and the Republic*, for example, the most frequently repeated thesis was the identification of democracy with force. Mrs. Johnson, too, appealed to history. She pointed out that women voted in aristocratic countries the governments of which gave representation not to individuals but to property. An estate must not be deprived of its power in government merely because its owner happened to be a woman. The argument "No Taxation without Representation!" originated, she added, in societies in which voting was connected with property ownership. But when taxation of property ceased to be the basis for voting, women lost the vote. Government came to rely solely on the strength of individual men for its defense. Before, when kings ruled nations, men and women were taxed to pay a hired soldiery to defend the

---

[3] Carrie Chapman Catt in speech (1896?) quoted in clipping in Catt Collection, NYPL (the clipping, from the Oakland *Tribune*, is in scrapbook labeled "Personal"); Susan B. Anthony in the San Francisco *Examiner*, June 21, 1896; Austin and Martin, *Suffrage and Government*, pp. 3–4; Addams, "Women, War and Suffrage," *The Survey*, November 6, 1915, p. 148.

established order; at a later and more enlightened time, when every man became a king, each man became liable for the defense of the government he helped rule. Consent never replaced force and never would. A time came when men agreed to vote instead of fight, but behind the voting must stand the democratic force of the majority of men even in our enlightened American society.[4] This theory contradicted that of the suffragists in regard not only to the facts of history but, more importantly, to political and social theory. The suffragists disapproved of rule by force; the antis believed rule by force of the majority of men to be the sign of true democracy.

The suffragists agreed with the antis that a government based on the ballots of both men and women could not rest on force.[5] Inevitably, therefore, they postulated a necessary interrelation among consent, democracy, woman suffrage, and the type of government that concerned itself primarily with social welfare rather than with defense against invasions and rebellions. The stage of evolution a given society had reached, they believed, could be inferred from the degree to which consent had replaced force in government. This might be measured by the extent to which women participated in the govern-

[4] This was so because, as explained on p. 28, a vicious minority that had lost an election might resort to force to achieve its ends if half the electorate were incapable of taking up arms to enforce the majority's mandate. See Johnson, *Woman and the Republic*, chaps. II, III, and X.

[5] This assumption is particularly clear in Ellen Battelle Dietrick, "The Errors of Mr. John Fiske," *Woman's Journal*, December 30, 1893, in which she wrote that "the point at present is to warn the public not to accept as gospel truth the opinions of teachers who preach that government rests on physical force," implying that an assertion that government did rest on physical force would *ipso facto* constitute an argument against woman suffrage.

ment. Such evolution was both natural and inevitable.[6]

The women took pride in the fact that their movement was in the mainstream of American history, seeking
to realize and further the ideals of the Founding Fathers,
but not to replace those ideals or overthrow the government of the glorious republic brought forth by their ancestors.[7] In 1917 they announced proudly that suffragism
was "A Bourgeois Movement," marching down the middle
of the road, with reaction to one side and radicalism to
the other. An article in the *Woman Citizen* declared:

Quite the worst epithet the mind of the radical can conjure
up, in castigation for the less radical, quite the smelliest rose
of yesterday he can pin on you, is *"bourgeois."* To be neither
very conservative nor very radical, to be plain every-day,
middle-class average, is to be just too awful for language,
take it from the radical who is one degree more so than the
last one. . . . So far as the suffrage is concerned the accusa-
tion might as well be faced and admitted. That is exactly
what the suffrage movement is today—bourgeois, middle-
class, a great middle-of-the-road movement; evidence of a
slow-come mass conviction; representative of that most coherent, tightest-welded, farthest-reaching section of society—
the middle.[8]

[6] Carrie Chapman Catt expressed this thought repeatedly. See: "Evolution and Woman's Suffrage," carbon of typed manuscript speech,
1893, Catt Collection, NYPL; speech quoted in *Woman's Journal*, February 23, 1901; *President's Annual Address*, 1902, p. 3 (copy in Catt
Collection, NYPL); "An Address to the Congress of the United States,"
NAWSA, *Proceedings*, 1917, pp. 50-52.

[7] Putnam-Jacobi, *"Common Sense" Applied to Woman Suffrage*, chap.
VIII; Alice Stone Blackwell in *Woman's Journal*, April 25, 1903;
NAWSA, *Proceedings*, 1904, p. 19, quoting "Declaration of Principles"
prepared by Mrs. Catt, Miss Shaw, Miss Blackwell, and Mrs. Harper
and adopted by the convention; Catt, "An Address to the Congress
of the United States," NAWSA, *Proceedings*, 1917, p. 50.

[8] "A Bourgeois Movement" was the title of this unsigned editorial
in the *Woman Citizen*, July 7, 1917. The *Woman Citizen* was a weekly
begun in mid-1917, incorporating the former *Woman's Journal*, *Woman*

In placing their movement in the middle of the road, the suffragists were perfectly correct. They exhibited both the strengths and the weaknesses of other reform movements in American history, especially when in justifying their demand for the vote they voiced principles too extreme for their own consistent allegiance. The pioneers of the suffrage movement, living in a time when victory for their cause seemed eons away, did not have to concern themselves too much with tactics. They could afford to state their ideals in ringing declarations on democracy that would admit of no qualifications or exceptions. In fact, they had to do so, for only ideals that could inspire a martyr's dedication could sustain these women through the physical violence and almost unbearable ridicule to which they were subjected. Later, when victories could be won here and there at the cost of small concessions to political expediency, the hard facts of political life and the equivocal position in American society of these middle-class women exerted a pull away from the high ideals and ringing declarations. To win support from needed allies they compromised with those principles perhaps more than the requirements of the alliances dictated. More often than not they voiced the ideals and advocated the compromises at the same time.

In a sense, however, they were perfectly consistent. When they demanded the vote on the basis of justice and the consent of the governed, they could not intend absolutely universal suffrage, which would have given

Voter, and *National Suffrage News*. The new paper was the official organ of the NAWSA. The article noted here appeared in the sixth issue, when the editor, it may be assumed, was still carefully explaining the association's nature and policy to the public.

the vote to every human being. Having conceded that children, lunatics, and felons must be excluded, they had to define those categories. Such definitions, necessarily containing an element of arbitrariness, would have to be justified as serving the "good of society," and other limitations of the franchise for the same reason would appear logical enough. The right to political liberty was then identified with capacity to exercise it. In an association primarily of white, native-born, middle-class American women between 1890 and 1920, capacity for political liberty was almost automatically equated with Anglo-Saxon ancestry.[9] This assumption constitutes a unifying thread linking their anti-Negro,[10] antiforeign, frequently antilabor attitudes[11] with their defense of American democracy and the principles of the Declaration of Independence.[12] Even their Americanization programs for immigrants during and after World War I, which the suffragists themselves believed to be motivated by a new positive attitude toward the foreign born,[13] were actually programs to transform the immigrants so far as possible into Anglo-Saxons and "therefore" into desirable voters.[14]

[9] Sometimes the equation was conscious. See chap. VII for examples of the common contrast they made between the old and new immigrations. They frequently declared that only the older immigrants, from England and northern Europe, could govern themselves. See also Putnam-Jacobi, *"Common Sense" Applied to Woman Suffrage*, chap. III; Harriot Stanton Blatch in *Woman's Journal*, January 18, 1896; Catt, *President's Annual Address*, 1902, p. 10.

[10] See chap. VI.   [11] See chap. VII.   [12] See chap. III.

[13] See chap. VII.

[14] See "Program of the National American Woman Suffrage Association," *National Municipal Review*, IX (January, 1920), 56-57, and various speeches of Mrs. Catt in the same period, proposing that English be made the language of instruction in all public and private schools; that an educational qualification for the vote be imposed in all states after a certain date; direct citizenship for women so that a foreign-born woman could not vote simply because her more Americanized

The coexistence within the suffrage movement of strong reformist motives, alleged to be proof of the movement's democracy,[15] along with undemocratic attitudes such as white supremacy, suggests a comparison with another reform movement of the period, the Progressive party of 1912. At the founding convention, Roosevelt and the other leaders decided that the party in the South must be lily-white. They calculated that the number of Southern white votes attracted by this policy would more than compensate for the number of Northern Negro votes the party would lose. Jane Addams searched her soul anxiously and sincerely, and finally concluded that in the long run American Negroes would benefit from a Progressive party with a nationwide base, even though such a party could be built only if its Southern wing for a time excluded Negroes.[16] Most suffragists accepted racism

husband became a citizen; and citizenship schools to teach Americanism to adults to make imported radicalism less attractive to them.

[15] See, for example, FitzGerald, *What Is a Democracy?*: "Do you know what people are most against women's voting? It is the women of means, in comfortable circumstances, who do not need it for the good of their bodies, and do not realize that they need it for the good of their souls, and who are *afraid* to let their working sisters have it. Why? Because they are afraid of the *people*, afraid of the *workingman*, afraid of *democracy*. They think that the women's vote will strengthen the workingman's vote, the popular vote, and they are *afraid*. And they may well be afraid, if they do not trust the people, for the real people are going to *win*, and the day of their victory will be hastened when women can vote."

[16] See August 1912 folder in Jane Addams Papers, FHL; Addams, "The Progressive Party and the Negro," *The Crisis*, V (November, 1912), 30-31; Mowry, "The South and the Progressive Lily White Party of 1912," *Journal of Southern History*, VI (May, 1940), 237-47. Woodward, "Progressivism—For Whites Only," chap. XIV, in *Origins of the New South*, discusses the actual compatibility of Progressivism with racism. William E. Leuchtenburg, in "Progressivism and Imperialism," *Mississippi Valley Historical Review*, XXXIX (December, 1952), 483-504, shows that the same compatibility existed in other sections of the country too. Thus the suffrage movement was in the mainstream

within the NAWSA much more easily than Miss Addams
accepted it in the Progressive party, but both the Progressives and the suffragists could at the same time advocate
white supremacy and democratic reforms and accept the
organizational reflections of this fact.[17] When Southern
suffragists coupled the "consent of the governed" argument with appeals to white supremacy, they showed that
they simply did not include Negroes in "the people";
when Miss Addams accepted a lily-white Progressive
party, she did not believe she was betraying the Negroes'
interests, but felt she was bringing nearer the time when
Negroes would have the right to consent to the laws by
which they were governed.

This coexistence of reformist and humanitarian motives
with undemocratic attitudes links the woman suffrage
movement with the Progressive movement in still another way. Progressivism may be seen as a broad humanitarian cause, and it may be seen as a convergence of
several distinct self-interested movements challenging en-

---

of American intellectual history in this respect, just as its demand for
the vote placed it in the mainstream of American political and social
history.

[17] See, for example, "Statement of Purpose," of a conference of
Southern suffragists held in Memphis in 1906 (copy in Clay Papers,
UK), in which Laura Clay played a leading role. Note the proximity
of democracy, white supremacy, and justice to workers: "Declaring our
adherence to the principles of political liberty, guaranteed to the American people by the fundamental principles of our government, we affirm
that they should not be limited by sex. . . . If the women of the South
were enfranchised, it would insure a permanent and enormous preponderance of the white race in politics, and would preclude the
necessity for any doubtful expedients to minimize the negro vote.

"We ask for the ballot because students of industrial conditions
affirm that the lack of direct political power is a factor in the comparatively low wages of the six million wage-earning women in our country.

"We ask for the ballot as the strongest insurance against child-labor
under conditions destructive to the best development of the men and
women of the future."

trenched political or economic powers. Suffragism may be interpreted as one of these self-interested movements. It may also be interpreted in this dual manner, since it contained women who wanted the vote to enact a broad humanitarian program, as well as women who participated in the humanitarian movement in order to achieve their primary goal of political equality. Just as progressives of both types (those whose main interest was broad humanitarianism and those whose main interest was the achievement of specific changes in the economic or political structure) found common ground in their demand for what they called democratic reform, so did the suffragists.

The suffragists, then, saw in the long sweep of history consent replacing force in government. The United States represented the finest expression of this progress toward universal consent. This was proved by the Declaration of Independence promulgated at its birth. Since the American Revolution, new portions of the population had received the vote in each generation. Sometimes the suffragists admitted that the sense of justice of the already-enfranchised men could not account for the enfranchisement of new groups and that political expediency exerted the decisive influence,[18] but in the long view the women emphasized the pattern of steady progress toward the ideal of true "government by consent of the governed." The last step would be the enfranchisement of women.[19]

---

[18] See, for example, Susan B. Anthony in National Council of Women, *Transactions*, 1891, pp. 229-30; Laura Clay, "Counterparts," *Woman's Journal*, June 15, 1901; Mrs. Harper in House *Hearing*, 1912, pp. 70-71.

[19] In two major respects, they believed, woman suffrage was not analogous to previous extensions of the franchise. First, they declared that no other group that had won the vote had won it as much

The progress, however, although inevitable, was obviously not automatic. No one knew better than the suffragists the long years of work and struggle they must contribute to their cause before it could triumph. No one knew better than they (although the antis knew it too and frequently reminded them of it) that one of their greatest obstacles was the indifference of the majority of women to their own political equality. They consoled themselves and answered their critics in two ways. First, as Mrs. Stanton had repeatedly argued, the dulling of the desire for freedom through long centuries of suppression was the best proof of its desirability. Second, progress was always made by forward-looking minorities in the face of majority hostility or indifference.[20] This theory supported suffragist morale, particularly in the days when they were indeed a very small minority and even later when, as always, the antis confronted them with theories of woman's sphere that defined the natural as the customary. If progress was always due to the minority that saw further than the majority, then the customary was never the natural, nor the natural customary. Here again the suffrage movement proved itself a "bourgeois movement," that is, reformist rather than

through its own efforts as the women would. Second, they occasionally complained that the enfranchisement of other groups (Negro men, foreign-born men, Indian men) had erected new obstacles to the enfranchisement of women, inasmuch as these new voters were allegedly against woman suffrage and inasmuch as the enfranchisement of "unfit" men had made many people unwilling to extend the franchise still further. Hence, although in suffragist thinking, their movement was in the mainstream of gradually broadening American democracy, that stream turned out to have a few rapids and sharp bends.

[20] Elizabeth Cady Stanton to Clara B. Colby, 1894 letter quoted in Lutz, *Created Equal*, p. 292; speech of Mrs. Catt in 1900, quoted in Anthony and Harper, eds., *History of Woman Suffrage*, IV, 369-70; Harper in her 1902 introduction to *ibid.*, p. xxii.

revolutionary, for although the theory of progress that they developed seems to imply unending change, the suffragists did not visualize any further extensions of the franchise after women had secured the vote. Nor did they approve of the efforts of other minorities to effect changes in those areas of American life in which the suffragists themselves equated the customary with the natural.[21]

Two recent historians describe the essentially conservative position of the class to which most suffragists belonged:

While maturing industrialism was responsible for the growth of many social evils, it was also responsible for producing wealth and leisure for groups that could attack such evils. Ministers, teachers, writers, and thousands of prosperous women had no large financial stake in child and female labor, long hours, sweat-shops, saloons, tenements, and slums. . . . This class had no unity, but its members suffered in common the fear of having their independence abridged by monopolizing Titans from above or else engulfed by a surge of socialism from the ranks of labor below. Truly conservative, they opposed equally the collectivism of the great trusts and the collectivism of trade unions; and they shared a profound belief in free capitalism, equal economic opportunity, fair trade practices and the protection of property. Inheritors of the victory of the English Parliament over the Stuart kings, they insisted also upon the supremacy of laws over men or institutions, and they had a naïve belief in the efficacy of legislation to achieve their ends.[22]

[21] See Anna Howard Shaw's comments on anarchism and McKinley's assassination, in *Woman's Journal*, September 21, 1901; Grace Bagley in *Woman Citizen*, June 30, 1917; "A Bourgeois Movement," in *ibid.*, July 7, 1917; NAWSA, *Proceedings*, 1919, p. 59, quoting sixth resolution passed.

[22] Cochran and Miller, *The Age of Enterprise*, pp. 274-75, quoted by permission of The Macmillan Company which originally published the work in 1942. The order of the two passages has been reversed.

Working-class women certainly needed the vote more than did leisured women, if the suffragists were correct in their opinion that the ballot represented power, self-protection, and the means whereby many wrongs could be righted. But it was the middle-class women who had, in the course of the nineteenth century, acquired education, leisure time, and the opportunity to participate in activities ·outside their homes, all of which made them aware of the gap between their social standing and economic status on the one hand and their political power on the other. This awareness bred a sense of grievance and a motive for the struggle to secure redress. The political power of working-class women of course lagged behind their needs, and in the last few years many such women became active suffragists, but their sense of grievance, where it existed, generally focused on more urgent demands than that for the vote. Moreover, since there was no gap between their educational and social standing and their political power, they lacked one of the motives that led the middle-class women to demand the vote.[23] When workingwomen did demand the suffrage,

[23] Thorstein Veblen commented on the same phenomenon from a different point of view: "It is among the women of the well-to-do classes, in the communities which are farthest advanced in industrial development, that this sense of grievance to be redressed is most alive and finds most frequent expression. That is to say, in other words, there is a demand, more or less serious, for emancipation from all relations of status, tutelage, or vicarious life; and the revulsion asserts itself especially among the class of women upon whom the scheme of life handed down from the regime of status imposes with least mitigation a vicarious life, and in those communities whose economic development has departed farthest from the circumstances to which this traditional scheme is adapted. The demand comes from that portion of womankind which is excluded by the canons of good repute from all effectual work, and which is closely reserved for a life of leisure and conspicuous consumption.

"More than one critic of this new-woman movement has misap-

their arguments rarely mentioned justice or the Declaration of Independence, not because justice or democracy carried less appeal to workers than to middle-class women, but because workingwomen did not simply *want* the vote; they found they *needed* it for the same reasons as they had organized their unions. Working-class women, however, never constituted more than a small minority of organized suffragists.

The ballot was for some suffragists an end and for others a means to other ends. To Mrs. Stanton, Mrs. Gilman, and Miss Addams, it was never more than a means toward woman's all-round development or toward social regeneration. One might infer that to Miss Anthony it was an end, but only because she believed that no other reform could be achieved without women's equal participation.[24] It therefore loomed so large in her writ-

---

prehended its motive. The case of the American 'new woman' has lately been summed up with some warmth by a popular observer of social phenomena: 'She is petted by her husband, the most devoted and hard-working of husbands in the world. . . . She is the superior of her husband in education, and in almost every respect. She is surrounded by the most numerous and delicate attentions. Yet she is not satisfied.' . . . The grievance of the new woman is made up of those things which this typical characterization of the movement urges as the reasons why she should be content. She is petted, and is permitted, or even required, to consume largely and conspicuously—vicariously for her husband or other natural guardian. She is exempted, or debarred, from vulgarly useful employment—in order to perform leisure vicariously for the good repute of her natural (or pecuniary) guardian. These offices are the conventional marks of the un-free, at the same time that they are incompatible with the human impulse to purposeful activity." *Theory of the Leisure Class* (New York, Mentor Books, 1958), pp. 231-32, quoted by permission of The Viking Press, Inc. See also pp. 120-22, 229-30, and 233.

[24] See, for example, Susan B. Anthony to "Mr. Bowman," September 7, 1894, Anthony Family Collection, HL: "I am as deeply and keenly interested in the many reforms in city, State & National government as any one can possibly be— but knowing that no right solution of any great question can be reached until the whole people have a voice in

ings and speeches that it could appear to be her one
goal. To many later suffragists the vote was indeed the
main goal; the possibility of arguing that women's votes
could help reform society made the vote seem, in their
writings, a means to reform. These differences among
suffragists are instructive. When Mrs. Stanton was in her
prime, women had not yet won many of the rights they
took for granted by 1900. To her the vote then seemed
to be a means to the acquisition of precisely those rights,
to their entrance into professions and graduate schools,
to equal guardianship of their children, and so on. Those
later suffragists to whom these rights seemed almost the
sum of the equality they desired in the most desirable
society imaginable could not visualize the vote as a means
because it was virtually the only right they aspired to
that they had not yet won. Hence it stood alone and
appeared to be the "end." To Mrs. Gilman and Miss
Addams, both of whom belonged to the last generation
of suffragists and who in different ways were deeply
dissatisfied with the society in which they lived, many
rights were still to be won. The suffrage in their view
remained a mere means, among others, to the achievement of these rights. The more satisfied a middle-class
suffragist was with her personal lot, in the later years of
of the suffragist agitation, the more important the vote
would probably be to her, simply because it stood alone
and was not sought as a means to any drastic change
in the status quo.

As women obtained one new right after another, the

---

it— I give all of myself to the getting the whole people inside the body
politic, so as to be able to begin making even the first equation of any
of the problems—"

rights of men and women became more and more similar, just as other changes were causing their spheres to draw closer together. The social, economic, and political separation that had encouraged different ways of thinking, that had given plausibility to the assertion that innate psychological differences between the sexes were so great that women must be kept in their customary sphere, melted away. Disfranchisement itself had bred differences in thinking and social roles between enfranchised and disfranchised that had provided arguments for maintaining the political separation. Those differences led both men and women to expect women, if and when they obtained the ballot, to vote differently from men. They gave antisuffragists an argument for keeping women out of politics; they gave women reformers an argument why men reformers should give them the vote. But when women won the ballot and in other ways continued to close the gap between their sphere and men's, all those arguments lost their plausibility. The differences produced by that very disfranchisement and exclusion from the male sphere evaporated.

The pattern of women's voting since 1920 shows that the diversity of thinking within the movement, noted at the beginning of this study, has persisted. Just as the suffragists differed among themselves in religion, politics, even the reasons for wanting the vote, they have continued to differ as voters. The addition of women to the electorate has not significantly altered American voting patterns as the suffragists predicted it would. But it would not be correct for that reason to deny that an enormous change took place with the enactment of the Nineteenth Amendment. Even those many suffragists who wanted the vote primarily to enact reforms became suffragists partly because of the intense shame they felt at being thought unfit to help govern their country. When they acquired that right they felt a new pride in American democracy and a new respect for themselves.

Appendix: Biographical Data

Twenty-six suffragists are described in the following pages. The list comprises: all those women who held national office in the NAWSA for three or more years between 1890 and 1918 with the exception of two on whom insufficient data were found; the four chief leaders of the CU and WP between 1914 and 1920; and two women—Harriot Stanton Blatch and Charlotte Perkins Gilman—whose opinions were extremely important to the suffrage movement. The twenty-six are listed in order of their birth years.

ELIZABETH CADY STANTON, 1815-1902, is discussed in Chapter I. Daughter of a judge and relative of abolitionist Gerrit Smith, she acquired a broad education without attending college. A provocative and wide-ranging thinker, she adhered to no formal church and held unorthodox views on many subjects, although she agreed with most reformers of her day in favoring prohibition. Of her seven children, one daughter, Harriot, became an outstanding suffrage leader.

LUCY STONE, 1818-1893, receives little attention in the foregoing chapters because she died soon after the beginning of the thirty-year period discussed. She was, however, one of the most important of the first generation of suffragists. She was born in Massachusetts, the daughter of farmers descended from English immigrants of the seventeenth century. Her antislavery activities caused her expulsion from the Congregational Church, although she continued to consider herself a member. Her marriage to Henry B. Blackwell is famous for its joint statement by the newlyweds that they were to be equals in all things, Mr. Blackwell renouncing the superior rights the law granted him as husband. His wife kept her maiden name throughout their married life. Their only child, Alice Stone Blackwell, became the foremost suffragist propagandist. Mrs. Stone was an eloquent speaker, and much of her life was spent in traveling from one lecture to another, speaking on abolition, temperance, or woman suffrage.

SUSAN B. ANTHONY, 1820-1906, was born in Massachusetts of Quaker stock. Her first career was that of a schoolteacher. In that capacity and as a temperance lecturer she encountered such prejudice against women's participation in public activities that she soon became an ardent exponent of equal rights for women. She was undoubtedly the most traveled suffragist, within the United States, criss-crossing the country on speaking and organizing tours virtually every year.

ANNA HOWARD SHAW, like Miss Anthony, is discussed in Chapter I. Born in England in 1847, she was brought to America as a child and grew up in the back woods of Michigan. She eventually acquired a D.D. and an M.D., although most of her life was spent as a lecturer, a profession for which her magnificent gift for oratory especially fitted her and in which she earned a very comfortable living. In addition to the NAWSA, the WCTU claimed her allegiance throughout her life. She died in 1919.

LAURA CLAY, 1849-1941, was the daughter of Cassius Clay, Kentucky abolitionist. She was educated at a New York finishing school and the University of Michigan, as well as a Kentucky college, although she evidently received no degree. She was active in the Kentucky WCTU, serving as State Superintendent of Franchise, and was a devoted member of the Protestant Episcopal Church. She earned her living by renting her Bluegrass farm to sharecroppers and supervised the management of the farm herself. Her suffrage arguments frequently stressed religion and the Bible.

ALVA BELMONT (Mrs. Oliver H. P. Belmont), 1853-1933, was born in Alabama to cotton planter Murray Forbes Smith and Phoebe Ann Desha Smith. In 1875 she married William K. Vanderbilt and embarked on a campaign to persuade Mrs. Astor to accept her into New York's "400." A $3 million chateau on Fifth Avenue and a $2 million mansion in Newport—the furnishing of which cost $9 million—as well as a lavish ball, eventually proved persuasive enough, and Mrs. Vanderbilt was admitted into society's inner circles. In 1895 the Vanderbilts were divorced; Mrs. Vanderbilt received custody of their three children. She soon married Belmont, who died in 1908. Mrs. Belmont turned to suffrage; she showed genuine interest in the cause and gave generously of money and leadership to it. After the Congressional Union was formed she joined it and for the rest of her life was a top-level leader in the CU and its successor, the Woman's Party, although she spent her last years in France. Her philanthropies included hospitals for children. She had a natural talent for architecture and designed her own homes as well as other buildings.[1]

HARRIET TAYLOR UPTON, 1854-1945, was the daughter of an Ohio judge who later became chairman of the House of Representatives Judiciary Committee. In that capacity he met Susan B. Anthony and brought Harriet into contact with the suffrage movement. At first, however, she was an anti; later she publicly acknowledged her change of heart. Such honesty was characteristic of Mrs. Upton, who was known for her good nature, loud laugh, and ability to end arguments with compromises. In 1884 she married George W. Upton, a lawyer. Her education was limited to the public schools of Warren, Ohio. She was a member of the Daughters of the American Revolution, was active in the Warren Board of Education, and belonged to the WCTU, Women's Relief Corps, and the Episcopal Church. After the suffrage victory she became a vice-chairman of the Republican National Executive Committee. She was the NAWSA's national treasurer from 1891 to 1909. Mrs. Upton also wrote a number of historical works and children's stories.[2]

HARRIOT STANTON BLATCH, 1856-1940, was the daughter of Elizabeth Cady Stanton. She was born in Seneca Falls, New York. Twenty-two years later, she was graduated from Vassar College with honors in mathematics

[1] Data on Mrs. Belmont may be found in Harris E. Starr, ed., *Dictionary of American Biography*, Supplement One (New York, Charles Scribner's Sons, 1944); *Equal Rights*, February 18, 1933; and John William Leonard, ed., *Woman's Who's Who of America, 1914-1915* (New York, the American Commonwealth Company, 1914).

[2] Data on Mrs. Upton may be found in *Woman's Who's Who, 1914-1915; Who Was Who in America*, II (Chicago, The A. N. Marquis Company, 1950); Durward Howes, ed., *American Women* (1939-1940) (Los Angeles, American Publications, Inc., 1939); and New York *Times*, November 4, 1945.

and was elected to Phi Beta Kappa. Mrs. Blatch then studied at the Sorbonne and in Berlin and, in 1894, received her M.A. from Vassar. She married an Englishman in 1882; he died in 1913. During her twenty-year residence in England, Mrs. Blatch joined the Fabian Society. Soon after the turn of the century she returned to America to find the suffrage movement in a rut of tea parties and innocuous ladylikeness. Drawing on her experience in the British suffrage movement, she began organizing street meetings and parades in New York City. Later she joined the CU, although she did not agree with all of Miss Paul's policies and never found it easy to work with others. One of Mrs. Blatch's two daughters, Nora, became an active suffragist. In 1921 Mrs. Blatch ran for Comptroller of New York City on the Socialist ticket.[3]

ALICE STONE BLACKWELL, daughter of Lucy Stone, was born in 1857 in New Jersey and died in 1950 in Massachusetts. Her long life was completely devoted to reforms of various natures. Until 1917 she was editor of the *Woman's Journal*, from 1890 to 1908 was the NAWSA's recording secretary, and in 1909 and 1910 one of the national auditors. She was also prominent in WCTU affairs. In 1881 she was graduated with honors from Boston University, a member of Phi Beta Kappa. At various times she belonged to the American Peace Society, New England Anti-Vivisection Society, National Association for the Advancement of Colored People, Massachusetts Total Abstinence League, Free Trade League, Women's

[3] Mrs. Blatch is listed in the *Woman's Who's Who, 1914-1915*. See also New York *Times*, November 21, 1940. The best source, of course, is *Challenging Years*, her memoirs.

Trade Union League, and Committee Against Repeal of
the Eighteenth Amendment. Her chief activity uncon-
nected with reform movements was translating poetry;
her translations include works from the Armenian, Rus-
sian, Yiddish, Hungarian, Spanish, French, Italian, Latin,
German, and Bohemian. A letter to her from Laura Clay
in 1934 [4] mentions that in a previous letter Miss Blackwell had called herself a Socialist.[5]

RACHEL FOSTER AVERY was born in Pennsylvania in 1858
and lived most of her life in Swarthmore. She served the
NAWSA from 1890 to 1900 as corresponding secretary and
from 1907 to 1909 as a vice-president. She was educated
in Philadelphia schools and engaged in special studies
in political economy in the University of Zürich. A
wealthy philanthropist, she was an accomplished linguist
and accompanied Susan B. Anthony on the latter's trip
to Europe in 1883. Her main talent seems to have been
organizing conventions, and she served both the NAWSA
and the International Congress of Women (1888) in that
manner. Mrs. Avery had three daughters, one of whom
was adopted. She favored prohibition but would not support the Prohibition party until she had the right to vote.[6]

FLORENCE KELLEY, 1859-1932, served the NAWSA as a
vice-president from 1905 to 1909, although other causes
claimed her strongest allegiance. She was born in Philadelphia, daughter of Rep. William D. (Pig-Iron) Kelley,

---

[4] June 16. The letter is in Box 164, Suffrage Archives, LC.

[5] Data on Miss Blackwell are in *Woman's Who's Who, 1914-1915*,
New York *Times*, January 10, 1936, and Hays, *Morning Star*.

[6] See Avery to C. W. McCulloch, April 27, 1909, McCulloch Papers,
RWA; *Woman's Who's Who, 1914-1915* (there are errors in this article,
however); Frances E. Willard and Mary A. Livermore, eds., *A Woman
of the Century* (Buffalo, Charles Wells Moulton, 1893), a biographical
dictionary.

and studied at Cornell University. After graduation she studied law in Zürich and practiced in Illinois for two years. Later she became an agent for the United States Department of Labor and investigated slum conditions. In 1893 she was appointed the first woman Chief Inspector of Factories in Illinois. While in Chicago she lived at Hull-House. In 1897 she moved to New York to become secretary of the newly organized National Consumers' League and lived at the Henry Street Settlement. This descendant of Irish, English, and Huguenot forebears, whose childhood was spent in a Quaker home, grew up to become a well-known Socialist. She translated Friedrich Engels' *Condition of the Working Class in England in 1844* in the 1880s and in 1884 married a Polish-Russian Socialist, Dr. Lazare Wischnewetzky. They were divorced in 1891. Mrs. Kelley resumed her maiden name and received custody of their three children.[7]

CARRIE CHAPMAN CATT, 1859-1947, the general of the suffrage movement, was born in Wisconsin, daughter of Lucius and Maria Clinton Lane, descendants of seventeenth-century immigrants to Massachusetts. After college graduation she taught school and became Superintendent of Schools in Mason City, Iowa. Her first husband, Leo Chapman, died in 1886 soon after their marriage. In 1890 she married George Catt, a well-to-do engineer and suffragist, with whom she made an arrangement that

[7] Data on Mrs. Kelley may be found in New York *Times*, February 18, 1932 (obituary); and Josephine Goldmark, *Impatient Crusader: Florence Kelley's Life Story* (Urbana, University of Illinois Press, 1953). The *Times* spells her husband's name "Wischwetzky"; Goldmark's version is "Wishniewski." The spelling I have chosen is the one that appeared in print during her own lifetime, on the title pages of the works of Marx and Engels that she translated (in addition to the Engels book, see Karl Marx, *Free Trade*).

permitted her to devote several months a year to suffrage work. In 1895 Mrs. Catt, an excellent speaker and organizer, became chairman of the NAWSA's new Organization Committee, and in 1900 she succeeded Miss Anthony as national president. Her husband's ill health caused her to withdraw two years later, but in 1915 she resumed the presidency and led the organization to victory. In the same years Mrs. Catt was very active in the international suffrage movement, traveling all over the world, organizing and speaking for the cause, and retained leadership in the International Woman Suffrage Alliance until 1923.

CHARLOTTE PERKINS GILMAN, 1860-1935, was born in Hartford, great-granddaughter of Lyman Beecher and relative of Henry Ward Beecher and Harriet Beecher Stowe. Her early years were spent in painting and drawing, and her first husband was an artist. She soon turned to writing poetry, novels, and essays and eventually became a widely known lecturer. Difficulties arose in her marriage which in her autobiography she finds hard to explain; she found she suffered periods of depression that prevented her from writing. Feeling that her daughter's happiness as well as her own mental balance required her separation from her husband, she obtained a divorce. They remained good friends, however. Later she married her distant cousin, George Houghton Gilman. Mrs. Gilman believed that life meant growth and activity; when cancer made life as she defined it impossible, she committed suicide.

JANE ADDAMS, like Mrs. Gilman, was born in 1860 and died in 1935. Her life story is too well known to need detailed recounting here. Among the lesser-known facts is that she was the NAWSA's first vice-president from 1911 to 1913. Social work, however, was always her main interest. Her biographer notes that her father was a Quaker by sympathy, although not a member of the Society of Friends. Miss Addams joined the Presbyterian Church at the age of twenty-five, but later became a Congregationalist; however, she was never a strict adherent to the doctrines of any sect. She was a college graduate.[8]

KATE M. GORDON, c. 1861-1932, was a member of a prominent New Orleans family who, with her sister Jean, devoted her life and fortune to support for virtually every reform movement in her native Louisiana. The Era Club which they organized in New Orleans was instrumental in obtaining a sewer system for the city. After the suffrage victory, Miss Gordon established the first tuberculosis hospital in Louisiana. I have not been able to obtain information on her education or other relevant data.[9]

HELEN RICHARDS GUTHRIE MILLER (Mrs. Walter McNab Miller) was an auditor of the NAWSA in 1914 and 1915 and a vice-president the following year. She was born in 1862 in Ohio, daughter of Stephen Hand and Mary Annette Strong Guthrie. She was educated in a seminary in her home town of Zanesville and later studied at universities in Missouri and Nevada, at Stanford University, and in European institutions. Her husband was a doctor. The mother of two sons, Mrs. Miller taught school for several years and was a member of the Missouri State Board of Charities and Corrections; the Executive Board of the State Conference of Charities; chairman of the

[8] See James Weber Linn, *Jane Addams* (New York, D. Appleton-Century Company, Incorporated, 1935).

[9] See New York *Times*, August 25, 1932; and *Woman's Journal*, July 20, 1901.

Public Health Department; chairman of the Anti-Tuberculosis Nurse Committee of Columbia, Missouri; chairman of the Missouri School Patrons' Department of the National Education Association; and other committees. Her principal activity, however, was directed toward securing pure food and drug legislation. As a leader in the nationwide pure-food movement, she organized and wrote articles. She was an Episcopalian and a Daughter of the American Revolution. She died in 1949.[10]

CATHARINE WAUGH MCCULLOCH, 1862-1945, was an auditor of the NAWSA from 1897 to 1900 and a vice-president in 1910. In the early years of this century she became the first woman to be elected to a judicial office in the United States, serving as a justice of the peace. She was born in Ransomville, New York, the daughter of A. Miller and Susan Gouger Waugh, and received her B.A. and M.A. degrees from Rockford College. In 1886 she was graduated from Northwestern University Law School and practiced on her own until 1890 when she became a member of McCulloch & McCulloch; she had just married Frank McCulloch, also a lawyer. They had four children. Living in Evanston, Mrs. McCulloch was active in community affairs in that town and in Chicago. She belonged to the WCTU, Immigration Aid Society, Evanston Woman's Club, and other societies. A Congregationalist, she was an independent in politics, but in 1916 supported Wilson and served as a presidential elector on the Democratic ticket in Illinois. She played an important role in securing the presidential suffrage for Illinois women in 1913 and for twenty-two years was in charge

[10] See *Woman's Who's Who, 1914-1915*; and *Who Was Who in America*, II.

of legislative work of the Illinois Equal Suffrage Association. She wrote a number of pamphlets explaining the legal disabilities of women and their consequences.[11]

EMMA WINNER ROGERS (Mrs. Henry Wade Rogers) was national treasuer of the NAWSA from 1914 to the end of the amendment campaign. She was born in Plainfield, New Jersey, the daughter of a Methodist minister, the Rev. John Ogden Winner, and Sarah J. Taylor Winner. Mrs. Rogers was graduated from the University of Michigan in 1891. In 1890 she moved to Evanston. There her husband was president of Northwestern University from 1890 to 1900, after which he joined the faculty of Yale, first as a teacher of law and then as dean of the Law School. He became a United States Circuit Judge in 1913. Mrs. Rogers was interested in social and economic questions and in the arts and crafts movement. She was president of the Northwestern University Settlement Association from 1894 to 1900, president of the University Art Guild in Chicago and Evanston from 1895 to 1900, and a member of the American Economic Association, the Association of Collegiate Alumnae, and other societies.[12]

ELLA SEASS STEWART (Mrs. Oliver W. Stewart) was the NAWSA's recording secretary in 1909 and 1910 and an auditor in 1908. She was born in Illinois in 1871, the daughter of Levi and Elizabeth A. Powell Seass. She received a B.A. from Eureka (Ill.) College in 1890, an M.A. in 1892, and another B.A. from the University of Michigan, the same year. She served as president of the

[11] See New York *Times*, April 21, 1945 (some of its dates are unreliable, however); Beldon, "A History of the Woman Suffrage Movement in Illinois," pp. 34-41; *Woman's Who's Who, 1914-1915.*
[12] See *Woman's Who's Who, 1914-1915;* and *Woman of the Century.*

Illinois Equal Suffrage Association from 1906 to 1913. An ardent supporter of prohibition, she was also active in the WCTU. Her other associations included the Chicago Woman's Club and the Association of Collegiate Alumnae. She belonged to the Disciples of Christ.[13]

SUSAN WALKER FITZGERALD (Mrs. Richard Y. FitzGerald), 1871-1943, was the recording secretary of the NAWSA from 1911 to 1914. She was born in Jamaica Plain, Massachusetts, the daughter of Admiral John Grimes Walker (former chairman of the Isthmian Canal Commission after his retirement from the Navy) and Rebecca W. Pickering Walker. She was graduated from Bryn Mawr in 1893 and remained to do graduate work. From 1898 to 1901 she was head of Fiske Hall at Barnard College, from 1901 to 1904 head worker of the West Side Branch of the University Settlement of New York City, and for a year was a truant officer in New York. Her husband was a Boston lawyer and author. They had three daughters. After she moved to Boston she became a leader in Massachusetts suffragist circles as well as secretary of the School Voters' League.[14]

MARY WARE DENNETT, 1872-1947, was born in Worcester, Massachusetts, daughter of George Whitfield and Livonia Ames Ware. She studied at the Boston Art Museum School of Art and in 1900 married Hartley Dennett, an architect. They had two sons. At various times in her career as a professional house decorator she served as head of the School of Design and Decoration at the

[13] Stewart to C. W. McCulloch, February 22, 1906, McCulloch Papers, RWA; Folder 18 in Stewart Papers, RWA; *Woman's Who's Who, 1914-1915.*
[14] See *Woman's Journal,* February 5, 1910, and January 6, 1912; and *Woman's Who's Who, 1914-1915.*

Drexel Institute, Philadelphia; director of the Handicraft Shop, Boston; director of Boston Arts and Crafts Society. From 1910 to 1913 she was the NAWSA's corresponding secretary. In 1914 she wrote a twenty-four-page pamphlet designed to teach the facts of sex to her two sons. After securing the warm endorsement of eminent doctors, clergymen, and others, and seeing it reprinted in the *Medical Review of Reviews,* she continued to distribute it. In 1930 Mrs. Dennett was convicted of sending obscene literature through the mails, fined $300, and sentenced to three hundred days in prison. The American Civil Liberties Union defended her, raised money, publicized the cause it felt was at stake, and eventually secured a reversal of the conviction. In 1915 Mrs. Dennett was one of the three organizers of the National Birth Control League. Her other activities included work in 1916 in the antipreparedness campaign and for the reelection of Wilson, membership on the board of the Women's Peace Party in 1918, and helping to found the World Federalists in 1941.[15]

HARRIET BURTON LAIDLAW, a national auditor for the NAWSA from 1911 to 1913 and a director thereafter, was born in Albany, New York, in 1873. She was the daughter of George Davidson and Alice Davenport Wright Burton and a descendant of Scotch, Dutch, and English immigrants to New York of the seventeenth and eighteenth centuries. She received B.A. and M.A. degrees from Albany Normal College and taught high school English for twelve years in New York City. Meanwhile

[15] See *Woman's Who's Who, 1914-1915; The Prosecution of Mary Ware Dennett for "Obscenity"* (New York, American Civil Liberties Union, 1929); New York *Times,* March 4, 1930, and July 26, 1947.

she studied at Barnard College—from which she received a B.A.—and at several other universities during summer vacations. In 1905 she married wealthy New York banker James Lees Laidlaw, an active suffragist. They had one daughter. Mrs. Laidlaw was most active in New York suffrage campaigns and spoke frequently on street corners and in parks. In addition she belonged to organizations to fight prostitution, worked in behalf of a home for wayward or homeless girls, favored prohibition, and contributed time and energy to the Women's Trade Union League, Social Hygiene Association, English Speaking Union, and many other organizations. After suffrage was won she devoted most of her time to work for peace and international understanding. She was a remarkably beautiful woman.[16]

ANNE MARTIN, the first chairman of the Woman's Party, was born in Empire City, Nevada, in 1875, the daughter of William O'Hara and Louise Stadtmuller Martin. Her ancestors had left Northern Ireland to settle in the American West; her father was a Nevada state senator, president of the Washoe County Bank, and prominent in a number of industrial corporations in Reno. Miss Martin studied at the University of Nevada and also received B.A. and M.A. degrees from Stanford. While studying in Cambridge, she joined the English militant suffrage movement and was arrested in the course of this activity. In England she also belonged to the Fabian Society and the Women's Social and Political Union—the militant suffragists. Her other organizations included the

[16] See *Who's Who in New York: 1947* (New York, Lewis Historical Publishing Company, Inc., 1947); *Who's Who in New York: 1929* (New York, Who's Who Publications, Inc., 1929); *Who Was Who in America,* II.

American Historical Association, the Nevada Historical Society, and the Nevada Equal Franchise Society. She was founder and first head of the history department at the University of Nevada from 1897 to 1901. Her hobbies were tennis and mountain-climbing; she was Nevada woman's tennis champion in 1893 and 1894 and for the next two years was the tennis champion at Stanford University. Her athletic talents were put to good use in the suffrage campaign, which she had to conduct largely on horseback, traveling from one nearly inaccessible mining camp to another.[17]

KATHERINE DEXTER MCCORMICK (Mrs. Stanley McCormick) was the national treasurer of the NAWSA in 1912 and 1913 and a vice-president thereafter. She was born in Michigan in 1876, the daughter of Wirt and Josephine Moore Dexter. Her father was a prominent Boston lawyer. She was graduated from the Massachusetts Institute of Technology. Her husband was the son of Cyrus McCormick. The McCormicks were prominent in Boston society, but Mrs. McCormick found time to become vice-president of the Massachusetts Woman Suffrage Association and of the Massachusetts branch of the National College Equal Suffrage League.[18]

ALICE PAUL, the grand strategist of the semimilitant suffragists in the United States, was born in 1885 in Moorestown, New Jersey, the daughter of William M. and Tacie Perry Paul, Quakers. She received her B.A. from Swarthmore in 1905, her M.A. from the University

[17] *Woman's Who's Who, 1914-1915; Suffragist*, March 19, 1918; Anne Martin, *The Story of the Nevada Equal Suffrage Campaign* (Reno, University of Nevada, 1948), p. 3.
[18] *Woman's Journal*, September 28, 1912; *Woman's Who's Who, 1914-1915*.

of Pennsylvania in 1907, and a Ph.D. from the latter institution in 1912. After receiving the M.A. she went to England to study at Birmingham and London and while there did settlement work and engaged in militant activity in behalf of woman suffrage. In the course of this activity she, along with other women, served three prison terms, went on a hunger strike, and was forcibly fed, an ordeal to which she was later subjected in the United States also. She returned to this country in 1910 to write her dissertation on the legal status of women and then to put new life into the moribund federal amendment campaign. Her co-workers regarded her with enormous respect; she seems to have inspired deep devotion and a willingness to work intensely for the cause. Her pictures show a short, frail young woman with piercing eyes and abundant brown hair piled on the top of her head.

LUCY BURNS was Miss Paul's chief lieutenant. She was born in Brooklyn, New York, and received her B.A. in 1902 from Vassar. She then did graduate work in Yale and at the Universities of Berlin and Bonn. In the three years before her European sojourn she taught in a Brooklyn high school. After leaving Germany she went to Scotland, where she became an organizer of the militant Women's Social and Political Union in Edinburgh. It was in the course of this activity that she met Miss Paul, although she did not return to the United States until two years after her friend. As far as is now ascertainable, she was the only nationally prominent suffrage leader of Irish-Catholic ancestry, a fact undoubtedly connected to the additional fact that she was either the youngest or the second youngest of the women on this list of twenty six.[19]

[19] I have not been able to ascertain her birth year. Irwin, in *Angels*

A number of tentative generalizations may be made from the above information, although it is not complete, and the biographical dictionaries from which many of the data are drawn contain errors.

Of the twenty-six, sixteen were college graduates and three more attended college. Information is missing on one (Miss Gordon). The six who evidently never attended college must nevertheless be considered better educated than the average. The unusually high percentage of college-educated women among suffrage leaders is notable.

Of the twenty-six, seventeen were married. Three were divorced, of whom two remarried and remained married to their second husbands. The nine of twenty-six who never married represent a higher percentage than in the general population. At least part of the explanation for this must be that these women were prominent in a movement that aimed at changing the role of women in society, an objective not shared by most men and, for a long time, by most women. It must be assumed that this association would decrease the matrimonial chances of a single woman even more than association with another unpopular cause. Furthermore, there are in suffragist records a number of instances in which local leaders married and then withdrew from activity because of family responsibilities. It may be assumed, therefore, that those who did not have such responsibilities were more avail-

---

and Amazons, p. 354, writes that she was a few years younger than Miss Paul. Inasmuch as she received her B.A. in 1902, when Miss Paul was seventeen, this seems unlikely. Data on Miss Burns may be found in *Angels and Amazons,* pp. 354-55 and 382-87; Irwin, *The Story of the Woman's Party,* chaps. II-III; Stevens, *Jailed for Freedom, passim* (photo is opposite p. 178); *Woman's Who's Who, 1914-1915.* These works also furnish data on Miss Paul; the two women are usually discussed together.

able for leadership positions. For this reason one would expect the percentage of married women to be higher among the rank and file than in the leadership.

It appears that those suffragist leaders born before 1859 tended more to be WCTU'ers and for prohibition than those born after 1859.

Every individual listed was of Anglo-Saxon derivation except for two whose ancestors came from Ireland. Of these two, one was descended from natives of Northern Ireland, probably Protestant. All these individuals whose religious affiliations were definitely ascertained were members or daughters of members of Protestant sects, except for the one Catholic who was one of the two youngest.

Of the twenty-six, at least sixteen at some time in their lives earned their own livings, each in a middle-class occupation. This high percentage of breadwinners sets this group off from the average of American women of their generations, as does the completely middle-class character of their occupations. It is directly related to the suffragist leaders' high educational level, and both their education and their financial independence are probably causally related to their suffragism and generally wider mental horizons than the generality of American women.

Most of these twenty-six participated in activities in behalf of schools, sanitation, public health, and other aspects of social welfare.

Bibliography

MANUSCRIPT COLLECTIONS

Bancroft Library. University of California. Berkeley, California:
Anne Martin Papers
Mabel Vernon Papers
Friends Historical Library of Swarthmore College. Swarthmore, Penna.:
Jane Addams Papers
Huntington Library. San Marino, California:
Anthony Family Collection
Clara Bewick Colby Papers
Ida Husted Harper Collection
Alice Locke Park Papers
Library of Congress, Manuscript Division. Washington, D.C.:
Susan B. Anthony Papers
Olivia B. Hall Papers
National Woman's Party Collection
Elizabeth Cady Stanton Papers
Suffrage Archives (recent gift of Mrs. Edna L. Stantial)
Mary Church Terrell Papers
Margaret I. King Library. University of Kentucky. Lexington, Kentucky:
Laura Clay Papers
New-York Historical Society. New York, N. Y.:
Harriet Burton Laidlaw Scrapbooks
New York Public Library. New York, N.Y.:
Carrie Chapman Catt Collection
Smith Family Papers (letters of Elizabeth Cady Stanton and Susan B. Anthony)
Woman Suffrage Scrapbooks

Sophia Smith Collection. Smith College Library. Northampton, Mass.:
    Casement Collection
    Ethel E. Dreier Papers
    Garrison Family Papers
    Miscellaneous Newspapers Collection
    Suffrage Collection
Women's Archives, Radcliffe College. Cambridge, Mass.:
    Blackwell Family Papers
    Olympia Brown Papers
    Carrie Chapman Catt Papers
    Elizabeth Boynton Harbert Papers
    Harriet Burton Laidlaw Papers
    Catharine Waugh McCulloch Papers
    Leonora O'Reilly Papers
    Caroline I. Reilly Papers
    Anna Howard Shaw Papers
    Ella Seass Stewart Papers
    Sue Shelton White Papers

GOVERNMENT PUBLICATIONS

South Carolina. Governor. Annual Message of Richard I. Manning, Governor, to the General Assembly of South Carolina at the Regular Session, beginning January 8, 1918. Columbia, S.C., Gonzales & Bryan, State Printers, 1918.
United States. Congressional Record. Vols. L-LIII.
────── Congress. Hearing before the Committee on Woman Suffrage of the House of Representatives, 1918. Washington, D.C., Government Printing Office, 1918.
────── Congress. Hearing before a Senate Joint Committee of the Committee on the Judiciary and the Committee on Woman Suffrage. . . . Washington, D.C., Government Printing Office, 1912.
────── Congress. Hearings of the Committee on Rules of the House of Representatives, 1914 and 1917, on resolutions proposing establishment of a Committee on Woman Suffrage. Washington, D.C., Government Printing Office, 1914 and 1917.

—————— Congress. Hearings of the House Judiciary Committee, 1892, 1898, 1900, 1902, 1904, 1910, and 1912. Washington, D.C., Government Printing Office, various dates. Titles vary from year to year; the resolutions on which the hearings were held vary in number, but "Woman Suffrage" appears somewhere in each of the titles.

—————— Congress. Hearings of the Senate Committee on Woman Suffrage, 1898, 1904, 1908, and 1916. Washington, D.C., Government Printing Office, various dates. Titles vary from year to year; the resolutions on which the hearings were held vary in number and slightly in purpose, but "Woman Suffrage" appears in all the titles.

—————— Department of Commerce and Labor. Bureau of the Census, S.N.D. North, Director. Statistics of Women at Work. Based on unpublished information derived from the schedules of the Twelfth Census, 1900. Washington, D.C., Government Printing Office, 1907.

PERIODICALS

New York *Daily Tribune*, 1896-1903.

New York *Sun*, 1899-1903 (Sundays).

New York *Times*, 1913-19.

Remonstrance (Boston), 1890-1919.

San Francisco *Examiner*, 1896 (Sundays).

The Suffragist (Washington, D.C.), 1914-18.

The Woman Citizen (New York), 1917-19.

The Woman's Journal (Boston), 1890-1917.

The Woman's Protest (New York), 1912.

The Woman's Tribune (Washington, D.C., and Beatrice, Neb.), 1890-91.

OTHER

Abbott, Edith. "Are Women a Force for Good Government?" *National Municipal Review*, IV (July, 1915), 437-47.

—————— "The Woman Voter and the Spoils System in Chicago," *National Municipal Review*, V (July, 1916), 460-65.

Abbott, Lyman. "The Assault on Womanhood," *The Outlook*, April 3, 1909, pp. 784-88.

————— "The Profession of Motherhood," *The Outlook*, August 10, 1909, pp. 836-40.

————— "Why the Vote Would Be Injurious to Women," *Ladies' Home Journal*, XXVII (February, 1910), 21-22.

————— "Why Women Do Not Wish the Suffrage," *Atlantic Monthly*, XCII (September, 1903), 289-96.

Adams, Mary Dean. Wages and the Ballot. New York, New York State Association Opposed to Woman Suffrage, 1909.

Addams, Jane. A Centennial Reader. Edited by Emily Cooper Johnson. New York, Macmillan, 1960.

————— "If Men Were Seeking the Franchise," in A Centennial Reader. New York, Macmillan, 1960. Reprint of parts of article in *Ladies' Home Journal*, June, 1913.

————— "The Larger Aspects of the Woman's Movement," in Women in Public Life. *Annals of the American Academy of Political and Social Science*, LVI (November, 1914), 1-8.

————— The Modern City and the Municipal Franchise for Women. Warren, Ohio, National American Woman Suffrage Association, n.d.

————— "The Progressive Party and the Negro," *The Crisis*, V (November, 1912), 30-31.

————— Quotation in *The Survey*, October 23, 1915, p. 85.

————— The Second Twenty Years at Hull-House. New York, Macmillan, 1930.

————— "Significance of Organized Labor," *Machinists' Monthly Journal*, X (September, 1898), 551-52.

————— Twenty Years at Hull-House. New York Macmillan, 1910.

————— "Utilization of Women in City Government," in A Centennial Reader. New York, Macmillan, 1960. Reprint of parts of Newer Ideals of Peace (New York, Macmillan, 1907).

————— "Why Women Should Vote," in A Centennial Reader. New York, Macmillan, 1960. Reprint of parts of article in *Ladies' Home Journal*, January, 1910.

————— "Women, War and Suffrage," *The Survey*, November 6, 1915, pp. 148, 150.

Allen, Lee N. "The Woman Suffrage Movement in Alabama, 1910-1920," *Alabama Review*, XI (April, 1958), 83-99.

Anthony, Katharine. Susan B. Anthony: Her Personal History and Her Era. Garden City, N.Y., Doubleday, 1954.

Anthony, Susan B. "Address of Miss Susan B. Anthony to the Convention, Saturday, January 13," *The Bricklayer and Mason* (Official Journal of the Bricklayers' and Masons' International Union of America), II (February, 1900), 19-21.

——— "Fifty Years of Work for Women," *Independent*, February 15, 1900, pp. 414-17.

——— "The Outlook for Woman Suffrage," *Cosmopolitan*, XXVIII (April, 1900), 621-23.

——— "The Status of Women, Past, Present, and Future," *The Arena*, XVII (May, 1897), 901-8.

Anthony, Susan B., and Ida Husted Harper, eds. History of Woman Suffrage. Vol. IV (1883-1900). Rochester, N.Y., Susan B. Anthony, 1902.

Austin, Mary, and Anne Martin. Suffrage and Government. New York, National American Woman Suffrage Association, 1914.

Aylesworth, Leon E. "The Passing of Alien Suffrage," *American Political Science Review*, XXV (February, 1931), 114-16.

Bashford, Bishop J. W. The Bible for Woman Suffrage. Warren, Ohio, National American Woman Suffrage Association, n.d.

Beard, Charles A. "The Woman's Party," *The New Republic*, July 29, 1916, pp. 329-31.

Beard, Charles A., and Mary R. Beard. Rise of American Civilization. Vol. II. New York, Macmillan, 1927.

Beard, Mary R. "The Legislative Influence of Unenfranchised Women," in Women in Public Life. *Annals of the American Academy of Political and Social Science*, LVI (November, 1914), 54-61.

——— Woman as Force in History. New York, Macmillan, 1946.

—— "Woman's Work for the City," *National Municipal Review*, IV (April, 1915), 204-10.

Beldon, Gertrude May. "A History of the Woman Suffrage Movement in Illinois." Unpublished M.A. thesis, University of Chicago, 1913.

Bissell, Emily P. A Talk with Women on the Suffrage Question. New York, New York State Association Opposed to Woman Suffrage, 1909.

Björkman, Frances M., and Annie G. Porritt, eds. Woman Suffrage: History, Arguments and Results. New York, National Woman Suffrage Publishing Co., Inc., 1915.

Blackwell, Alice Stone. A Bubble Pricked: A Reply to "The Case against Woman Suffrage." Boston, *The Woman's Journal*, 1916.

—— The Division of Labor. Warren, Ohio, National American Woman Suffrage Association [1906?].

—— "Do Teachers Need the Ballot?" *Journal of Education*, July 1, 1909, pp. 8-9.

—— The M.A.O.F.E.S.W. Warren, Ohio, National American Woman Suffrage Association, n.d.

—— "An Object Lesson," *Independent*, July 21, 1906, pp. 198-99.

—— Why Women Should Vote. Warren, Ohio, National American Woman Suffrage Association, n.d.

Blake, Katherine Devereux, and Margaret Louise Wallace. Champion of Women: The Life of Lillie Devereux Blake. New York, Fleming H. Revell, 1943.

Blatch, Harriot Stanton, and Alma Lutz. Challenging Years: The Memoirs of Harriot Stanton Blatch. New York, Putnam, 1940.

Blatch, Harriot Stanton, and Theodore Stanton, eds. Elizabeth Cady Stanton as Revealed in Her Letters, Diary and Reminiscences. Vol. II. New York, Harper, 1922.

Bly, Nellie. "Champion of Her Sex," New York *World*, February 2, 1896, p. 10. Interview with Susan B. Anthony.

Bowman, Nelle E. "A Short History of Woman Suffrage in California." Unpublished M.A. thesis, University of Chicago, 1913.

Bronson, Minnie. The Wage-Earning Woman and the State. Boston, Massachusetts Association Opposed to the Further Extension of Suffrage to Women, 1910.

Brown, Ira V. "The Higher Criticism Comes to America, 1880-1900," *Journal of the Presbyterian Historical Society*, XXXVIII (December, 1960), 193-212.

Brown, Olympia, ed. Democratic Ideals: A Memorial Sketch of Clara B. Colby. N.p., Federal Suffrage Association, 1917.

Buckley, J. M. "The Wrongs and Perils of Woman Suffrage," *The Century*, XLVIII, new series XXVI (August, 1894), 613-23.

Cadogan-Etz, Anna. Some Reasons Why. Warren, Ohio, National American Woman Suffrage Association, n.d.

Caldwell, Martha B. "The Woman Suffrage Campaign of 1912," *Kansas Historical Quarterly*, XII (August, 1943), 300-18.

Carpenter, Mrs. Elbert L. (Member of Minneapolis Association Opposed to the Further Extension of Suffrage to Women). "The Disadvantages of Equal Suffrage." Papers and Proceedings of the Eighth Annual Meeting of the Minnesota Academy of Social Sciences. *Publications of the Minnesota Academy of Social Sciences*, VIII (1915), 186-98.

Caswell, John E. "The Prohibition Movement in Oregon: II. 1904-1915," *Oregon Historical Quarterly*, XL (March, 1939), 64-82.

Catt, Carrie Chapman. "Do You Know?" in Björkman and Porritt, eds., Woman Suffrage: History, Arguments and Results. New York, National Woman Suffrage Publishing Co., Inc., 1915; also published as pamphlet, in Catt Papers, NYPL. Published a number of times by various suffrage groups, including the South Dakota Universal Franchise League.

——— "The Home and the Higher Education," *Journal of Proceedings and Addresses* of the Forty-First Annual Meeting of the National Educational Association, held at Minneapolis, Minnesota, July 7-11, 1902, pp. 100-10.

——— Mrs. Catt's International Address. Delivered June 15, 1908, to the Congress of the International Woman Suffrage

Alliance in Amsterdam. Warren, Ohio, National American Woman Suffrage Association, n.d.

———— The Nation Calls: An Address to the Jubilee Convention of the National American Woman Suffrage Association. New York, National Woman Suffrage Publishing Co., Inc., 1919.

———— President's Annual Address (1902). Washington, D.C., Hayworth Publishing House, n.d.

———— President's Annual Address (1904). N.p., n.d.

———— "Ready for Citizenship," *The Public*, August 24, 1917, pp. 817-18.

———— "Women Voters at the Crossroads," *The Public*, May 31, 1919, pp. 569-70.

———— The World Movement for Woman Suffrage, 1904 to 1911, being the Presidential Address delivered at Stockholm to the Sixth Convention of the International Woman Suffrage Alliance, 1911. June 13, 1911. London, International Woman Suffrage Alliance, 1911.

Catt, Carrie Chapman, and Nettie Rogers Shuler. Woman Suffrage and Politics. New York, Scribner's, 1926.

Clark, Charles Worcester. "Woman Suffrage Pro and Con," *Atlantic Monthly*, LV (March, 1890), 310-20.

Clarke, Ida Clyde, compiler. Suffrage in the Southern States: A Brief History of the Progress of the Movement in Fourteen States. . . . Nashville, Williams Printing Co., 1914.

Cleveland, Grover. "Woman's Mission and Woman's Clubs," *Ladies' Home Journal*, XXII (May, 1905), 3-4.

———— "Would Woman Suffrage Be Unwise?" *Ladies' Home Journal*, XXII (October, 1905), 7-8.

Cochran, Thomas C., and William Miller. The Age of Enterprise: A Social History of Industrial America. Rev. ed. New York, Harper (Harper Torchbooks), 1961.

Collier's, April 20, 1912, p. 27.

Copy of Preamble and Protest. Brooklyn, N. Y., Committee on Protest against Woman Suffrage, 1894.

Crannell, Mrs. W. Winslow (Chairman of the Executive Committee of the Anti-Suffrage Association of the Third Judicial District of the State of New York). Address before the

Committee on Resolutions of the Democratic National Convention, at Chicago, July 8, 1896. Albany [Albany Anti-Suffrage Association, 1896].

———— Wyoming. Albany, Albany Anti-Suffrage Association, 1895.

Cuyler, The Rev. Theodore L. Shall Women Be Burdened with the Ballot? Brooklyn Auxiliary of the New York State Association Opposed to the Extension of Suffrage to Women, n.d.

Debs, Eugene V. "Susan B. Anthony," *Pearson's Magazine* (New York), XXXVIII (July, 1917), 5-7.

Degler, Carl N. "Charlotte Perkins Gilman on the Theory and Practice of Feminism," *American Quarterly*, VIII (Spring, 1956), 21-39.

Deland, Margaret. "The Change in the Feminine Ideal," *Atlantic Monthly*, CV (March, 1910), 289-302.

Dell, Floyd. Women as World Builders: Studies in Modern Feminism. Chicago, Forbes, 1913.

Diggs, Annie L. "The Women in the Alliance Movement," *The Arena*, VI (July, 1892), 161-79.

A Discussion of Woman Suffrage. Yale University Debating Association Handbook No. 1. New Haven, Yale University Press, 1914.

Dix, Dorothy. Dorothy Dix on Woman's Ballot. Warren, Ohio, National American Woman Suffrage Association, n.d.

Doane, The Rt. Rev. William Croswell, D.D., Bishop of Albany. Extracts from Addresses to the Classes graduated from St. Agnes' School, Albany, June 6, 1894 and June 6, 1895. Albany, Albany Anti-Suffrage Association, 1895.

———— "Why Women Do Not Want the Ballot," *North American Review*, CLXI (September, 1895), 257-67.

Dodge, Mrs. Arthur M. (President of the National Association Opposed to Woman Suffrage, New York). "Woman Suffrage Opposed to Woman's Rights," *Annals of the American Academy of Political and Social Science*, LVI (November, 1914), 99-104.

Dorr, Rheta Childe. Breaking into the Human Race. New York, National American Woman Suffrage Association, n.d.

———— Susan B. Anthony. New York, Frederick A. Stokes, 1928.

———— A Woman of Fifty. New York, Funk & Wagnalls, 1924.

Dos Passos, John R. Equality of Suffrage Means the Debasement Not Only of Women But of Men. New York, National Association Opposed to Woman Suffrage, n.d.

"Do You, as a Woman, Want to Vote?" *Ladies' Home Journal*, XXVIII (January, 1911), 17.

Drinker, Sophie H. "Votes for Women in Eighteenth-Century New Jersey," *Proceedings of the New Jersey Historical Society*, LXXX (January, 1962), 31-45.

Duniway, Abigail Scott. Path Breaking: An Autobiographical History of the Equal Suffrage Movement in Pacific Coast States. Portland, Ore., James, Kerns & Abbott, 1914.

Dunne, F. P. "Mr. Dooley on Woman's Suffrage," *The American Magazine*, LXVIII (June, 1909), 198-200.

Dwight, Frederick. Taxation and the Suffrage. New York, New York State Association Opposed to Woman Suffrage [published between 1900 and 1910].

Earhart, Mary. Frances Willard: From Prayers to Politics. Chicago, University of Chicago Press, 1944.

Eminent Opinions on Woman Suffrage. N.p., n.d.

Faulkner, Harold U. The Quest for Social Justice, 1898-1914. New York, Macmillan, 1931.

Finch, Edith. Carey Thomas of Bryn Mawr. New York, Harper, 1947.

Fiske, John. Civil Government in the United States. Boston, Houghton Mifflin, 1890.

FitzGerald, Susan W. What Is a Democracy? Warren, Ohio, National American Woman Suffrage Association [1908?].

———— Women in the Home. Warren, Ohio, National American Woman Suffrage Association [1908?].

Flexner, Eleanor. Century of Struggle: The Woman's Rights Movement in the United States. Cambridge, Mass., The Belknap Press of Harvard University Press, 1959.

Frothingham, O. B. "The Real Case of the 'Remonstrants' against Woman Suffrage," *The Arena*, II (July, 1890), 175-81.

Frothingham, The Rev. O. B., and others. Woman Suffrage Unnatural and Inexpedient: Views of Rev. O. B. Frothingham, Prentiss Cummings, Esq., John Boyle O'Reilly, Prof. W. W. Goodwin, Richard H. Dana, Esq., and Rev. J. P. Bodfish, Chancellor, Cathedral of the Holy Cross. Boston, 1894.

Gehlke, C. E. "On the Correlation between the Vote for Suffrage and the Vote on the Liquor Question. A preliminary Study," *American Statistical Association Journal*, XV (March, 1917), 524-32.

George, Mrs. A. J. Address before the Brooklyn Auxiliary, April 30, 1909. New York, New York State Association Opposed to Woman Suffrage [1909].

Gibbons, J. Cardinal. "The Restless Woman," *Ladies' Home Journal*, XIX (January, 1902), 6.

Giele, Janet Zollinger. "Social Change in the Feminine Role: A Comparison of Woman's Suffrage and Woman's Temperance, 1870-1920." Ph.D. dissertation, Radcliffe College, 1961.

Gilfillan, Lavinia Coppock (Member of Minneapolis Association Opposed to the Further Extension of Suffrage to Women). "The Disadvantages of Equal Suffrage." Papers and Proceedings of the Eighth Annual Meeting of the Minnesota Academy of Social Sciences. *Publications of the Minnesota Academy of Social Sciences*, VIII (1915), 170-85.

Gilman, Charlotte Perkins. The Living of Charlotte Perkins Gilman: An Autobiography. New York, Appleton-Century, 1935.

—— Women and Economics: A Study of the Economic Relation between Men and Women as a Factor in Social Evolution. Boston, Small, Maynard, 1898.

Ginger, Ray. Altgeld's America: The Lincoln Ideal versus Changing Realities. New York, Funk & Wagnalls, 1958.

Goldman, Eric F. Rendezvous wtih Destiny. New York, Vintage, 1958.

Goldmark, Josephine. Impatient Crusader: Florence Kelley's Life Story. Urbana, University of Illinois Press, 1953.

Gompers, Samuel. "'Labor and Woman Suffrage," *American Federationist*, XXVII (October, 1920), 936-39.

Goodman, Clavia. Bitter Harvest: Laura Clay's Suffrage Work. Lexington, Ky., Bur Press, 1946.

Harper, Ida Husted. The Life and Work of Susan B. Anthony. 3 vols. Indianapolis, Hollenbeck Press, 1898 and 1908.

———— "Men versus Women: An Indictment," *Independent*, April 2, 1908, pp. 741-44.

———— "The Passing of Elizabeth Cady Stanton," *Independent*, November 6, 1902, pp. 2622-25.

———— "The Passing of Susan B. Anthony," *Collier's*, March 31, 1906, p. 22.

———— "Present Status of Woman Suffrage," *The World To-Day* (Chicago), XI (December, 1906), 1264-68.

———— "Status of Woman Suffrage in the United States," *North American Review*, CLXXXIX (April, 1909), 502-12.

———— "Suffrage—a Right," *North American Review*, CLXXXIII (September, 1906), 484-98.

———— "What Do the Newport Suffrage Meetings Mean?" *Independent*, September 9, 1909, pp. 575-79.

———— "What the Suffragists Are Doing," *Harper's Bazar*, LXIII (February, 1909), 201-3.

———— "Why Women Cannot Vote in the United States," *North American Review*, CLXXIX (July, 1904), 30-41.

———— "Woman Suffrage: Is It a Waning Issue?" *Collier's*, August 25, 1906, pp. 28-30.

———— "Woman Suffrage throughout the World," *North American Review*, CLXXXVI (September, 1907), 55-71.

———— "The Woman Suffrage Movement," *Harper's Bazar*, LXIII (January, 1909), 99-101.

———— "Would Woman Suffrage Benefit the State, and Woman Herself?" *North American Review*, CLXXVIII (March, 1904), 367-74.

Harper, Ida Husted, ed. History of Woman Suffrage. Vols. V and VI (1900-20). New York, National American Woman Suffrage Association, 1922.

Harper, Ida Husted, and Susan B. Anthony, eds. History of

Woman Suffrage. Vol. IV (1883-1900). Rochester, Susan B. Anthony, 1902.

Harvey, Alexander. "The American Woman Peril," *Sewanee Review,* XVIII (July, 1910), 300-16.

Haworth, Paul Leland. America in Ferment. Indianapolis, Bobbs-Merrill, 1915.

Hays, Elinor Rice. Morning Star: A Biography of Lucy Stone, 1818-1893. New York, Harcourt, 1961.

Hecker, Eugene A. A Short History of Women's Rights. New York, Putnam, 1910.

Henry, Alice. "The National American Woman Suffrage Association and Machine Politics," *Life and Labor,* II (February, 1912), 51-54.

Higham, John. Strangers in the Land. New Brunswick, N. J., Rutgers University Press, 1955.

Hoar, Senator George F. Woman in the State. Warren, Ohio, National American Woman Suffrage Association [1909?].

Hofstadter, Richard. Age of Reform. New York, Knopf, 1956.
——— Social Darwinism in American Thought. Rev. ed. Boston, Beacon, 1955.

Holland, Robert Afton. "The Suffragette," *Sewanee Review,* XVII (July, 1909), 272-88.

Howe, Frederic C. Frederic C. Howe on Suffrage. Warren, Ohio, National American Woman Suffrage Association [1908?].

Illinois Association Opposed to Extension of Suffrage to Women. To the Voters in the Middle West: Bulletin No. 1. Chicago, Illinois Association Opposed to Extension of Suffrage to Women, 1909.

In Memory of Anna Howard Shaw. New York, National Woman Suffrage Publishing Co., Inc. [1919].

International Woman Suffrage Alliance. Reports of Annual Conferences, 1906, 1908, 1909, 1911, 1913.

Irwin, Inez Haynes. Angels and Amazons: A Hundred Years of American Women. Garden City, N. Y., Doubleday Doran, 1934.
——— The Story of the Woman's Party. New York, Harcourt, 1921.

Jamison, Heloise. The Wrong of Suffrage: From an Article in the *American Woman's Journal,* for May, 1894. N.p., n.d.

"Jane Addams Points to the Progressive Party as Hope for Woman Suffrage," Indianapolis *Star,* October 27, 1912.

Johnson, Helen Kendrick. Woman and the Republic. New York, Appleton, 1897.

Jones, Mrs. Gilbert E. (Chairman, National League for the Civic Education of Women, New York). "The Position of the Anti-Suffragists," Supplement to the *Annals of the American Academy of Political and Social Science,* XXXV (May, 1910), 16-22.

———— "Some Facts about Suffrage and Anti-Suffrage," *Forum,* XLIII (May, 1910), 495-504.

Katzenstein, Caroline. Lifting the Curtain: The State and National Woman Suffrage Campaigns in Pennsylvania as I Saw Them. Philadelphia, Dorrance, 1955.

Kelley, Florence. Letters to the editor, *The Outlook,* March 17, 1906, p. 622; July 21, 1906, pp. 675-76; October 16, 1909, p. 363.

———— "One Kind of Child Labor," *Woman's Era* (New Orleans), I (March, 1910), 89-90. Copy in Clay Papers, University of Kentucky.

———— Persuasion or Responsibility? Warren, Ohio, National American Woman Suffrage Association, n.d.

———— Some Ethical Gains through Legislation. New York, Macmillan, 1905.

———— Woman Suffrage: Its Relation to Working Women and Children. Warren, Ohio, National American Woman Suffrage Association [1906?].

———— "Women and Social Legislation in the United States," in Women in Public Life. *Annals of the American Academy of Political and Social Sciences,* LVI (November, 1914), 62-71.

Laidlaw, Harriet Burton. Organizing to Win by the Political District Plan: A Handbook for Working Suffragists. New York, National Woman Suffrage Publishing Co., Inc., 1914.

———— Review of My Little Sister, *The Survey,* May 3, 1913, pp. 199-202.

———— "The Woman's Hour," *Forum,* LVI (November, 1916), 531-43.

Leonard, Priscilla. "The Ideal of Equality for Men and Women," *Harper's Bazar,* LXII (November, 1909), 1169-70.

Levine, Daniel. "Jane Addams: Romantic Radical, 1889-1912," *Mid-America,* XLIV (October, 1962), 193-210.

Linkugel, Wilmer Albert. "The Speeches of Anna Howard Shaw." Ph.D dissertation, University of Wisconsin, 1960.

Lippmann, Walter. Drift and Mastery. New York, Mitchell Kennerley, 1914.

Livermore, Mary A. Mrs. Livermore on Suffrage. Warren, Ohio, National American Woman Suffrage Association [1906?].

Louis, James P. "Sue Shelton White and the Woman Suffrage Movement, 1913-20," *Tennessee Historical Quarterly,* XXII (June, 1963), 170-90.

Lubove, Roy. "The Twentieth Century City: The Progressive as Municipal Reformer," *Mid-America,* XLI (October, 1959), 195-209.

Lutz, Alma. Created Equal: Elizabeth Cady Stanton, 1815-1902. New York, John Day, 1940.

———— Susan B. Anthony: Rebel, Crusader, Humanitarian. Boston, Beacon, 1959.

Lutz, Alma, and Harriot Stanton Blatch. Challenging Years: The Memoirs of Harriot Stanton Blatch. New York, Putnam, 1940.

McCulloch, Catharine Waugh. Bridget's Sisters: A Play. Chicago, Catharine Waugh McCulloch, 1911.

M'Intire, Mary A. J. Of No Benefit to Woman. Letter to the editor, Boston *Sunday Herald,* reprinted as a pamphlet. N.p., n.d.

MacLean, Annie Marion. Wage-earning Women. New York, Macmillan, 1910.

McVickar, Mrs. Robert (President of New York State Consumers' League). Address on Opposition to Woman Suffrage, before the Joint Senate and Assembly Judiciary Committee, March 9, 1910. New York, New York State Association Opposed to Woman Suffrage [1910].

Mann, Arthur. Yankee Reformers in the Urban Age. Cambridge, Mass., The Belknap Press of Harvard University Press, 1954.

Man-Suffrage Association. The Case against Woman Suffrage: A Manual for Speakers, Debaters, Writers, Lecturers, and Anyone Who Wants the Facts and Figures. New York, The Man-Suffrage Association, 1915.

Martin, Anne. The Story of the Nevada Equal Suffrage Campaign. Reno, *University of Nevada Bulletin*, Vol. XLII (August, 1948).

Massachusetts Association Opposed to the Extension of Suffrage to Women. Annual Report, 1896.

Massachusetts Anti-Suffrage Committee. The Case against Woman Suffrage. Boston, Massachusetts Anti-Suffrage Committee [1915].

Merk, Lois B. "Boston's Historic Public School Crisis," *New England Quarterly*, XXXI (1958), 172-99.

———— "Massachusetts and the Woman-Suffrage Movement." Ph.D. dissertation, Radcliffe College, 1958. Rev. ed., 1961.

Merriam, Charles Edward. A History of American Political Theories. New York, Macmillan, 1928.

Meyer, Annie Nathan. "Woman's Assumption of Sex Superiority," *North American Review*, CLXXVIII (January, 1904), 103-9.

Morris, Monia Cook. "The History of Woman Suffrage in Missouri, 1867-1901," *Missouri Historical Review*, XXV (October, 1930), 67–82.

Mowry, George E. The Era of Theodore Roosevelt, 1900-1912. New York, Harper, 1958.

———— "The South and the Progressive Lily White Party of 1912," *Journal of Southern History*, VI (May, 1940), 237–47.

———— Theodore Roosevelt and the Progressive Movement. New York, Hill & Wang, 1960.

"Mrs. Stanton to President Roosevelt," *Independent*, November 6, 1902, pp. 2621-22.

Nathan, Maud. The Wage Earner and the Ballot. Warren, Ohio, National American Woman Suffrage Association [1908?].

National American Woman Suffrage Association. Proceedings of Annual Conventions, 1893-1919. Titles and places of publication vary. Full publication data on each volume are given in the text in the first footnote in which it is cited.
——— Victory: How Women Won It: A Centennial Symposium, 1840-1940. New York, H. W. Wilson, 1940.

National Anti-Suffrage Association. The Case against Woman Suffrage. Boston, National Anti-Suffrage Association [1916].

National Council of Women. Transactions. Philadelphia, 1891.

Neu, Charles E. "Olympia Brown and the Woman's Suffrage Movement," *Wisconsin Magazine of History*, XLIV (Summer, 1960), 277–87.

"Newspapers on Woman Suffrage," *Harper's Bazar*, LXI (March, 1907), p. 304. A press survey.

New York *Advertiser*, April 16, 1894.

New York State Association Opposed to the Extension of Suffrage to Women. Annual Report of the Chairman of the Executive Committee. New York, April, 1896.

New York State Woman Suffrage Party. Annual Reports, 1916 and 1917.

New York *Telegram*, May 4, 1894.

New York *World*, April 29, 1894, and May 4, 1894.

Nottingham, Elizabeth K. "Toward an Analysis of the Effects of Two World Wars on the Role and Status of Middle-Class Women in the English-Speaking World," *American Sociological Review*, XII (December, 1947), 666–75.

Obenchain, Lida Calvert. "Captivated Calves." Warren, Ohio, National American Woman Suffrage Association [1906].
——— The "Unanswerable Argument." Warren, Ohio, National American Woman Suffrage Association [1908].

Osborne, Duffield. "Xanthippe on Woman Suffrage," *Yale Review*, new series, IV (April, 1917), 590–607.

Ostrander, Gilman M. The Prohibition Movement in California, 1848-1933. University of California Publications in

History, Vol. LVII. Berkeley and Los Angeles, University of California Press, 1957.

O'Sullivan, Mary Kenney. Women and the Vote. Warren, Ohio, National American Woman Suffrage Association [1908?].

The Outlook, April 28, 1894, pp. 738, 760; March 10, 1900, pp. 573–74; June 8, 1901, pp. 353-55; August 3, 1912, pp. 767–68.

Park, Maud Wood. Front Door Lobby. Ed. by Edna Lamprey Stantial. Boston, Beacon, 1960.

Parkhurst, The Rev. Charles H. "The Inadvisability of Woman Suffrage," in Significance of the Woman Suffrage Movement. Supplement to the *Annals of the American Academy of Political and Social Science,* XXXV (May, 1910), 36–37.

Parkman, Francis. Some of the Reasons against Woman Suffrage, N.p., n.d.

Paxson, Frederic L. "The Question of Suffrage," letter to the editor, *The Nation,* February 8, 1912, p. 132.

Peck, Mary Gray. Carrie Chapman Catt. New York, H. W. Wilson, 1944.

——— "Rise of the Woman Suffrage Party," *Life and Labor,* I, (June, 1911), 166–69.

——— "Some American Suffragists," *Life and Labor,* I (December, 1911), 368–73.

Philbrook, Mary. "Woman's Suffrage in New Jersey prior to 1807," *Proceedings of the New Jersey Historical Society,* LVII (April, 1939), 87–98.

Porter, Kirk H. A History of Suffrage in the United States. Chicago, University of Chicago Press, 1918.

Potter, Francis Squire. The Direct Way. Warren, Ohio, National American Woman Suffrage Association [1909?].

"Program of the National Woman Suffrage Association," *National Municipal Review,* IX (January, 1920), 56–57.

Putnam-Jacobi, Mary. "Common Sense" Applied to Woman Suffrage. New York, Putnam, 1894.

Quarles, Benjamin. "Frederick Douglass and the Woman's

Rights Movement," *Journal of Negro History*, XXV (January, 1940), 35–44.

Ray, P. Orman. "The World-Wide Woman Suffrage Movement," *Journal of the Society of Comparative Legislation and International Law* (London), third series, I (July, 1919), 220–38.

Revised Record of the Constitutional Convention of the State of New York, May 8, 1894, to September 29, 1894. . . . Vol. II. Albany, 1900.

Richardson, Anna Steese. "The Work of the 'Antis,'" *Woman's Home Companion*, XXXVIII (March, 1911), 15, 70–71.

Robinson, Helen Ring (Colorado state senator). "What about the Woman's Party?" *Independent*, September 11, 1916, pp. 381–83.

Roessing, Jennie Bradley. "Federal Suffrage in a Dynamic State," *The Public*, August 24, 1917, pp. 814–15.

Rogers, Mrs. Henry Wade. "Win-the-War Women," *The Public*, August 24, 1917, pp. 815–17.

Root, Elihu. Address Delivered before the New York State Constitutional Convention, on August 15, 1894. New York, New York State Association Opposed to Woman Suffrage, n.d.

Schaffer, Ronald. "The New York City Woman Suffrage Party, 1909-1919," *New York History*, XLIII (July, 1962), 268–87.

Schain, Josephine. Women and the Franchise. Chicago, A. C. McClurg, 1918.

Schlesinger, Arthur M. "A Critical Period in American Religion, 1875-1900," *Proceedings of the Massachusetts Historical Society*, LXIV (June, 1932), 523–47.

Scott, Anne Firor. "The 'New Woman' in the New South," *South Atlantic Quarterly*, LXI (Autumn, 1962), 473–83.

Scott, Francis M. Address to Meeting of the Committee on Suffrage of the New York Constitutional Convention at Albany, New York, on June 14, 1894, in regard to Amendment under Consideration to Eliminate the Word "Male" from Article III, Section I, of the Constitution. N.p., n.d.

Scott, Mary Semple, ed. "History of Woman Suffrage in Missouri," *Missouri Historical Review,* XIV (April-July, 1920), 281–384.

Scott, Mrs. Francis M. Extension of the Suffrage to Women: Address Delivered before the Judiciary Committee of the New York Senate, April 10, 1895. Boston, Massachusetts Man Suffrage Association, n.d.

Scott, Mrs. William Forse. "Woman's Relation to Government," *North American Review,* CXCI (April, 1910), 549–58.

Sewall, May Wright. Women, World War and Permanent Peace. San Francisco, John J. Newbegin, 1915.

Shaw, Anna Howard. An Address by Dr. Anna Howard Shaw. Delivered December, 1915. New York, National Woman Suffrage Publishing Co., Inc., n.d.

——— "Equal Suffrage—A Problem of Political Justice," in Women in Public Life. *Annals of the American Academy of Political and Social Science,* LVI (November, 1914), 93–98.

——— "Men of America on Trial for Democracy," *The Public,* August 24, 1917, pp. 813–14.

——— Passages from Speeches of Dr. Anna Howard Shaw. New York, National Woman Suffrage Publishing Co., Inc., 1915.

——— A Speech by Doctor Anna Howard Shaw. Delivered April 16, 1915. New York, National Woman Suffrage Publishing Co., Inc., 1915.

——— Story of a Pioneer. New York, Harper, 1915.

Sherwood, Mrs. M. E. W., article in the New York *Herald,* May 6, 1894.

Shuler, Marjorie. For Rent—One Pedestal. New York, National Woman Suffrage Publishing Co., Inc., 1917.

Shuler, Nettie Rogers, and Carrie Chapman Catt. Woman Suffrage and Politics. New York, Scribner's, 1926.

"Significance of the Woman Suffrage Movement," Supplement to the *Annals of the American Academy of Political and Social Science,* XXXV (May, 1910).

Slosson, Preston W. The Great Crusade and After, 1914-1928. New York, Macmillan, 1931.

Smith, Gerald Birney, ed. Religious Thought in the Last Quarter-Century. Chicago, University of Chicago Press, 1927.

Smith, Goldwin. Woman Suffrage. Reprinted from Essays on Questions of the Day. New York, Macmillan, 1894.

Smith, Munroe. "The Consent of the Governed," *Proceedings of the Academy of Political Science*, V (1914), 82–88.

Smith, T. V. The American Philosophy of Equality. Chicago, University of Chicago Press, 1927.

Smuts, Robert W. Women and Work in America. New York, Columbia University Press, 1959.

Spencer, Anna Garlin. Woman's Share in Social Culture. New York, Mitchell Kennerley, 1913.

Sprague, William Forrest. Women and the West: A Short Social History. Boston, Christopher Publishing House, 1940.

Stanton, Elizabeth Cady. "Are Homogeneous Divorce Laws in All the States Desirable?" *North American Review*, CLXX (March, 1900), 405–9.

—— "Divorce Versus Domestic Warfare," *Arena*, V (April, 1890), 560–69.

—— Eighty Years and More (1815-1897): Reminiscences. Vol. II. New York, Harper, 1898.

—— Letter to the editor, *The Critic* (New York), March 28, 1896, pp. 218–19.

—— "Patriotism and Chastity," *Westminster Review* (London), CXXXV (January, 1891), 1–5.;

—— "Progress of the American Woman," *North American Review*, CLXXI (December, 1900), 904–7.

—— "Reading the Bible in the Public Schools," *The Arena*, XVII (June, 1897), 1033–38.

—— Suffrage a Natural Right. Chicago, Open Court, 1894.

—— "Wyoming Admitted as a State," *Westminster Review* (London), CXXXIV (September, 1890), 280–84.

Stanton, Elizabeth Cady, and others. The Woman's Bible. Two parts. New York, European Publishing Company, 1895 and 1898.

Stanton, Theodore, and Harriot Stanton Blatch, eds. Elizabeth Cady Stanton as Revealed in Her Letters, Diary and Reminiscences. Vol. II. New York, Harper, 1922.

Stevens, Doris. *Jailed for Freedom*. New York, Liveright, 1920.

Stewart, Ella Seass. "Woman Suffrage and the Liquor Traffic," in Women in Public Life. *Annals of the American Academy of Political and Social Science*, LVI (November, 1914), 134–52.

Taylor, A. Elizabeth. "The Last Phase of the Woman Suffrage Movement in Georgia," *Georgia Historical Quarterly*, XLIII (March, 1959), 11–28.

—— "The Origin of the Woman Suffrage Movement in Georgia," *Georgia Historical Quarterly*, XXVIII (June, 1944), 63–79.

—— "Revival and Development of the Woman Suffrage Movement in Georgia," *Georgia Historical Quarterly*, XLII (December, 1958), 339–54.

—— "The Woman Suffrage Movement in Arkansas," *Arkansas Historical Quarterly*, XV (Spring, 1956), 17–52.

—— "The Woman Suffrage Movement in Florida," *Florida Historical Quarterly*, XXXVI (July, 1957), 42–60.

—— "The Woman Suffrage Movement in North Carolina (concluded)," *North Carolina Historical Review*, XXXVIII (April, 1961), 173–89.

—— The Woman Suffrage Movement in Tennessee. New York, Bookman, 1957.

—— "The Woman Suffrage Movement in Texas," *Journal of Southern History*, XVII (May, 1951), 194–215.

Terrell, Mary Church. A Colored Woman in a White World. Washington, D. C., Ransdell, 1940.

Thomas, M. Carey. Dr. Thomas on Woman's Ballot. Warren, Ohio, National American Woman Suffrage Association [1907?].

Trout, Grace Wilbour. "Side Lights on Illinois Suffrage History," *Journal of the Illinois State Historical Society*, XIII (July, 1920), 145–79.

A Tribute to Woodrow Wilson. New York, National American Woman Suffrage Association, 1919. In Rare Book Room, New York Public Library.

Turner, Edward Raymond. "Woman's Suffrage in New Jersey, 1790-1807," *Smith College Studies in History*, I (July, 1916), 165–87.

Twenty-Five Answers to Antis: Five-Minute Speeches on Votes for Women by Eminent Suffragists. New York, National Woman Suffrage Publishing Company, Inc., n.d.

"Votes for All," A Symposium, *The Crisis* (New York), XV (November, 1917), 19–21.

Votes for Women on the Home Stretch. N.p. [1913].

Wallace, Margaret Louise, and Katherine Devereux Blake. Champion of Women: The Life of Lillie Devereux Blake. New York, Fleming H. Revell, 1943.

Walsh, The Rev. Father (of Troy). Protest against Woman Suffrage: Address delivered at a mass meeting called by the Anti-Women's Suffrage Association of Albany, N. Y. N.p., n.d.

Ward, Lester Frank. "Our Better Halves," *Forum*, VI (November, 1888), 266–75.

Watkins, Ann. "For the Twenty-Two Million: Why Most Women Do Not Want to Vote," *The Outlook*, May 4, 1912, pp. 26–30.

Wells, Mrs. Kate Gannett. An Argument against Woman Suffrage, delivered before a special legislative committee. Brookline, Massachusetts Association Opposed to the Extension of Suffrage to Women, n.d.

Wheeler, Everett P. Home Rule. Brief on Argument before Judiciary Committee, House of Representatives, March, 1914, against Proposition for Constitutional Amendment Compelling the States to Adopt Woman Suffrage. New York, Man Suffrage Association, n.d.

Why Should Suffrage Be Imposed on Women? Boston, Massachusetts Man Suffrage Association, n.d.

Williams, Mattie L. "History of Woman Suffrage in Arizona and the Nation," *Arizona Historical Review*, I (January, 1929), 69–73.

"Woman and the Ballot," Chicago Sunday *Record-Herald,* October 6, 1912.

The Woman Movement in America. [Chicago], Illinois Association Opposed to the Extension of Suffrage to Women [1902].

"Woman Suffrage," *Harper's Weekly,* June 16, 1894. An editorial.

"Woman Suffrage and Party Politics," *The New Republic,* December 9, 1916, pp. 138–40. An editorial.

Woman Suffrage and the Liquor Interests. New York, National Woman Suffrage Publishing Co., Inc., 1916.

"Women Demand Equal Suffrage in New Chicago Quarter," Chicago Sunday *Record-Herald,* April 1, 1906.

Women in Public Life. *Annals of the American Academy of Political and Social Science,* LVI (November, 1914). Symposium of nineteen articles.

Women Remonstrants of the State of Illinois. To the Honorable the Senate and House of Representatives of the State of Illinois. Chicago, June 1, 1891.

"Women Who Want to Vote," New York *Times,* December 20, 1908.

Zangwill, Israel. Mr. and Mrs. Sapsea. Warren, Ohio, National American Woman Suffrage Association [1909?].

Index